HOMO POLITICUS

HOMO POLITICUS

The Strange and Barbaric Tribes
of the Beltway

DANA MILBANK

DOUBLEDAY
New York London Toronto Sydney Auckland

PUBLISHED BY DOUBLEDAY

Copyright © 2008 by Dana Milbank

All Rights Reserved

Published in the United States by Doubleday, an imprint of
The Doubleday Broadway Publishing Group,
a division of Random House, Inc., New York.
www.doubleday.com

DOUBLEDAY and the portrayal of an anchor with a dolphin are
registered trademarks of Random House, Inc.

Library of Congress Cataloging-in Publication Data

Milbank, Dana.
Homo politicus : the strange and barbaric tribes of the beltway / Dana Milbank. — 1st ed.
p.   cm.
1. Political culture—Washington (D.C.). 2. Politicians—Washington (D.C.)—Social life and
customs. 3. Washington (D.C.)—Social life and customs. I. Title.
JK1726.M575 2008
306.209753—dc22
2007019456

ISBN 978-0-385-51750-8

PRINTED IN THE UNITED STATES OF AMERICA

1   3   5   7   9   10   8   6   4   2

First Edition

TO TOM DELAY

Contents

Homo Politicus

Introduction

I should have known something was amiss when Jack Abramoff told me about the kosher pigs.

The Republican superlobbyist and I were dining a few years ago at the high-end restaurant he owned, Signatures, across the street from the National Archives. Abramoff was a well-connected source who gave me newsy tips about presidential adviser Karl Rove and House majority leader Tom DeLay. On this day, however, we were talking about a second restaurant he planned to open, a kosher Jewish deli called Stacks. He said he had just located a species of swine in Asia that chews its cud—as required by the Jewish dietary laws. Thus, Abramoff said, would he operate the first kosher restaurant to serve bacon and pork sausage.

Alas, the kosher pigs turned out too good to be true—as did just about everything else about Abramoff. To date, Abramoff and eleven of his friends and associates have pleaded guilty in a sprawling corruption scandal in which Indian tribes were bilked for tens of millions of dollars and federal officials were bribed with golf trips and skyboxes. Signatures and Stacks are gone, and kosher pork continues to elude us.

As I thought about the crimes that sent Abramoff to jail, it occurred to me that they had much in common with his cud-chewing-pig scheme. Abramoff believed that if you were powerful enough, the rules—federal statutes or Jewish dietary laws—didn't apply to you. In this view, Abramoff was typical of the peculiar species that inhabits the capital: *Homo politicus,* or, in the native tongue, Potomac Man. Homo politicus is unlike other members of his genus because he strives for power for its own sake. For him, fame and fortune are only vehicles to obtain power or are by-products of power; it matters little how or to what end the power is exercised, only that it is possessed.

I came to live in political Washington—Potomac Land, if you will—twelve years ago. For most of that time, I have lived among the natives as if I were one of them: working, eating, dressing, and socializing as they do and wearing the same government-issued ID cards and BlackBerry devices. As I gained their trust over time, they allowed me to join them in their homes, war rooms, and tribal councils. Seeing them that way, I felt like a Spanish explorer witnessing an Aztec human sacrifice for the first time. In his natural state, Homo politicus was so defined by tribalism that he placed tribe, or party, above even family and nation-state. Though he was equipped with the tools of modern civilization, his work proved to be less efficient—and his rituals more bizarre—than those of even the most primitive cultures.

As I write this, the events of recent weeks in Potomac Land must confound those who have not lived among Homo politicus. Senator Larry Craig of Idaho was arrested for lewd conduct in an airport men's room after touching an undercover policeman in a neighboring stall. (The officer was not impressed when Craig handed him his Senate business card and said, "What do you think about that?") The deputy secretary of state, Randall Tobias, has resigned and Senator David Vitter of Louisiana has issued a public apology because they used an escort service alleged to be a prostitution ring run by the "D.C. Madam."

Meanwhile, Paul Wolfowitz, who, after championing the disastrous Iraq war, was rewarded with the presidency of the World Bank, lost that job for getting his girlfriend a raise. The former number two official at the Interior Department was sentenced for lying to

Congress about one of several girlfriends he used his office to assist. The FBI raided the home of Senator Ted Stevens of Alaska and businesses associated with two congressmen, John Doolittle of California and Rick Renzi of Arizona. Congressman William Jefferson was indicted for taking bribes, the president commuted a thirty-month perjury sentence given to the vice president's former chief of staff, and the attorney general resigned after being accused of perjury and witness tampering.

None of these tales, however, causes much surprise in Potomac Land. While the names of the offenders change, and the plot details vary slightly, the theme is universal: Potomac Man will do almost anything to amass and to flaunt his power and that of his tribe. The same character trait can be found in many of the subjects of this study: the former national security adviser who hid classified documents in his clothing, the senator who handed out bingo cards at a confirmation hearing for chief justice of the United States, the congressman who wrote a menu listing exactly how large a bribe he required for various official acts, the Supreme Court justice who made an obscene gesture leaving church, the chairmen of the Iraq Study Group who paused in deliberations for a photo shoot for *Men's Vogue,* the attorney general who ordered a drape to cover the exposed breast of the *Spirit of Justice* statue, and the family-values lawmaker who settled a lawsuit with a young mistress who accused him of trying to strangle her.

To understand such behavior, I followed Potomac Man through his daily rituals: the morning "Gaggle" at the White House, the lunchtime reading of *Hotline,* the afternoon viewing of Wolf Blitzer, and the evening fund-raiser. I learned of his weekly rhythms: the Sunday morning shows that are more popular than church, the lawmakers' Thursday afternoon rush to National Airport, and the administration's Friday evening "dump" of bad news. I observed his seasonal festivals at each stage of the biennial electoral cycle: the winter budget battle, the summer recess, and the fall campaign. And I explored the Potomac rites of passage: election, the accumulation of seniority, and, finally, the ascent to lobbyist.

Admittedly, even intensive research cannot thoroughly explain why a senior White House official would shoplift from Target or why a member of Congress would stash bribe money in food containers in his freezer or strike a police officer with her cell phone. Neither can such a study adequately account for the senator who calls man-made global warming the "greatest hoax ever perpetrated" or the Senate candidate who explained a low turnout at an airport rally by making up a story about a tree falling on a hangar. Such Potomac Land mysteries may never be solved. But they are well worth contemplating over a kosher ham sandwich.

One

STATUS

Among the many paradoxes of Potomac Land is that it is, ostensibly, the capital of the most egalitarian people on the planet, and yet it has embraced a status system that is both hierarchical and byzantine. In substance, it is most similar to the varna caste system that has divided India for millennia. But while the caste system has become increasingly irrelevant and anachronistic in India—driven out by educated urbanites who dismiss it as primitive—the antiquated system grows ever more powerful in the mind of status-conscious Homo politicus, ever on the prowl for ways to demonstrate his power.

In India, there is the priestly caste (Brahmans) for teachers and scholars, the warrior caste (Kshatriyas) for kings and landowners, the trading caste (Vaishyas) of merchants and artisans, and a lower class (Sudras) of farmers and service workers who do not read the sacred texts. Below all the castes are the untouchables, those considered too filthy even to live among others in a village. Each caste is further subdivided into jati, or gotra, a band of people in a similar occupation; by performing daily rituals, members of a gotra allow their sect to survive.

In Potomac Land's highest caste are the top appointees and advisers to the president and congressional leaders, as well as justices who interpret the sacred texts and prominent strategists who use their shamanic powers to keep officials in power. Next are the rank-and-file lawmakers, who are in a constant state of aggression; though the kings and landowners of Potomac Land, they are in status inferior to the top strategists who put them into office and keep them there. Journalists, lobbyists, and bureaucrats form the various gotra that are part of the Vaishyas, the third caste responsible for the daily transactions that keep Potomac Land functioning. Finally, there are the backward castes, the Sudras and the untouchables—those who live in and around Potomac Land but have no interest in politics. They are by far the largest group in number, but they are invisible to the upper castes.

The crucial difference between varna castes and Potomac castes is that Potomac Man has a severe shortage of indigenous wise men and scholarly figures and therefore must draw Brahmans from other levels of status or from outside Potomac Land entirely. By simply attaching oneself to a rising political star, a Sudra can easily become a Brahman—as illustrated by young and unknown Dan Bartlett's ascent to a top position in the White House because he got a job out of college with Karl Rove. Others, such as George Soros, can propel themselves to higher castes by spending large sums of money. Rock star Bono, embraced by the White House, has found that his musical fame has a certain reciprocity in Potomac Land. Then there is just plain luck: in the 1994 Republican landslide, a man with a history of homelessness, unemployment, and drug charges was elected to Congress from Texas. Still others, such as Barack Obama, a Democratic senator from Illinois, have gained status through good looks and oratorical gifts; Obama surged in popularity and announced his presidential candidacy shortly after a photo appeared in *People* magazine of him in a bathing suit as part of a "Beach Babes" spread also showing Catherine Zeta-Jones and Penelope Cruz.

BECOMING OUTCASTE

It is not uncommon for a prominent member of Potomac Land to become outcaste—evicted from his caste and denied privileges to associate with his former peers. In the nasty, brutish, and short life of Potomac Man, it is possible for a perfectly upstanding member of the community to become, within a matter of days, the punch line of a joke. This is in part because partisan opponents will use any excuse to bring down a foe and in part because members of Potomac Land's ever-present Greek chorus—"the press" in the local dialect—take great enjoyment in these campaigns. Thus a powerful Potomac Man can be destroyed by what would be, by common criminal standards, fairly minor transgressions.

Sometimes the cause of the hasty social demotion is entirely self-inflicted. There were, for example, few people predicting a rapid comeback for Claude Allen. He resigned his job as White House domestic policy adviser in February 2006, using the familiar line that he wished to spend more time with his family. A month later, word got out that Allen had been arrested—for shoplifting.

While Potomac Man is often willing to condone high crimes such as perjury or obstruction of justice, he rarely tolerates the misdemeanors associated with the common criminal. And Allen was positively petty. He stole some $5,000 from Target and Hecht's stores—Bose speakers, a Kodak printer, a jacket, and knickknacks worth as little as $2.50—by requesting refunds for items he had not, in fact, returned. Potomac Land was agog at this discovery, and nobody accepted his lawyers' denials. Allen entered his inevitable guilty plea in August.

"Something did go very wrong," he confessed, with a lawyer at his side who had previously represented Bill Clinton and Ted Kennedy. Allen wept in court as he blamed the hard work of responding to Hurricane Katrina. "I lost perspective and failed to restrain myself." His wife concurred that "this was not the man I married." She blamed "fourteen-hour workdays" and a stretch of three months with fewer than two hours of sleep each night.

He got away with two years of probation, a small fine, and community service—but for Potomac Man, admitting such low behavior might as well have been a death sentence. "You are a classic example," the judge told him, "a fresh and enlightening example, that shame is not dead."

Another former high White House official turned outcaste is Sandy Berger, who as Bill Clinton's national security adviser was one of the most powerful in Potomac Land. In 2003, this man, who once controlled the fate of millions, walked out of the National Archives with documents related to his performance on terrorism. Berger said he merely walked off inadvertently—twice—with copies of classified documents and then lost them. His political opponents alleged that he carried them off in his underwear, or even ate them. In either case, he was clearly trying to avoid an embarrassing write-up in the 9/11 Commission's report of his actions, or inaction, on the rising threat of terrorism.

A report by the National Archives' inspector general, issued in December 2006, described Berger's crime: "He headed towards a construction area on Ninth Street. Mr. Berger looked up and down the street, up into the windows of the Archives and the DOJ, and did not see anyone." He folded the notes "in a V shape," then "walked inside a construction fence and slid the documents under a trailer." Later, "Mr. Berger left the building, retrieved the documents and notes from the construction area, and returned to his office."

In 2005, he accepted a three-year suspension of his security clearance and paid a fine. And he had to admit that he didn't misplace the missing documents; he shredded them. And things would only get worse. Two days after that court plea, he got in more legal trouble, this time for reckless driving. He was going eighty-eight in his Lexus on a fifty-five miles per hour part of I-66 in Virginia. For ordinary men, it would have been an annoying matter but not an embarrassing one. For Berger, it meant another round of news stories. If people missed those stories, they probably caught the ones about House Republicans demanding a congressional investigation into Berger's document heist or the ads from a conservative group alleging Berger "stole and ate classified documents that exposed the failures of the Clinton antiterrorism policies."

The cases of Berger and Allen, however, must be contrasted with that of Harriet Miers, who did nothing wrong but, over a fortnight in October 2005, saw her reputation destroyed anyway. Miers's sin: rising too high, too quickly in Potomac Man's status structure.

When Miers, who had been the Texas lottery commissioner and Bush's lawyer in Texas, came to the White House with President Bush as staff secretary, nobody was surprised. When, at the start of Bush's second term, she became White House counsel, people thought it was a bit of a stretch for the lottery commissioner but did not protest. Then, when William Rehnquist died and Bush nominated Miers for a Supreme Court seat, all hell broke loose.

First, conservative commentators and interest groups protested that Miers was insufficiently conservative. Then they protested that she was insufficiently intelligent. Then the State of Texas was forced to release dozens of painfully fawning messages Miers wrote to Bush when he was Texas governor. "You are the best governor ever—deserving of great respect," she wrote in 1997. She pronounced the Bushes to be "cool" and said that Bush and his wife were "the greatest!" She advised, "Keep up the great work. Texas is blessed." "Texas has a very popular governor and first lady!" Miers gushed at one point. She also wished: "Hopefully Jenna and Barbara recognize that their parents are 'cool'—as do the rest of us."

The White House, trying to rebuild Miers's status as more than a cheerleader, had supporters hold a conference call vowing that Miers would overturn Roe v. Wade. But by then, observations had turned to the excessive use of eyeliner by the unmarried Miers. She went to the Hill to meet with senators and quickly wound up in a dispute with Arlen Specter over birth-control law. The Judiciary Committee complained that Miers was late submitting the standard questionnaire, then called her responses "inadequate" and "insufficient." Miers was forced to acknowledge that, in 1989, her Texas bar license was suspended because she didn't pay her dues.

Her courtesy calls on the Hill made her look more out of her depth. She talked about the weather with senators. Comedians adored her. David Letterman devised a "Top Ten Signs Your Supreme Court Pick Isn't Qualified" (8. "Her legal mentor: Oliver Wendell Redenbacher"). Others recalled then-senator Roman Hruska's 1970 defense of doomed Supreme Court nominee G. Harrold Carswell: "[T]here are a lot of mediocre judges and people and lawyers. Aren't they entitled to a little representation and a little chance?"

Bush, growing desperate, hauled in some Texas jurists who backed Miers and called reporters into the Oval Office to remind everybody of her "high character" and "integrity." John L. Hill, Jr., a former chief justice of the Supreme Court of Texas, gave it his all. "I would trust her with my wife and my life," he announced.

But by then, senators weren't even arriving on time when Miers visited their offices. She dodged their questions with phrases such as "I need to sort of bone up on this a little more." Three weeks after her nomination, Miers finally bowed to the inevitable and withdrew. She returned to the White House counsel's office—still a competent lawyer but now also a Potomac Land joke.

It surprised nobody when, shortly after the Democrats took control of Congress in late 2006, Bush eased Miers out of her job as White House counsel and sent her packing in favor of former Reagan and Nixon administration lawyer Fred Fielding. The woman Bush once called the most qualified person in America to serve on the Supreme Court was not qualified enough to protect him from the expected congressional subpoenas. Within a few months, Congress was indeed approving subpoenas—to Miers herself, for her bungled effort to fire federal prosecutors and replace them with more loyal "Bushies."

INHERITED STATUS

Though Potomac Land is ostensibly meritocratic, the accident of birth is still a powerful indicator of status for Potomac Man. Dozens of members of Congress and one in five senators are there because their parents, spouses, or other relatives held the position before them. The offices are not technically inherited, but because the kin of an officeholder often benefit from broad name recognition (and perhaps confusion) among voters, the effect is the same.

Lisa Murkowski, an Alaska Republican, was elected to the Senate after being appointed to that position by her father, who vacated the seat to become governor. And in Illinois, Democratic congressman William O. Lipinski announced his retirement too late for a primary to be conducted, allowing him to persuade party elders to select his son,

Daniel, to represent the comfortably Democratic district. Likewise, four days after the funeral of California Democrat Robert Matsui, his widow, Doris, announced her candidacy for his seat in Congress.

This happens at the very highest level. After President Bush won his office because he shares a name with his father, the former president (himself the son of a senator), he began to populate his administration with former aides to his father. He also appointed his secretary of state's son as the chairman of the Federal Communications Commission, the chief justice's daughter as a top official at the Health and Human Services Department, another justice's son as a Labor Department official, a senator's wife as labor secretary, and the vice president's daughter and her husband to positions in the State and Justice departments.

Likewise, Hillary Clinton parlayed her marriage with President Clinton into a Senate seat and her own presidential run. The Speaker of the House, Nancy Pelosi, is the daughter of the late congressman and Baltimore mayor Thomas D'Alesandro, Jr. John Sarbanes won his seat in the House at the same moment his father, Paul, retired from the Senate; young Sarbanes joined scions Connie Mack, Dan Boren, Russ Carnahan, William Clay, John Sununu, Chris Dodd, Mark Pryor, Robert Bennett, Judd Gregg, Mary Landrieu, John Rockefeller, and many others in a club of the children of former officeholders.

The powerful in Potomac Land have mechanisms to perpetuate the family influence. Senators Al Gore and Birch Bayh, for example, enrolled their children in St. Alban's School in northwest Washington; the scions, bred to lead, followed their fathers to the Senate. The most successful at perpetuating dominance has been the family of Congressman Rodney Frelinghuysen, a New Jersey Republican who is the sixth generation of Frelinghuysens to represent New Jersey in Congress, dating from 1793. "You sort of get it in your blood," he explained.

Powerful clans compete for Potomac Land dominance. The last of the powerful line of Cabot Lodges, for example, was defeated by the first representative of a new line, John F. Kennedy. Kennedy's brother Teddy used his president brother's name to get a Senate seat of his own in 1962 and has kept it to this day. The name has permitted him to withstand scandals that would have destroyed those from lesser lines, from the monstrous (Chappaquiddick) to the simply amusing (Kennedy's speech referring to the nuclear Stockpile Stewardship Program as the "Stockpile Stewardess Program"). In fact, the name even allowed Ted Kennedy's son Patrick to win election to Congress and to survive his own slate of scandals.

The younger Kennedy, a Rhode Island Democrat, crashed his Mustang convertible into a Capitol Police barrier in the wee hours one spring day in 2006. The thirty-eight-year-old lawmaker, his speech slurred and his eyes watery, announced to the surprised cops that he was late for a vote—even though the House was not in session. Police drove him home without demanding a breath test.

After the usual range of written denials and hiding from the press, Kennedy finally paid a visit to the House television gallery, confessing to an addiction to prescription drugs such as Ambien. His hands trembling, he began to speak, but something sounding like "argh" came out and he cleared his throat and began again.

"The incident on Wednesday evening concerns me greatly," he said, tripping over the last word. "I simply do not remember getting out of bed, being pulled over by the police, or being cited for three driving infractions." As he spoke, he began to shake more noticeably. Perspiration built on his upper lip. "I need to seek expert help," he continued. "This afternoon, I'm traveling to Minnesota to seek treatment at the Mayo Clinic." On the decorative bookshelf behind the lectern where he spoke, there was a copy of the Warren Commission's report on his uncle's assassination.

The I-have-an-addiction speech! It was, as one of the reporters there put it, a "get-out-of-jail-free card." Another Kennedy would survive yet another scandal.

Kennedy was not new to the role. He admitted past treatment for cocaine addiction. In 2000, he was caught on film shoving an airport security guard in Los Angeles when she told him his bag was too big for the X-ray machine. That same year, his insurance company settled a claim from a charter boat company that said he did $28,000 of damage to one of their yachts and abandoned it off Martha's Vineyard. The

Coast Guard rescued a woman who had been Kennedy's date from the boat after she had an argument with Kennedy and called for help.

Kennedy was not harmed politically, and he was not cowed. In 2004, Democrats called off a Grateful Dead fund-raiser he planned for the national convention. On the campaign trail, he collapsed during a health-care event at a hospital—and was caught by an emergency room doctor. At another event, Kennedy told young Democrats at a nightclub: "I don't need Bush's tax cut. I have never worked a fucking day in my life."

Nor, evidently, did he take driver's ed. Sometime after the nightclub incident, in Rhode Island an eyewitness said Kennedy was weaving and appeared impaired when he drove against traffic and crashed into another car in a CVS parking lot. Kennedy provided a nearly illegible written statement. This was the same month he required six stitches on his lip after a demonstration in his office involving a hammer went awry.

Kennedy deflected some of the scandals with humor. When Lincoln Chafee, who succeeded his father in the Senate, admitted to using cocaine, Kennedy noted, "Now when I hear someone talking about a Rhode Island politician whose father was a senator and who got to Washington on his family name, used cocaine, and wasn't very smart, I know there is only a fifty-fifty chance it's me."

About the Coast Guard incident and the damaged yacht, Kennedy wrote a song to the tune of the *Gilligan's Island* theme song, and the *Providence Journal-Bulletin* dutifully transcribed it:

> *Just sit right back and you'll hear a tale,*
> *a tale of a fateful trip,*
> *that started in Connecticut,*
> *aboard a damaged ship.*
> *I'd asked a gal whom I had met*
> *to take an evening cruise.*
> *Little did I know that it*
> *would make the evening news.*
> *And, boy, did I get bruised.*

But after the drug-induced Capitol Hill crash, Kennedy needed more than laughs and his surname to save him. After a month at Mayo, he put himself in the care of Jim Ramstad, a Republican congressman and recovering addict. As Kennedy's sponsor, Ramstad visited Kennedy at Mayo, went to court with him, and landed on the front page of the *New York Times* with him. It was a touching, bipartisan tale—and the Kennedy line would live to see the next scandal.

TOTEM POLES

Potomac Man jealously guards his gotra with various rites and rituals. He has developed a wide array of symbols that instantly convey his high place within and among the castes.

At the White House or in the Capitol complex, a person's rank is displayed by the proximity of his parking spot to the building. A person's true rank can be found not in the person's title but by how near the front of Air Force One that person's seat is when the president travels. To make status comparisons simpler across agencies, government bureaucrats are sorted by fourteen grades that determine their salary and clout—and all fourteen are of a lesser grade than the political appointees serving at the president's pleasure.

Among the highest ranking of Potomac Men, status distinctions can be made by gauging the size of the motorcade: just one car for a minor cabinet official, and up to twenty plus motorcycles and a helicopter for the president. Among diplomats, status can be determined by the frequency of visits to the White House, Camp David (better), or the president's ranch (best). Among the lowest of Potomac Men, trinkets show some element of status: a wooden egg from the White House Easter Egg Roll, a Christmas party photo with the president and first lady, or perhaps M&Ms or cuff links with the presidential seal or a certificate stating the bearer flew aboard Air Force One. The most tragic of Potomac Men attempt to display their status by wearing their security badges around their necks during lunch or after work at bars.

Clothing, though important in many cultures, has proven to be an unreliable gauge of Potomac status. During his confirmation interviews, for example, Supreme Court nominee Samuel Alito—automatically one of the most important of Potomac Men—wore an ill-fitting suit, had a shoelace untied, and moved his head in a disconcerting bobblehead motion. The chairman of the Federal Reserve, Ben Bernanke, trying to reassure Wall Street with his testimony before a House committee in 2007, wore a large Band-Aid on one finger and brown socks with his black shoes; his suit jacket was bunched up like a life vest around his neck, and his sleeves were too short. Likewise, journalists, even prominent ones, wear the frayed chinos, blue blazers, and rubber-soled shoes that are the uniform of the trade, while even the lowest White House aide, earning $20,000 a year, wears a sharp business suit every day. On the other hand, nobody was fooled by Bill Reynolds, chief of staff to Senator Arlen Specter, when he attempted to inflate his status by sucking on a cigar in committee meetings as if it were Tammany Hall. And even Potomac Men are unsure what to make of Rob Woodall, who, as chief of staff to a backbench Republican, lived in an office supply closet in a House office building. Mary Ann Akers, who wrote a gossip column for a Capitol Hill newspaper called *Roll Call,* found that the man slept in a storage space known as the cage and had furnished the five-foot-by-ten-foot space with a cot, towel, blanket, and decorative throw pillow.

The need for symbols has made Potomac Man exceedingly vain. Members of Congress—even the men—routinely get plastic surgery and risk public embarrassment by regular trips to the manicurist. Some exhibit their status by appearing busy, as when Bobby Jindal, a Republican congressman from Louisiana, was caught by *Roll Call* sending e-mails from his BlackBerry while attending Ash Wednesday services. Others use symbols to their financial advantage: Rebecca Cox, the wife of a congressman, wore her "spouses pin" on a necklace while visiting the Capitol to lobby for Continental Airlines; this allowed her to reach lawmakers where the public was forbidden.

Even in death, the powerful can demonstrate clout: an Arlington Cemetery burial, a funeral at the National Cathedral (the highest ranking have former senator John Danforth preside), perhaps followed by a reception at the Cosmos Club. The most prestigious of three eating clubs—along with the Metropolitan Club and the University Club—the Cosmos Club takes itself extremely seriously. Haughtily, its members say that the Cosmos is for those with brains, the Metropolitan is for those with money, and University is for those with neither. After the September 11 attacks, the Cosmos Club tasked a committee with developing a continuity of operations plan so that the club could continue to function after a terrorist attack. Its Web site lists the number of Nobel Prize winners and Medal of Freedom winners who have paid dues there. And when the District of Columbia government banned smoking, the Cosmos Club debated whether to seek a hardship exemption for its annual cigar dinner.

One of the best displays of Potomac Land's status obsession, and the role of the Cosmos in it, was uncovered by the Senate committee examining the Jack Abramoff affair. Abramoff wrote an e-mail to a friend who was a rabbi. "I hate to ask you for your help with something so silly but I've been nominated for membership in the Cosmos Club, which is a very distinguished club in Washington, D.C., comprised of Nobel Prize winners, etc.," he wrote. "Problem for me is that most prospective members have received awards and I have received none. I was wondering if you thought it possible that I could put that I have received an award from Toward Tradition with a sufficiently academic title, perhaps something like Scholar of Talmudic Studies? Indeed, it would be even better if it were possible that I received these in years past, if you know what I mean."

The rabbi, conservative radio host Daniel Lapin, gave his blessing. "I just need to know what needs to be produced," he replied. "Letters? Plaques?"

Even among the one hundred members of the Senate, there is a craving for symbolic displays of status. The leading symbol is the chairman's gavel, which entitles the holder to preside over committee meetings and boss around other senators. A chairmanship is, in fact, an anachronism. In the modern Senate, the chamber's leaders determine how legislation will be written and whether it will pass; actions taken by the committee are largely symbolic and are easily overridden if the leadership does not like the results.

Still, the vestigial status of the chairmanship has a powerful appeal to some senators. In 2004, Republican Arlen Specter of Pennsylvania was so keen to become chairman of the Senate Judiciary Committee that he went through a humiliating hazing ritual just to win what was little more than a title.

Specter's saga began the day after he won reelection in 2004 and was next in line to become the committee chairman. Momentarily forgetting that committee chairmen have no actual clout, he called a press conference in Philadelphia and attempted to display his status by warning President Bush not to send his committee judicial nominees who would make abortion illegal. "When you talk about judges who would change the right of a woman to choose, overturn *Roe v. Wade*, I think that is unlikely," he taunted. "And I would expect the president to be mindful of the considerations which I am mentioning."

Conservatives, infuriated by Specter's effrontery, demanded that as punishment he not be given the gavel. "For the social conservatives who just elected Republicans to office for the very purpose of getting sound judges confirmed," the *National Review* thundered, "Specter's elevation would not just be a symbolic slap in the face but an actual betrayal. Find the man another sinecure." The Family Research Council accused Specter of the "height of arrogance and ingratitude."

Specter suddenly realized his precious symbol might be taken away. The next day, he issued a statement reassuring that "I did not warn the president about anything and was very respectful of his constitutional authority on the appointment of federal judges." This wasn't sufficient. Conservatives wanted a full grovel.

"We are looking at a variety of ways to keep the gavel from going to Arlen Specter," a committee staffer told the *Washington Times*.

Specter became frantic. He went on CBS's *Face the Nation* and pleaded, "I have supported all of President Bush's nominees in committee and on the floor. I have never applied a litmus test." While confessing that he was "pro-choice," he assured the world that "I have supported many pro-life nominees." He did a flurry of radio and television interviews pleading the same case.

Specter spent days meeting privately with his colleagues to apologize for his loose tongue. For ninety minutes in Majority Leader Bill Frist's office, Specter begged party leaders to let him have the gavel.

"Arlen has done a tremendous job reaching out to senators over the phone and in person," said Frist, who was not yet offering support. In fact, he stripped Specter of another perk—serving on an ad hoc committee working out a spending deal with the House.

The ten Republicans on the Judiciary Committee held a closed-door meeting to see if Specter had done sufficient groveling. He had not. "I expect him to have the support of the committee," teased the outgoing chairman, Orrin Hatch of Utah. But not just yet. More remorse was required.

While antiabortion forces protested outside, one of the committee Republicans, Jeff Sessions, warned pointedly, "I haven't announced any decision." Said another, Mike DeWine, "I'm just not going to comment."

After more negotiations, Specter and the other senators agreed that he would need to make a more thorough show of contrition in the form of a new and more humiliating statement. "I'm working on it," he said after his private talks.

Finally, two weeks after his offense, Specter offered the full monty. At a press conference with his fellow Republicans, he read a lengthy statement reminiscent of a hostage video. "I have not and would not use a litmus test to deny confirmation to pro-life nominees," he pleaded. "I have voted to confirm Chief Justice Rehnquist after he voted against *Roe v. Wade*. Similarly, I have voted to confirm pro-life nominees Justice Scalia, Justice O'Connor, Justice Kennedy. And I led the successful fight to confirm Justice Thomas, which almost cost me my Senate seat in 1992." Promising "quick committee hearings" for all nominees, he vowed, "I have no reason to believe that I'll be unable to support any individual President Bush finds worthy of nomination. I believe I can help the president get his nominees approved just as I did on confirmation of two controversial Pennsylvania circuit court nominees." The groveling went on and on—and this time, Specter's colleagues were satisfied.

"He deserves to be chairman of this committee and he's going to be," Hatch said. Specter had lost his dignity—but he would get his gavel. In his campaign for the symbolic title, he had lost whatever trace of actual power that might have come with the chairmanship.

Over the next two years, he approved two Supreme Court justices opposed to abortion rights. And while he frequently clashed with the White House or fellow Republicans on matters of policy—over gay marriage, a shield law, immigration, habeas corpus, and wiretapping—in each case he either surrendered or lost the fight.

FALLING STATUS: THE BLOWHARD

The arrival of television cameras in the chambers of power—the House in the late 1970s, the Senate in the 1980s, and the White House briefing room in the 1990s—has given Potomac Man another way to demonstrate, and possibly enhance, his status. It is the notion of face time. The more hours one appears in front of the television cameras, the theory goes, the higher one's Q rating, or public recognition and support. Potomac Men now compete for face time not just in legislative debates but on Sunday network talk shows and, for the lesser officials, cable news. To keep track of this competition, *Roll Call* created a face time list that ranks political figures by the number of appearances on Sunday shows such as *Meet the Press* and *Face the Nation.*

The use of face time to enhance status, however, is double-edged. While face time increases a Potomac Man's profile among people outside Potomac Land, excessive use of the technique can brand the user a publicity whore or a blowhard among his fellow Potomac Men—and cause him to lose the social status of his caste. This leads to a situation in which a Potomac Man can be returned to office repeatedly by voters of his home state but become a subject of ridicule among others in his gotra.

This leads to the cautionary tale of Joe Biden, a Democratic senator from Delaware, who won *U.S. News & World Report*'s "most talkative" award and was first runner-up in *Washingtonian* magazine's "biggest windbag" category. Biden's lungs are legendary. When it was rumored that John Kerry might tap Biden as his secretary of state, journalists joked that Foggy Bottom would no longer need to schedule daily briefings: Biden's daily briefing would merely end when the next day's briefing was ready to begin. Biden used so many words that he briefly ran out and had to use somebody else's; he quit the 1988 presidential race after it was discovered that he had plagiarized remarks by British politician Neil Kinnock.

As a fixture on the Judiciary and Foreign Relations committees, Biden was known for his rambling, self-referential questioning of witnesses. During the confirmation of Chief Justice John Roberts, Biden warned the nominee to give "short answers" and then proceeded to talk for twelve of his allotted twenty minutes. After Biden fired off a series of questions without allowing Roberts to answer, the nominee finally replied, "Well, I was about to lay it out. You said you didn't want to hear about it." Everybody laughed except Biden. Biden reacted to Roberts's answers so theatrically—with pouts, glares, and face in hands—that colleague Lindsey Graham rolled his eyes.

But that was just a prelude to Biden's performance during Samuel Alito's confirmation to the Supreme Court. Given thirty minutes to question the nominee, Biden got off just one question in the first twelve minutes and four in the remaining eighteen minutes. Instead of grilling the nominee, he used his time to speak about his own ethnic roots, his grandfather, his son, his views of the nominee's college, and another senator's eyeglasses.

Following this performance, Biden showed up for the next day's questioning with a Princeton baseball cap.

"I understand, Judge, I am the only one standing between you and lunch. So I'll try to make this painless," he began, then offered to say "a few very brief things." Among them: a speech Biden made in the 1970s and his friendship with Bill Bradley, the former basketball star and senator. Five hundred forty-five words later, Alito tried to interrupt the senator. But Biden continued, for another 1,390 words.

"Here I was, a University of Delaware graduate, a sitting United States senator," he continued. "I didn't even like Princeton. No, I mean, I *really* didn't like Princeton. Yeah, I was an Irish Catholic kid who thought it hadn't changed like you concluded it had. I mean, you know, I admit I have a little—you know, one of my real dilemmas is I have two kids who went to Ivy League schools. I'm not sure my grandfather Finnegan would ever forgive me for allowing that to happen. But all kidding aside, I wasn't a big Princeton fan."

Biden moved on to discuss legal cases, pretending he was an employer and using his colleague Dianne Feinstein as his prop. "Ms. Feinstein, I am not going to hire you because the person seeking the job has a Rhodes Scholarship and I like him better," he said. "And it turns out he wasn't a Rhodes scholar. The real reason is I just don't like your glasses, I don't like the way you look. I'm not being facetious."

Feinstein looked surprised. "I like them," reassured Senator Pat Leahy. "I like the way you look, Dianne. You look okay."

Another monologue followed, before Biden finally closed. "I want to note for maybe the first time in history Biden is forty seconds under his time," he said. Final tally: Biden, 3,673 words; Alito, 1,013.

The reviews were savage and unanimous. "The man has no speed bumps between his brain and his mouth," David Brooks noted in the *New York Times*. *Newsweek* quoted a Democratic committee aide, calling Biden "a blowhard among blowhards." Richard Cohen judged in the *Washington Post*: "The only thing standing between Joe Biden and the presidency is his mouth."

"I deserved a lot of it," Biden confessed later. "I do talk too much."

It only got worse when he assumed the chairmanship of the Senate Foreign Relations Committee in 2007. Holding a much-anticipated hearing on Iraq, his horrified colleagues watched as he ran the hearing as if he were a talk show host. He opened the hearing with a three-thousand-word statement in which he used the word "I" eighty-eight times. Finally, the committee's ranking Republican got a chance to speak. Then Biden spoke again. Senator Chris Dodd, a Connecticut Democrat, introduced an amendment. Biden interrupted him four times, the last time stating, "I don't want to belabor the point."

By this point, Senator John Sununu, a New Hampshire Republican, had heard enough Biden. "We're going to be here a long time, and I'd certainly like to speak," he announced with irritation. Biden yielded the floor to Sununu but then interrupted him, too—five times.

"Senator," Sununu eventually pleaded, "you've had a wonderful opportunity to express your views. I think many on the committee would at least like to express their own views, and I'm sure you'll have ample opportunity to respond."

A week later, Biden announced that he was running for the Democratic nomination for president in 2008—but his mouth destroyed his candidacy before he even had the chance to launch it. On the very day of his presidential announcement, the *New York Observer* published an interview with Biden in which he described one of his presidential opponents, Barack Obama, as being the first black presidential candidate "who is articulate and bright and clean and a nice-looking guy." It was meant as a compliment, but, as frequently happens between Biden's brain and his mouth, something went badly wrong.

REGAINING STATUS

As easy as it is to become outcaste in Potomac Land's caste system, such social shunning is not necessarily permanent. Because of the singular importance of party, anybody who can demonstrate that his skills are useful to the advancement of the party will find that sins and transgressions can be forgiven quickly. Potomac Land relishes a comeback story almost as much as a disgrace, and the streets and halls are full of people who have undergone successful purification rituals.

One of the most notable recoveries in recent years has been that of Manuel Miranda, who in less than two years went from being a fired and disgraced congressional staffer to a key party strategist and hero of religious conservatives—even as he remained under federal investigation.

Between 2001 and 2003, two Republican staffers on the Senate Judiciary Committee hacked into the computers of committee Democrats and downloaded some four thousand files. Miranda, the more prominent of the two staffers, leaked the memos, which showed cooperation between Democrats and liberal interest groups, to conservative newspapers and groups in hopes of damaging the Democratic senators for opposing President Bush's judicial nominees. Before the "memogate" scandal became public, Miranda had worked his way up to being the Senate majority leader's top adviser on judicial nominees. The Senate sergeant at arms concluded in early 2004 that federal laws regarding theft and false statements could have been violated.

"A sad chapter," pronounced then-chairman Orrin Hatch, the Utah Republican, also calling it "unethical" and "simply unacceptable." Bill Frist, the majority leader, offered no defense of Miranda, who was forced to quit. Democrats demanded a special prosecutor.

But Miranda recovered quickly, aided by inertia at the Justice Department (it apparently never took action against Miranda) and unwillingness by the Senate to turn over its findings. This allowed Miranda to be openly defiant. He said the Senate probe "fails to find any criminal hacking or any credible suggestion of criminal acts." A year after his forced resignation, he wrote a law journal article blaming Frist for mishandling his ouster and said Frist "should have stood by me." After he failed to get a lobbying job he sought, he even sent a letter to the Justice Department asking it to investigate the Democrats who had criticized him for violating federal extortion laws.

Meanwhile, Miranda went through an elaborate purification ritual. He got himself a visiting fellowship at the conservative Heritage Foundation, and formed a group called the Third Branch Conference dedicated to conservative judicial nominees. By cleverly uniting conservative groups and using his ties to the media, Miranda became one of the most visible agitators during Supreme Court confirmation battles and played a key role in forcing the withdrawal of Harriet Miers's nomination to the Court because of her insufficient conservatism. *The National Journal* dubbed him "a leading GOP activist" and did a Q&A with him about "re-establishing yourself as a player in Washington."

In his comeback, Miranda followed the model employed by David Bossie, who was forced out of his staff job in Congress in 1998 but reemerged as a vocal conservative leader. In 1998, during the investigation of Bill and Hillary Clinton's land deals, Bossie, as chief investigator for a House committee, edited recordings of telephone conversations to include only damaging information about the Clintons and removed any exculpatory information.

Bossie was fired, but—as Miranda would do later—the disgraced staff member fell into the loving arms of the conservative movement. He became chief of a well-funded advocacy group called Citizens United, which through regular press conferences kept Bossie's name in the news. Then he set out to produce documentary films as a right-wing Michael Moore—answering Moore's *Fahrenheit 9/11* with *Celsius 41.11* (the temperature at which the brain begins to die). The fallen staffer had become a movie mogul.

Rapid falls and rises are possible in Potomac Land because of Potomac Man's short attention span. As long as a person's scandal is in the news, he remains a pariah because his problems are still hurting his party. But once the news stories end, it becomes surprisingly easy for Potomac Man to regain his status.

A fine illustration of this phenomenon has been demonstrated by Trent Lott, Republican senator from Mississippi and one of the most affable of all Potomac Men. A former Ole Miss cheerleader, he created such Potomac institutions as the Singing Senators (a barbershop quartet of lawmakers that appeared with the Oak Ridge Boys) and seersucker Thursdays (in which a third of the Senate risks ridicule for wearing the lightweight stripes). He was also a celebrated deal maker, serving as Senate Republican leader for years. He was about to become Senate majority leader again in 2002 after Republican election victories but then lost his perch at the unlikeliest of places—a hundredth birthday party for a fellow senator, Strom Thurmond.

Recalling Thurmond's segregationist presidential campaign of 1948, Lott ad-libbed, "I want to say this about my state: When Strom Thurmond ran for president, we voted for him. We're proud of it. And if the rest of the country had followed our lead, we wouldn't have had all these problems over all these years, either."

Proud? Thurmond had said during that campaign: "All the laws of Washington and all the bayonets of the Army cannot force the Negro into our homes, our schools, our churches."

This was a problem. After a couple of days, the remarks blossomed into a front-page scandal. Lott apologized. "A poor choice of words conveyed to some the impression that I embraced the discarded policies of the past," he said in a written statement. That was obviously insufficient, so he appeared in the public and said his words were "terrible and insensitive." This didn't help much, and Republicans began to whisper about whether Lott had become a hindrance to the party.

The next day, Bush went to a mostly black audience in Philadelphia and cut Lott loose. "He has apologized, and rightly so," Bush said. "Every day our nation was segregated was a day that America was unfaithful to our founding ideals." The lowly Lott issued another statement: "Senator Lott agrees with President Bush that his words were wrong, and he is sorry." He worked the phones, apologizing to his fellow Republican senators for the harm done.

But the whispering wouldn't stop, and so eight days after his offense, Lott offered his third apology, this time in a news conference. "I'm asking for forbearance and forgiveness as I continue to learn from my own mistakes," he pleaded. He explained that he was "winging it" that night and confessed anew that his words were "totally unacceptable and insensitive, and I apologize for that."

Word came back from Potomac Land: not good enough. Lott gave his fourth apology the next day. "I only hope that people will find it in their heart to forgive me for that grievous mistake," he said. In a new low for groveling, he even announced that he would amplify his regrets on Black Entertainment Television. His staff sent out papers showing his support for African American causes. In the BET interview, he decried the "wrong and wicked" history of the South and stunned friend and foe alike by announcing his newfound enthusiasm for affirmative action.

The meek and obsequious route worked well for Specter, but it did not work at all for Lott; his transgression had been too visible for the party to ignore without serious political damage. Bush sent out word that he wanted Lott out, and he wanted a junior and relatively malleable senator, Frist, to replace him. A "senior Republican official" dropped the hint in the *Washington Post*: "The president is allowing the process to work itself out in a way that will seem natural and doesn't have a lot of fingerprints on it." In public, Bush aides refused to back Lott. With Bush's blessing, Frist began his campaign to oust Lott. The next day, Lott resigned his leadership position.

The controversy ended abruptly. Frist took over and quickly established himself as a weak leader. Lott, embracing Potomac Man's most tested recovery plan, wrote a book in which he called Frist's act "a personal betrayal." He took glee in punishing the White House and GOP leaders. Lott was one of the early detractors of Harriet Miers's nomination to the Supreme Court, and stood outside the Senate chamber the day she withdrew and sang "Happy Days Are Here Again." He suggested that Bush should dump his top strategist, Karl Rove; branded White House aides "all young and inexperienced"; and accused the president of "cronyism." And when lawmakers were furious about a national-security leak, Lott suggested they blame themselves. "We have met the enemy, and the enemy is us," he ventured.

While Lott threw bombs, colleagues pined for the orderly way in which he had run the Senate. Reporters went to him for quotes; senators went to him for advice. Three years after his fall, Lott dared to muse to reporters about a possible return to leadership. The *Chicago Tribune* called Lott the "shadow Senate leader" and had one Senate colleague calling Frist "a majority leader who can't run a conga line."

Senator Lindsey Graham, the South Carolina Republican, observed a Potomac Land truism: It's the man, not the position, that carries status. "Senator Lott is as relevant as ever," Graham said. "He has proved to me that leadership is more than just a title."

Finally, eight days after the Republicans' defeat in the 2006 midterm elections, Lott got his title—or some of it—restored. By one vote, his colleagues chose him to become the number two GOP leader in the Senate—in exchange for a promise by Lott to control his mouth. His vanquished opponent, Lamar Alexander, reasoned that "Senators, like Americans, like a comeback."

Lott's supporters, logs in their eyes, were willing to ignore his speck. "We all believe in redemption," Senator John McCain said after the vote. "Thank God."

THE ROLE OF FIGUREHEADS

Visitors to Potomac Land generally assume that those in the highest-ranking positions—president, Speaker, majority leader, cabinet secretary—are the most powerful figures. This assumption is as wrong as it is common. For Potomac Man prefers a government of figureheads, in which the truly powerful Potomac Men install genial, nonthreatening leaders to serve as the public face of power. The nominal head of a totemic clan—say, the House Republicans—is merely a symbol. The real, private face of power tends to be less attractive but far savvier.

While George Bush is the titular president, for example, he was put in that position largely by longtime adviser Karl Rove. Though Bush is typically described as "the most powerful man in the world," and this is technically true, he takes direction from Rove and from the vice president, Dick Cheney. Likewise, former Senate majority leader Bill Frist was installed by Rove and his colleagues in the White House after they orchestrated the ouster of Frist's predecessor, Trent Lott. Frist, a relative novice when he took the job, remained far from the most powerful Senate Republican even as the nominal leader; that role went to people such as John McCain of Arizona. A similar experience confronts members of the president's cabinet. Though they are, by title, in charge of massive agencies such as the Treasury and State departments, they in fact take orders from young White House aides who are unknown to the public. Forced to testify in federal court in 2007, Cathie Martin, a relatively junior White House official, described how she and colleagues coerced the head of the CIA, George Tenet, to take the fall for a scandal. After "delicate" talks with Tenet, who far outranked her, Martin told how Tenet agreed to issue a statement saying "I am responsible."

Perhaps the most readily identifiable figurehead in Potomac Land in recent years was Denny Hastert, who was nominally the Speaker of the House and thus third in line to the presidency. But it is commonly known among Potomac Men that Hastert was put in his position by—and served at the pleasure of—his underlings. He was routinely called the "accidental Speaker."

The son of an embalmer and a feed supply entrepreneur, Hastert was a high school history teacher and wrestling coach. He married a phys ed teacher. He got elected to the Illinois state house in 1980—by accident. He came in third place in the primary, but party elders chose him anyway after the incumbent died. Six years later, party leaders again installed Hastert on the ballot—this time for Congress when the local congressman was dying of cancer.

Hastert had an unremarkable career in Congress until 1994, when he agreed to be the campaign manager for Tom "the Hammer" DeLay, the Machiavellian Texan seeking to become House majority whip. DeLay won, and chose Hastert as his chief deputy; Hastert got an office inside DeLay's suite and shared his staff.

When the powerful House Speaker, Newt Gingrich, quit in 1998, Hastert ran for the number two position in the House, majority leader. Out of 221 votes cast, Hastert got 18, losing on the first ballot. "I don't feel bad," he said bravely. But just a few weeks later, when the heir to the speakership, Bob Livingston, resigned because of an adultery scandal, DeLay hatched a plan. DeLay knew he was too controversial to become Speaker himself, so he championed Hastert for the speakership, expecting that Hastert, known as "Coach," would do the Hammer's bidding.

Thus did Hastert, in 1999, become the accidental Speaker. He proved so inoffensive to his powerful handlers that he remained in his job for seven years, longer than any other Republican Speaker in history. Hastert, a huge and rumpled figure, became the public face of the House, even though the Potomac Men knew he was not truly in charge. The press found the lumbering Speaker clownish, as when he went to an energy-conservation event a few blocks from the Capitol—and was caught on film sneaking in and out of his Chevy Suburban. Publicly, DeLay said "Hastert is his own man." Privately, DeLay aides told reporters Hastert was DeLay's figurehead. When Hastert strayed, as when he backed gun-control legislation, DeLay reined him in.

This all worked well enough until DeLay was forced to resign in 2005 because of a series of scandals. Hastert had lost his protector, and ambitious Republicans turned on the figurehead. In 2006, somebody leaked a (false) report to ABC News that Hastert was under investigation in the Abramoff scandal, and Hastert blamed the White House. "This is one of the leaks that come out to try to, you know, intimidate people," he told Chicago's WGN Radio. "We're just not going to be intimidated on it." He suggested the White House was retaliating against him for an earlier disagreement.

"False, false, false," retorted White House spokesman Tony Snow.

In the House, Republican unity crumbled and GOP members openly condemned the party leadership as "clueless." When word broke in 2006 that a Republican congressman, Mark Foley of Florida, had been preying on teenage boys who had been House pages, Republican leaders blamed Hastert for the party's failure to hold Foley to account before the scandal became public.

Representative John Boehner of Ohio, who had replaced DeLay as the House's number two, told a hometown radio station that the blame was all Hastert's. "I believe I talked to the Speaker and he told me it had been taken care of," Boehner said. "And my position is, it's in his corner, it's his responsibility."

Not clear enough? "The clerk of the House, who runs the page program, the Page Board—all report to the Speaker," Boehner declared.

Representative Tom Reynolds of New York, the chairman of the National Republican Congressional Committee, also blamed Hastert for failing to act earlier to protect boys in the congressional page program from Foley's overtures. "I heard something; I took it to my supervisor," Reynolds said, as if he were a Wal-Mart associate.

Republican media outlets took up the cry. "Resign, Mr. Speaker," advised the *Washington Times* at the top of its editorial page. Hastert, the paper said, either (a) "was grossly negligent" or (b) "deliberately looked the other way." The *National Review* found Hastert and his team guilty of "serious sins of omission," while the magazine's Larry Kudlow joined the resignation calls and labeled Hastert "an ineffective leader." Republican talk radio host Neal Boortz said Hastert needed to find a "better excuse" for his handling of Foley.

As Hastert suffered the ignominy of going before a House Ethics investigation of the Foley matter, the figurehead went on the conservative airwaves to appeal for calm and understanding. The calls for his resignation eventually stopped—but only because people became convinced that Hastert would be stepping down in a few months anyway.

Hastert, his status shattered by the Foley affair, became a joke overnight. Days into the Foley scandal, Hastert was duped by a con man posing as a Christian evangelist. He talked his way into Hastert's home in Illinois by offering the Speaker spiritual counseling regarding the Foley crisis. Instead, the man, Indian-born K. A. Paul, who believes he is on a "crusade" to save America from Republicans, advised Hastert to step down. It later emerged that Paul had talked himself into similar audiences with Slobodan Milosevic and Saddam Hussein.

After the Republican defeat in the 2006 midterm elections, Hastert bowed to the inevitable and resigned his speakership. He took his place easily among the backbenchers. When Nancy Pelosi, a California Democrat, was sworn in as Speaker in January 2007, Hastert could be seen in the back row of the chamber, smoldering.

RESPECT FOR TRIBAL ELDERS

How, then, does the outsider gauge the status of a Potomac Man? One method is to count the number of staffers. In this sense, Potomac Land operates under the cattle complex that has been attributed to some East African cultures: the more animals in the herd, the higher the status of the owner. But this has limited use. The secretary of the interior, for example, has some eighty thousand employees, but his presence barely registers. By contrast, Senator John McCain has a mere twenty-five staffers in Washington, but there is no more powerful man in Potomac Land.

A better shorthand, though far from foolproof, is to judge a Potomac Man by his seniority. There was a time seniority was all important, particularly in Congress. Cardinals—the chairman of the various appropriations subcommittees—held firm control over the government's spending. The most ancient lawmakers led all the committees, and junior members deferred to their senior colleagues. That is rarely the case anymore: Charismatic figures such as Barack Obama become instant leaders, while those with previous Potomac Land experience (such as Congressman Rahm Emanuel, a former Clinton White House official) vault ahead of their more senior colleagues in leadership. And senior lawmakers such as Congressman Christopher Shays, a Connecticut Republican, are frequently passed over for chairmanships in favor of more junior officials who are more faithful to party leaders.

Potomac Land's vestigial traditions still favor those with the most extensive experience. This is particularly so in the Senate, where relatively young lawmakers nominally lead the chamber but older lawmakers, known as old bulls, invariably get things their way.

Outside Potomac Land, the name of Senator Ted Stevens, if it is said at all, is said with a smirk. The eighty-three-year-old Republican from Alaska, a fixture in the Senate for thirty-eight years, gained national attention in June 2006 when, as chairman of the Senate Commerce Committee, he delivered an eleven-minute lecture about the Internet.

"The Internet is not something you just dump something on. It's not a truck. It's a series of tubes," he explained. "And if you don't understand, those tubes can be filled. And if they are filled, when you put your message in, it gets in line and it's going to be delayed by anyone that puts into that tube enormous amounts of material."

The lecture was not done. "I, just the other day, got an Internet [that] was sent by my staff at ten o'clock in the morning on Friday and I just got it yesterday," he explained. "Why? Because it got tangled up with all these things going on the Internet commercially."

Stevens instantly earned himself a place of honor on the Web, where his rantings were remixed into a rap song, and on late night television. Web sites dedicated themselves to ridiculing him. But the laughter was muffled among the many Potomac Men who depend on Stevens for their livelihood. As a longtime member and former chairman of the Appropriations Committee, he used his thirty-eight years in the Senate to master the arcane spending process—eventually gaining almost complete mastery over it. He built himself into the undisputed champion pork barrel spender in Congress, eclipsing even Robert Byrd, the legendary West Virginia Democrat. It's no coinci-

dence that the two masters of pork are the ones with the greatest seniority; both Stevens and Byrd have served as Senate president pro
tempore, an honorary title reserved for the longest serving. The two
men are the main reason the "appropriators," as they are known, are
sometimes called Potomac Land's third political party.

In 2006, Stevens won an Oinker award from Citizens Against
Government Waste for directing $325 million in pork for Alaska.
Alaska that year got $490 in pork for every man, woman, and child in
the state (the national average is $30), and it has led all states in pork
receipts for years. The group Taxpayers for Common Sense similarly
calculated that Stevens beat all other senators in securing nearly $700
for every resident of Alaska in the 2005 defense spending bill. Stevens
himself has boasted about securing more than $5 billion for Alaska
projects since 2001. A grateful Alaska, which gets back $1.80 for every
$1 it sends to Washington in taxes, named the Anchorage airport after
Stevens. The FBI was less impressed with Stevens's largess: In 2007,
investigators asked him to preserve his records as part of their move
into an Alaska corruption investigation.

Stevens relies on his encyclopedic knowledge of the Senate's
quirky procedures—and his highly public temper tantrums. When fellow Republican Tom Coburn of Oklahoma tried to cut a $223 million
Bridge to Nowhere championed by Stevens (it linked an island inhabited by only fifty people), the old bull went to the Senate floor and
vowed that if Coburn prevailed, "I will resign from this body." He got
his money.

After a setback in his quixotic bid to open the Arctic National
Wildlife Refuge to oil drilling, he declared at a press conference: "I'm
really depressed. As a matter of fact, I'm seriously—I'm seriously depressed. Unfortunately, clinically depressed." He later told Alaska reporters that he had received no such diagnosis. When a newspaper
reported that he was helping fishing interests who hired his son,
Stevens threatened to investigate the newspaper chain's circulation
figures.

Stevens, who has called himself a "mean, miserable SOB," has
punished those who oppose him by denying them committee assignments and attempting to move federal funds out of their states. When

Maria Cantwell, a Washington Democrat, tried to get Stevens to put oil executives under oath at a hearing he was holding, Stevens stood by his oil friends. "It's the decision of the chairman, and I have made that decision," he lectured.

"I move that we swear in witnesses," Cantwell persisted.

"That's the last we're going to hear about that, because it's out of order," Stevens replied. He informed them that "I intend to be respectful of the position that these gentlemen hold."

Coburn, who defied Stevens on the Bridge to Nowhere, got worse treatment. When Coburn sponsored legislation to create more openness and "transparency" in the awarding of government contracts, Stevens stopped the bill by putting a secret hold on it. The irony evident to all—using a secret maneuver to block legislation devoted to openness—did not register in the tubes of Stevens's mind.

Ultimately, Stevens's earmarking found a more formidable foe than Coburn. In the summer of 2007, the FBI raided the senator's Alaska home as part of a probe into Stevens's earmarks. The feds took particular interest in his wine cellar.

Two

KINSHIP

Homo politicus sets himself apart from virtually all other people by adhering to a kinship system that is not based primarily on blood relationships. Potomac Man does honor the conventional family definitions of parent, child, sibling, and spouse, but these are not the overriding determinants of kinship. Rather, Potomac Man defines his kin by party affiliation. Consider the case of one of Potomac Land's most celebrated couples, Mary Matalin and James Carville. Though husband and wife, they belong to different tribes—she's a Republican and he's a Democrat—and this is a more important tie than matrimony. On election night in 2004, as reported by Bob Woodward, Matalin was with President Bush and Vice President Cheney when she took a call from her husband. He told her—in what couples in other cultures would assume to be a private, conjugal conversation—that John Kerry's campaign was going to challenge the results of the Ohio vote, which had gone to Bush. Matalin immediately told Bush and Cheney, giving their campaign crucial time to prepare its strategy and response in advance of Kerry's public announcement. Carville is her husband, but Bush and Cheney are her family.

This notion of fictive kinship—defining family by something other than bloodlines—is practiced elsewhere. On the Malaysian island of Langkawi, families often feed and shelter children who do not belong to them. In Nepal, likewise, teenagers of the Gurung people join youth associations, known as Rodi, in which children of different households prepare for adulthood in the home of an adoptive Rodi father and mother. But neither form of fictive kinship is as pervasive as Potomac Land's strict division into Republican and Democratic clans, which, more than family, determines the arc of Potomac Man's life. To keep these fictive ties close, both parties engage in regular rites of intensification and rites of solidarity—fund-raisers, voter registration drives, primaries, rallies, and the incessant repetition of talking points designed to make everybody in one party say the same words.

Party determines many of life's important choices in Potomac Land. Influential Republicans live in suburban Virginia, particularly McLean. Powerful Democrats live in upper northwest Washington or Montgomery County, Maryland. Establishment Republicans, such as the attorney general and numerous members of Congress, attend the Falls Church, which is Episcopalian, or the megachurch known as McLean Bible, home to the likes of Ken Starr and young Bush White House aides. Orthodox Jews from the Democratic side such as Joe Lieberman, find their way to Kesher Israel in Georgetown; observant Republican Jews seek the counsel of Rabbi Daniel Lapin, a radio talk show host. Republican Catholics attend Blessed Sacrament in Chevy Chase; Democratic Catholics prefer Holy Trinity in Georgetown. Elite Democrats, such as Bill and Hillary Clinton, send their children to Sidwell Friends School in northwest Washington; prominent Republicans, such as Antonin Scalia, send their children to Langley High or, in the case of the Cheney grandchildren, the Potomac School in McLean, Virginia.

FAMILY ESTRANGEMENT

Because Potomac Man regards party as the primary measure of kinship, estrangement from party can be particularly painful. While the people of Potomac Land can change their religions and even their spouses without arousing much notice, a change in party identification is a major event. David Brock, a writer for the conservative magazine *The American Spectator,* became a bestselling author by confessing, in a book titled *Blinded by the Right,* how he abandoned his life as a "right-wing hit man." He has since become a left-wing hit man. Likewise, Bruce Fein, a Reagan administration lawyer, has become a celebrity witness for congressional Democrats, who repeatedly invite him to testify because he will reliably condemn the Bush administration's actions.

The stakes are even higher when an elected Potomac Man turns against his kin. Jim Jeffords, a Republican senator from Vermont, quit the Republican Party in 2001 after the White House and fellow Republicans savaged him and the education programs he supported. This set off a serious round of domestic violence in the Republican family. The senator received death threats so worrisome that Capitol Police thought it necessary to assign Jeffords a security detail. At Republican National Committee headquarters, somebody put a photo of the apostate in one of the urinals. The defection, which shifted control of the Senate temporarily to the Democrats, earned Jeffords labels such as "extremist," "political dinosaur," "traitor," and "backstabber" in the conservative press.

The Republican Senate leader, Trent Lott, accused Jeffords of launching a "coup of one." The Vermont Republican Party labeled him "morally dishonest." A Republican congressman distributed Jim Jeffords barf bags as a fund-raiser. Karl Rove went on television to suggest Jeffords acted on ambition, not principle, citing "talk around town about committee chairs and deals and bargains."

"My colleagues, many of them my friends for years, may find it difficult in their hearts to befriend me any longer," Jeffords accurately predicted when he defected. Worse, they vowed revenge: To get at Jeffords, they would kill the New England dairy compact, which protected Vermont farmers. In Potomac Land, all policy is about loyalty.

Five years later, a defecting Democratic senator got even worse treatment from his colleagues. And Joe Lieberman, who became an Independent, did so only because he was forced to when he lost the Democratic primary to left-wing candidate Ned Lamont. But the moment Lieberman announced he would run for reelection as an Independent, Democrats denounced their newfound enemy. Forty of the forty-five Senate Democrats, spooked by left-wing bloggers who favored Lamont, announced that they would support Lamont over the man who, just six years before, was the party's vice presidential nominee.

John Kerry, the former Democratic presidential nominee for whom Lieberman campaigned actively in 2004, went on television to proclaim: "Joe Lieberman is out of step with the people of Connecticut." When Lieberman returned to the Senate floor after his primary defeat, Democratic leaders kept a distance from him; they discreetly turned their backs or, if cornered, offered him a perfunctory greeting. Even Chris Dodd, Lieberman's colleague from Connecticut, denounced his "friend" to reporters. "Joe made a decision to do what he wanted to do, and other people respect the decision by voters," he said angrily. "You don't just disregard that, okay?"

Even that didn't satisfy the left-wing bloggers. Arianna Huffington, who created the Huffington Post, demanded Democrats "do everything in their power—publicly and privately—to pressure Lieberman to drop his For the Sake of My Ego run." She also ordered them to strip Lieberman of his committee assignments and seniority and treat him like "a party-ditching, party-pooping, control-of-Congress-risking spoiler, i.e., a danger to the party."

Only the Republicans, hoping Lieberman would go all the way and join their party, embraced the apostate. "I'd be happy to have him in our party," offered Lott.

Lieberman tried to be philosophical. "Hey, you know, that's politics," the pariah told reporters. "I understand the rules of the game." Under those same rules, Lieberman won the general election a few months later—forcing his Democratic colleagues into a permanent state of sycophancy to prevent the Independent from joining the GOP.

On the other hand, it is perhaps even more dangerous for Potomac Man to keep an apostate in his party. Democrats learned this the hard way in 2004 when they continued to treat as kin a Democratic senator from Georgia, Zell Miller, who had quit the party in everything but name. After supporting Bush's legislative program, Miller wrote a book about the Democrats titled *A National Party No More*. Then he went to the Republican convention to give a speech endorsing Bush's re-election.

Glowering from the podium and shouting in a deranged fashion, Miller, an old Marine, denounced his party's nominee with a frightening bitterness. Attacking Kerry, in many cases falsely, for opposing weapons systems, Miller hollered, "This is the man who wants to be the commander in chief of our U.S. Armed Forces? U.S. forces armed with what? Spitballs?"

Further, the hysterical Miller yelled, "Kerry would let Paris decide when America needs defending," and Kerry "wants to outsource our national security." Kerry, Miller continued, gives the terrorists "a 'yes-no-maybe' bowl of mush that can only encourage our enemies and confuse our friends."

The speech was only the beginning of the insanity. After the tirade, he appeared on MSNBC with *Hardball* host Chris Matthews, where Miller was peppered with Matthews's typical rapid-fire questioning: "Do you believe that John Kerry and Ted Kennedy really only believe in defending America with spitballs? . . . You really believe that John Kerry and Ted Kennedy do not believe in defending the country? . . . That kind of rhetoric is not educational, is it?"

It wasn't unusual questioning, but Miller became livid. "I wish I was over there, where I could get a little closer up into your face," he told Matthews. "You are saying a bunch of baloney that didn't have anything to do with what I said up there."

Matthews pressed: "Do you believe, Senator, truthfully, that John Kerry wants to defend the country with spitballs?"

Miller informed Matthews that "we ought to cancel this interview," called him "hopeless," and advised him to "get out of my face" even though they were not in the same studio. Finally, the senator blurted out, "I wish we lived in the day where you could challenge a person to a duel." He also wondered if Matthews would "shut up."

"Well," Matthews said after the Miller assault ended, "that was an unexpected turn of events."

Miller—newly dubbed Godzella by alarmed Democrats—still wasn't finished. He wrote a memo to Democratic candidates in Georgia, leaked to the *Atlanta Journal-Constitution,* saying state Democratic leaders were "a Board of Deacons for Democratic Disaster." He advised them to "get Kerry from around your neck, and do it quickly and loudly."

"At least he didn't challenge me to a duel," one of the disaster deacons replied.

RITES OF PURIFICATION

Potomac Man operates under a principle stated most eloquently by Grover Norquist, a Republican activist. "Bipartisanship is another name for date rape," he told the *Denver Post* in 2003. "We are trying to change the tone," he continued, "toward bitter nastiness and partisanship."

Each clan in Potomac Land has several self-declared enforcers of loyalty. These men—unelected activists, for the most part—set standards for membership in the clan and seek to remove those who have been impure. Though they spend a good bit of time warring with those of the other party, they are at least as interested in setting kinship qualifications in their own.

These purification rites are dangerous business. After the Reverend Richard Cizik, policy director of the National Association of Evangelicals, spoke about the need to reduce global warming, prominent conservatives such as James Dobson and Tony Perkins, both enforcers of Republican purity, demanded he be dismissed or silenced. When the White House was aggravated by leaks from the CIA critical of Bush's actions in Iraq and gloomy about the prospects there, the president ordered in a new director, Republican congressman Porter Goss. Goss and several of his congressional aides, dubbed Gosslings by agency officials, purged the CIA of many of its top officials, reasoning that, even though they were mostly Republican, they were insufficiently loyal to Bush. But the professional spooks at the CIA proved resourceful, and managed within a couple of years to get Goss himself ousted in favor of a career military-intelligence man more to their liking.

In a similar instance, the Bush White House sought to purify the Justice Department by firing eight U.S. attorneys, its chief prosecutors, because they were insufficiently loyal to the Bush agenda; an e-mail from the department to the White House said they wanted to replace those who were not "loyal Bushies." The dismissals came even though the fired prosecutors had received high marks on their performance reviews. In one case, the U.S. attorney in Little Rock, Arkansas, was removed so that he could be replaced by a thirty-year-old military lawyer who worked for Karl Rove and the Republican National Committee. In other cases, the prosecutors were fired after Republican lawmakers' complaints that they weren't prosecuting more Democrats and seeking out more cases of pro-Democratic voter fraud. Investigators found that Justice officials hired career prosecutors based on their Republican bona fides—apparently in violation of federal law.

Among loyalty enforcers, Norquist, a short, bearded, troll-like figure, is perhaps the most accomplished. In 1986, Norquist, then a young man from Harvard, drafted a loyalty pledge directed primarily at Republican candidates for office. The candidate signs a pledge to "oppose any and all efforts to increase the marginal income tax rates for individuals and/or businesses" and to "oppose any net reduction or elimination of deductions and credits, unless matched dollar for dollar by further reducing tax rates."

Norquist's organization, Americans for Tax Reform, is quite proud of its pledge. Some 95 percent of House Republicans have signed on the dotted line, as have 85 percent of Senate Republicans, several governors, and more than 1,200 state legislators. Norquist runs a Hall of Shame for Pledge Breakers to keep the pressure on, and for egregious offenders he also keeps an Enemies of the Taxpayer list. Norquist notes with some glee that breaking the pledge is "career-ending" and likes to cite George H. W. Bush as the best example; his son, the current president, has stuck by his pledge.

The career-ending threat is not necessarily true, but the troll is very scary nonetheless. It was Norquist, after all, who said in 2001 that he would like to drag government "into the bathroom and drown it in the bathtub." When former Bush budget director Mitch Daniels, a pledge signer, decided to raise taxes as governor of Indiana, Norquist wrote to the state's legislators: "I urge you to prevent Governor Daniels from closing Indiana for business." Daniels couldn't believe how quickly he had been excommunicated. "Two years ago, Grover was giving me the Hero of the American Taxpayer Award," he marveled to the *Indianapolis Star*.

When another Norquist friend, Colorado governor and presidential aspirant Bill Owens, allowed a tax increase, Norquist scolded the Republican in the *New York Times,* calling him "beyond weak-kneed" and threatening: "He's finished nationally." Ohio's Republican governor, Bob Taft, was labeled "a serial tax increaser" by Norquist. When one Kentucky legislator asked Norquist to release him from the tax pledge, Norquist, according to a letter intercepted by *U.S. News & World Report,* wrote back in sorrow: "I do not have the power to release you. . . . Only your voters can do that."

Addressing College Republicans, Norquist branded three unreliable Republicans, Maine senators Olympia Snowe and Susan Collins and Arizona senator John McCain, as "the two girls from Maine and the nut job from Arizona." Norquist later joked that he should have called McCain "the gun grabbing tax increaser from Arizona."

When McCain helped negotiate a compromise with Democrats over Bush's judicial nominees, Norquist erupted: "When McCain brokered the deal to betray his Republican colleagues by negotiating a private surrender to the Democrats, he publicly declared he has no interest in the presidency. No Republican could expect to win the GOP nod after betraying his party's rank and file on one of their most central concerns."

To maintain unity—and purity—in the Republican Party, Norquist convenes a weekly breakfast meeting of movement conservatives at his offices downtown, known informally as the Wednesday meeting. Participants call it the Grand Central Station of conservatism, assembling religious conservatives, libertarians, gun owners, and establishment types under the umbrella of what Norquist calls the "leave us alone coalition." To the opposition, they resemble the cantina aliens in *Star Wars*.

Norquist, surrounded by one hundred conservatives, makes the sessions off the record, except in the frequent event that he is being profiled by a journalist. The group hears a plea from a representative of the Bush White House, and likely some congressional leaders, then discusses who's in, who's out, and what good Republicans should be saying about each issue on everything from the Supreme Court to foreign policy. Convener Norquist also cross-pollinates with his breakfast partners; he's on the board of the National Rifle Association.

Party members who run afoul of Norquist get punishments ranging from the label of RINO (Republican in name only) to a challenge in the GOP primary. Those supportive of Norquist's aims can find a lucrative lobbying position as part of Norquist's K Street Project, a help-wanted listing that encourages corporate groups to hire only Republicans, even as receptionists.

As a matter of policy, Norquist's efforts to cut the size of government have not had a huge impact: Spending has been growing at a record pace during the Bush years. But the experience has not been entirely bad for Norquist; the opponent of large government served as a paid agent of the Seychelles and its leftist leader, attempting to secure as much funding as possible to benefit the islands off Africa. Unfortunately for a man dedicated to purifying the party, Norquist also did business with his longtime friend from his days with the College Republicans, felonious superlobbyist Jack Abramoff.

Senate Finance Committee Democrats issued a report in 2006, sanctioned by the Republican chairman, concluding that Norquist's was one of five conservative groups that "appear to have perpetrated a fraud" on taxpayers by selling their influence to Abramoff. Norquist, they said, arranged White House meetings with the likes of Karl Rove or placed opinion articles—for a fee.

At Abramoff's direction, DH2, a mutual fund company, arranged to pay Norquist $50,000 in 2004 for an opinion piece arguing for tax breaks for its customers. "Get the money from [DH2] in hand," Abramoff wrote to one of his assistants, "and then we'll call Grover." Later, Abramoff wrote to Norquist: "I have sent over a $50K contribution from DH2 (the mutual fund client). Any sense as to where we are on the op-ed placement?"

"The *Wash. Times* told me they were running the piece," Norquist answered. "I will nudge again."

Even Abramoff knew such arrangements were shaky enough that he wrote to a colleague to keep it quiet. "We do not want the opponents to think that we are trying to buy the taxpayer movement," he wrote. Other Abramoff offers to Norquist were less lucrative: an "economic analysis" purchased for $3,000, another op-ed for $1,500. Abramoff advised a beverage company that Norquist would help it fight a tax if the company became "a major player in ATR." Norquist also served as a conduit for Abramoff to send more than $1 million of his tribal clients' money to operatives such as Ralph Reed. "Grover kept another $25K!" Abramoff wrote to himself in one e-mail complaining about Norquist's skimming.

At one point when Norquist was awaiting money from Abramoff's client, he wrote to the lobbyist: "What is the status of the Choctaw stuff? . . . I have a 75g hole in my budget from last year. Ouch."

Ouch was right. When word of his compromises came out, Norquist blamed politics—and an old foe, Republican presidential candidate John McCain, who had launched an investigation into Abramoff and his Norquist ties. "John McCain thinks he can't be president if I'm standing here saying he's got a problem with taxes," Norquist reasoned.

McCain's chief of staff, Mark Salter, retaliated: "Obviously, Grover is not well. It would be cruel of us to respond in kind."

Indeed, some of Norquist's old breakfast friends began to turn on the loyalty enforcer. "Grover's not that likable," one of them told the *Washington Post*. Another wondered "whose interests Grover is serving." A third posited that Norquist had ties to terrorist sympathizers. It was cruel treatment for the man who imposed Republican purity—but, then again, he hadn't made anybody sign a pledge promising to be nice.

Kin Selection

In Sarasota, Florida, in 2005, Jan Schneider was on her way to winning the Democratic Party's congressional nomination for a third straight time. But then Rahm Emanuel, chairman of the Democratic Congressional Campaign Committee, wrote a check for a Schneider opponent, Christine Jennings. Other national Democrats did the same. It wasn't much money, but it was a sign to Schneider: Get out. "They can't impose candidates on us from Washington," Schneider protested in the *Sarasota Herald-Tribune*.

Oh yes they can. A year later, Jennings trounced Schneider in the Democratic primary.

While evolution generally predicts the survival of the fittest, there is an exception known as kin selection. Under this theory, an animal will show self-sacrificing behavior toward relatives—not out of altruism but because this increases the likelihood that genes similar to his own will survive. Potomac Man offers strong confirmation of this theory. Members of both parties have demonstrated a willingness to sacrifice themselves—giving vast quantities of time and money, and surrendering ideological preferences—to secure the election of others from the same party.

Emanuel, is, at first glance, a misanthropic personality: The Democratic congressman from Chicago, a one-time ballet student, is known for his obscenity-laced speech; he engages in public fights and confrontations and is so rough in his ways that those who worked with him in Bill Clinton's 1992 presidential campaign came to call him Rahmbo. He once committed the tired cliché of sending rotten fish to a pollster who gave him bad advice. He lost part of his middle finger in a meat-slicer accident as a teenager, allowing him to press the stump into the chest of whomever he is arguing with. Always fighting with somebody, he confessed to his hometown *Chicago Tribune*: "I wake up some mornings hating me, too."

But Emanuel is a true believer in Democratic altruism. Taking over the Democratic Congressional Campaign Committee at the end of 2004, he decreed that each of the Democrats in Congress would have to pay $100,000 to $600,000 in dues to the party to spend on other Democrats' elections. Only Democrats in the party's Frontline program—those facing tough challenges themselves from Republicans—were exempt. After months of threats and pleading, and quarterly bills, Emanuel got all but sixteen of the two hundred

House Democrats to pay their dues. In some cases, he merely threatened to deny delinquents the use of phones, mailing lists, and party facilities; in extreme cases, he threatened to take the congressmen off plum committees. He also publicly humiliated the delinquents by sending a list of their names to all colleagues.

Members of the Congressional Black Caucus, who tend to represent poorer districts, complained of harassment by Emanuel and said that he hadn't hired enough black staffers. "I don't give a [expletive]," he responded, in the *Tribune*. Democratic leader Nancy Pelosi created an ad hoc group to ease the tension between Emanuel and black Democrats. In addition to bruised egos, Emanuel's harassment produced tens of millions of dollars in Democratic dues by the spring of 2006—double the amount the Republicans raised.

As head of the Democratic Congressional Campaign Committee, Emanuel also had the task of determining which candidates were the fittest to survive—and then giving them the dues money. In addition to Jennings in Florida, Emanuel and his colleagues forced his preferred candidates on Democratic primary voters across the country—in New Hampshire, New York, Illinois, Ohio, and elsewhere. In New Hampshire, local activists howled about being disenfranchised by Democratic kingmakers. In New York, after Emanuel decided on his preferred candidate, rival Democrat Les Roberts complained to *The Hill* newspaper that Emanuel and his committee "stopped answering our calls, and we can't get our brochure on their Web site."

Emanuel, a moderate by inclination, didn't care whether the candidates he recruited were liberal or conservative, reasoning, "I don't give a crap," as long as they could raise lots of money. If they hit their own targets, he sent his committee's money their way—a record $120 million in all. If they didn't, they were eliminated from the national committee's list.

When Howard Dean, the Democratic National Committee chairman, didn't direct enough of the party's money to the House campaign, Emanuel stormed out of Dean's office, shouting obscenities. Emanuel later told the *Tribune* he lectured Dean: "I know your field plan. It doesn't exist. . . . There's no plan, Howard." Emanuel then leaked a letter to Dean demanding $100,000 of DNC money for each tightly fought race. It's also no great coincidence that Alcee Hastings, a Florida Democrat who crossed Emanuel, was denied the chairmanship of the Intelligence Committee.

On the other hand, Emanuel could be downright solicitous when attempting to select his kin. Trying to convince Heath Shuler, a former pro football player, to run for Congress, Emanuel called him at all hours of the day until Shuler finally agreed. Shuler was an antiabortion, evangelical Christian—an ideology with almost nothing in common with Emanuel's—but for Emanuel, all that mattered was Shuler's party affiliation. The Democrat now represents the 11th district of North Carolina in Congress. The night that Shuler and two dozen other Democratic candidates gave the party control of the House for the first time in twelve years, Emanuel jumped on a desk and, in the company of his staff, colleagues, and a *Tribune* reporter, had some advice for the Republican Party: "They can go fuck themselves."

RITES OF SOLIDARITY

As a national capital, Potomac Land honors many of the solidarity rituals that bind other Americans: a pledge of allegiance; a national anthem; the copious display of flags on buildings, in photographs, and on lapels. But while he tolerates this symbolism because it plays so well outside Potomac Land, Potomac Man's genuine efforts at solidarity are within his own political party. Members of Congress meet Wednesday for breakfast with their party caucuses. Senators do the same over lunch on Tuesdays. The White House issues talking points to lawmakers so that each member of the party will be "on message" and deliver the same party line. Those who are the most adept at sticking to the talking points become known as surrogates for the president, meaning that what they say is a strong gauge of what the president would say.

There is no better surrogate in Potomac Land than John Cornyn, Republican senator from President Bush's home state of Texas. He voted with the president's wishes 98 percent of the time in 2003, slipped to 96 percent in 2004, then bounced back to 98 percent in

2005. And he has proven a tireless defender of the president's policies and nominees—sometimes even outdoing the White House in his defense of the White House's positions.

At 1:42 P.M. on July 19, 2005, Cornyn's office issued an embargoed speech in anticipation of President Bush's selection of a Supreme Court nominee. "Just minutes ago the president announced his nominee to the Supreme Court: Judge Edith Brown Clement, currently serving on the U.S. Court of Appeals for the Fifth Circuit," Cornyn wrote. "Judge Clement is an exceptional jurist, a brilliant legal mind, and a woman of outstanding character who understands her profound duty to follow the law. She has enjoyed a distinguished history of public service and professional achievement. It is clear to me that Judge Clement's history has prepared her well for the honor of serving this country on our nation's highest court, and I strongly support her nomination."

The statement went on to recite Clement's biography and demanded "personal respect for this fine nominee."

There was only problem. President Bush did not nominate Edith Clement. He selected John Roberts.

Cornyn, a flexible surrogate, quickly adjusted his talking points. "Judge Roberts is an exceptional judge, brilliant legal mind, and a man of outstanding character who understands his profound duty to follow the law," he said after learning of the true nominee. "I think clearly, Judge Roberts should be a consensus nominee."

Since arriving in the Senate in 2002, Cornyn has shown solidarity with the president on the full range of issues, as his press releases attest: "Cornyn Applauds President's Signing of Bill to Provide Tax Relief for Texans" . . . "Cornyn: President's Plan Will Make America Safer" . . . "Cornyn Praises Senate's Confirmation of Dr. Robert Gates" . . . "Cornyn Applauds Appointment of Cybersecurity Chief." Such constant applause almost certainly puts Cornyn at a high risk for a repetitive motion injury.

When Democrats delayed confirmation of Condoleezza Rice as secretary of state, Cornyn went to the Senate floor to condemn the "inappropriate partisan attacks" and said Democratic "foolishness" risked "adopting our enemy's view of the world." During battles to confirm Bush's judicial nominees, Cornyn said he could see how judicial rulings could lead people to "engage in violence."

When Roberts was nominated, Cornyn went to the cameras to proclaim Roberts probably "the most qualified nominee who has ever been put up for a Supreme Court vacancy." Though Democrats mounted no concerted opposition to Roberts, Cornyn nonetheless condemned them for having a "game plan" to do so. During the Judiciary Committee's hearings for Roberts, Cornyn distributed laminated cards labeled CRYING WOLF BINGO with words such as "Ideologue!" "Partisan!" "Far Right!" "Zealot!" "Extremist!" An accompanying news release chronicled "the sad history of attacks against previous nominees."

Even when fellow Republicans turned against a Bush nominee, as they did with Harriet Miers's nomination to the Supreme Court, Cornyn remained faithful. While conservatives labeled her unqualified, Cornyn pleaded with them to "reserve judgment" and promised that she has "ample qualifications" and is an "engaging person." He hosted the nominee in his office, where they discussed such legal matters as the weather in Austin. Cornyn looked around. "What else should we talk about?" he asked, as the cameras rolled. Miers sat silently and stiffly as Cornyn told the cameras, "She fills a very real and important gap" on a Supreme Court filled with Ivy Leaguers and Beltway intellectuals. Miers nodded when the senator called her a "real leader."

When Miers finally pulled out of consideration under pressure, Cornyn told reporters it was the fault of unnecessary contentiousness and partisanship. When a questioner pointed out that the objections came primarily from Republicans, Cornyn shouted back, incorrectly, "There is no Republican senator who opposed the nominee. Your statement was wrong!"

Nominees from the other party, naturally, received no such chivalry. Recalling the Clinton nomination of Ruth Ginsburg to the court, Cornyn alleged that she supported "prostitution and polygamy, and she opposed Mother's and Father's Days as discriminatory occasions."

When Karl Rove and other Bush aides were accused of unmasking a CIA operative for political reasons, Cornyn went before ABC News to proclaim the matter was "confined to a single individual." When Democatic senator Russ Feingold got former Nixon aide John Dean to testify at a hearing about abuses by President Bush, Cornyn denounced Dean as "a convicted felon" trying to sell a book—then left the hearing.

During the confirmation of Samuel Alito to the Supreme Court, Cornyn put his show of solidarity to verse, suggesting the other side would not give the nominee a fair hearing.

"Twas one month before the hearings, and all through the city," he wrote, "Not many Democrats were waiting, not even some on the committee."

New York Democrat Chuck Schumer reciprocated: "On Alito, they say, he deserves confirmation, but don't wait for hearings, just accept coronation."

Cornyn supported Bush's handling of the war in Iraq—a selfless gesture that even some hardened Bush surrogates refused. "We've got some very good news!" he proclaimed after the killing of a terrorist leader in Iraq. "The Democratic Party," he argued, is "looking success in the face and snatching defeat out of the jaws of victory."

Cornyn certainly is not the only Potomac Man to offer such conspicuous demonstrations of solidarity. When it was noted that President Bush appeared to have lost weight, his first chief of staff, Andy Card, reasoned: "I think what you might be seeing is a redistribution of weight. He's exercised with a little more vigor these days, because he's anxious to rout out the terrorists." Card was also the guy who, in 2004, went with White House counsel Alberto Gonzales to the hospital bed of Attorney General John Ashcroft and tried to get the ill and incapacitated man to overrule the Justice Department's objections to Bush's plan to conduct wiretaps without warrants.

Of course, Card was paid to defend Bush. In his selfless solidarity, Cornyn is more like Harry Whittington, the seventy-eight-year-old Texan who suffered a heart attack after he was shot in a hunting accident by Vice President Cheney. "My family and I are deeply sorry for all that Vice President Cheney and his family have had to go through this past week," the victim said, still full of bird shot.

Is there anything in it for Cornyn? Well, sometimes the president rewards the solidarity. And some have dared to talk about a John Cornyn nomination to the Supreme Court. Asked by reporters if he would accept, Cornyn melted: "Well, you know, if the president calls me, obviously I'll answer the phone or go see him, if he invites me to come to the White House," he said.

The phone call never came. Finally, in 2007, with Bush's standing below 30 percent in the polls, Cornyn broke with the White House over immigration legislation.

RITES OF INTENSIFICATION

Former Senate Republican leader Bob Dole once observed that the most dangerous place in Potomac Land is between Chuck Schumer and a television camera. And it's true: The Democratic senator from New York gives more press conferences than any other Potomac Man, sometimes three in a day.

Here he is giving a press conference on the minimum wage. There he is holding forth on Democratic election prospects. And Iraq and trade with China and taxes. And gas prices, cybersecurity, stem-cell research, student debt, port security, Jack Abramoff, Medicare, the CIA, Hurricane Katrina, contracting policies, and Supreme Court nominations.

Some of Schumer's fellow Democrats grumble about his efforts to insert himself into media coverage. But most realize that he is performing an important function for the party: the Rite of Intensification. Christians have confirmation, penance, anointing, and the Eucharist. The nearest equivalent in Potomac Land is the press conference—a time for the party faithful to reaffirm their beliefs in the presence of reporters and cameras. It helps the tribe to remain cohesive in times of strain.

In the summer of 2006, few in Potomac Land expected the Democrats would gain control of the Senate, where they had a five-seat deficit. Experts at the time could see a gain of four or five but not the necessary six. So Schumer called a press conference and announced his own forecast: a nine-seat gain. Even by usual standards of Potomac hyperbole, the message seemed absurd.

He was asked about Nevada, where Democrat Jack Carter trailed by twenty-one points. "Jack Carter has done a very good job. . . . Nevada is moving up on our radar screen. . . . We are getting more and more enthusiastic about Nevada."

And Arizona, where a poll found the Republican eighteen points ahead of Democrat Jim Pederson? "We're feeling better and better. . . . Our candidate Jim Pederson is running a great race. . . . The public seems to like what he says."

Asked if any races were not going well for Democrats, he was stumped. "Hmmmm," he replied.

"How about Maine?" a reporter offered. Polls showed Senator Olympia Snowe (a Republican) leading Democrat Jean Hay Bright by fifty points, and Democrats had likened Snowe's popularity in Maine to that of Jesus.

"Yeah," Schumer agreed. "Maine isn't going very well at all." But overall, he maintained, "We're doing amazingly well and better than we ever thought."

Nobody in the room actually believed Schumer. Nor did Schumer pay much attention to what he was saying; he mixed metaphors like a Cuisinart. "They're trying to find a new rabbit to pull out of the hat, but so far they've gone back to the old chestnuts," he said of the Republicans.

But that wasn't the point. Schumer's role in the intensification rite was not to be accurate but to demonstrate his faith. And in the end, Democrats gained six seats, not Schumer's nine, but enough for the majority.

CLAN TOTEMISM

Among certain aboriginals in Australia, it is common to be born into an animal clan that counts as its members both humans and furrier forms. Men in the kangaroo clan are responsible not just for the well-being of other people in the clan but for the kangaroo population. Same for the koala and the kookaburra. Each clan performs increase rituals to enhance reproduction of the kindred animal.

In Potomac Land, both Republicans and Democrats will go to extraordinary lengths to perform increase rituals for their totemic elephants and donkeys—even using foreign wars to grow their numbers.

There is a quaint aphorism in Potomac Land: "Politics stops at the water's edge." It's doubtful this was ever true, but it is, in any event, a rather comic notion to modern Potomac Man. In his view, foreign affairs are merely a way to extend the competition between Democrats and Republicans.

After the invasion of Iraq in 2003, the Pentagon screened applicants for jobs in Baghdad to make sure they were loyal Republicans. As the *Washington Post*'s Baghdad bureau chief, Rajiv Chandrasekaran, wrote in his book, *Imperial Life in the Emerald City*, a political appointee named Jim O'Beirne, husband of conservative commentator Kate O'Beirne, made sure applicants voted for Bush, inquired whether they supported Bush's policies, and in some cases ascertained that they opposed legal abortion. Instead of hiring experts who spoke Arabic and knew the region, the Pentagon sent children of friends, graduates of evangelical universities, and candidates submitted by Republican activists and members of Congress. To rebuild Iraq's health-care system, the administration decided to dismiss Frederick Burkle, a naval reserve officer and official at the U.S. Agency for International Development, with degrees in medicine and public health from schools including Harvard and Yale. Burkle was told a "loyalist" would take his place: a man who had been the community health director in Michigan for Governor John Engler, a top Bush fund-raiser. The loyalist's tenure was, predictably, disastrous: Instead of the emergency medical care Iraq desperately needed, he emphasized an antismoking program and an effort to revise the country's list of prescription drugs.

By law and custom, uniformed members of the military avoid politics. But this, like many other of the official edicts in Potomac Land, is widely ignored in practice. Increasingly, the top generals, the Joint Chiefs of Staff, are selected by political appointees in the Pentagon with an eye toward the generals' malleability. Just before Marine general Peter Pace was promoted to chairman of the Joint Chiefs, fellow Marine general James Jones, the NATO commander, warned him against taking the assignment. "You should not be the parrot on the secretary's shoulder," Jones said, according to Bob Woodward's account of events, which was not disputed by Jones.

The parrot problem surfaced almost immediately for Pace, as a number of retired generals complained about the disastrous situation in Iraq and demanded Defense Secretary Donald Rumsfeld's resignation. Jones himself, in Woodward's *State of Denial,* expressed his view that the Iraq war was a "debacle" and that "the Joint Chiefs have been systematically emasculated by Rumsfeld." Retired colonel Larry Wilkerson, former chief of staff at the State Department, accused Rumsfeld of participating in a "cabal" that had set new lows for "aberrations, bastardizations, perturbations, changes to the national security decision-making process."

Retired general John Batiste, the former commander of the Army's 1st Infantry Division in Iraq, went before Democratic members of Congress and labeled Rumsfeld "not competent" and surrounded by "compliant subordinates." He and other retired brass said pleas for more troops in Iraq were routinely ignored.

And Pace? Call him Polly. When the generals demanded Rumsfeld's ouster, Pace stood at a briefing lectern with Rumsfeld and pronounced "zero questions" about his leadership. "The fact of the matter is that the folks who are out doing this nation's business are appreciative of the leadership that's being provided," he attested. And Pace insisted that his commanders hadn't even dreamed of asking for more troops in Iraq. "Whatever troop level that commanders have asked for has been provided to them," he said, repeating Bush's formulation, on ABC News.

Just weeks before Rumsfeld was sacked, Pace went even further, saying Rumsfeld was divinely inspired. "He leads in a way that the good Lord tells him is best for our country," Pace said. Rumsfeld's "patriotism, focus, energy, drive, is exceeded by no one else I know." It wasn't soldierly—but it was loyal.

Alas, for Pace, the loss of his patron led to his own demise six months later, when Rumsfeld's successor, Bob Gates, declined to renominate Pace. "I've been told I'm done," the general reported.

Three

HUNTING AND GATHERING

In the tongue of the Piscataway Indians who first occupied Potomac Land, the word "Potomac" means "where the goods are brought in." The economy is little changed from the days when Native Americans inhabited modern-day Washington, and Homo politicus is still judged a failure or a success by his ability to bring in the goods.

Potomac Man's economy is primitive, prone to sharp swings between feast and famine depending on whether or not his tribe is in power. It is closest to the agrarian model of boom and bust: When your party is in control, there is unimaginable plenty; when your party is out of power, you may be forced to subsist on insects.

In this sense, Potomac Land's economy is closest in form to those of the native tribes of Melanesia, who organize themselves under something called the Big Man concept. These Pacific tribes are too small and disorganized even to be governed by chiefs. Rather, they are led by a collection of competing, ambitious Big Men: self-made figures who gain power by showering gifts on their followers. The Big Man has no actual authority; his power comes merely from his ability—usually fleeting—to influence others. The Big Man amasses the largest possible assortment of tangible wealth: shells, sheepskins, yams, wives. He demonstrates his wealth, and thereby gains clout, by favoring his fellow tribesmen with large *moka,* or gifts. Through this generosity, the Big Man wins the hearts and minds of his followers, who do as he tells them. The arrangement is inherently unstable, and it is common for Big Men to rise and fall in their relative power. While chiefs in nearby Polynesia have an inherited authority, the Melanesian Big Man secures his authority only through his largesse.

So it is in Potomac Land as well. The aspiring Big Man—"lobbyist," in Potomac Man parlance—seeks favors from elected officials while doubling as a fund-raiser for Potomac Man elections. These ambitious figures direct hundreds of millions of dollars in political contributions to elected officials in their respective parties, making it more likely that the officials remain in power. In a reciprocal gesture, officeholders then pass legislation enriching the lobbyists' clients, thereby enriching the Big Man, which in turn generates more campaign contributions for a larger number of lawmaker followers. In Potomac Land's economy, it is not the officeholder who is the true source of power but the Big Man who provides the funding that puts his followers into these positions.

Once Republicans gained unified control of the government in 2001—the White House, Senate, and House were all Republican— they expanded what they called the K Street Project to force companies and trade groups to hire Republican lobbyists. As the K Street Project reached its height in 2003, Republican Big Men earned thirty-three of thirty-six top-level lobbying positions. The few who dared to hire Democrats were threatened with retaliation. When the Motion Picture Association of America hired a Democrat, a K Street Project leader warned that the group's "ability to work with the House and Senate is greatly reduced." When Amgen did the same thing, the K Street group warned, ominously: "It's going to be treated seriously."

For the outside observer of Potomac culture, the K Street Project has had a greatly beneficial effect: the creation of the most elaborate and showy presentations of *moka* that Potomac Land has ever seen.

TRIBAL AFFAIRS

Perhaps the biggest of Big Men in Potomac Land in recent years was Jack Abramoff, whose *moka* would have impressed even a jaded Melanesian tribesman. Fortunately for those studying Potomac Man, Abramoff left anthropologists with extensive documentation as he became big among the Big Men.

"Let's get some more fucking money," he wrote in one e-mail.

"Can you smell money?" he wrote in another.

Abramoff could. In just nine months in 2002, he earned $12 million from Native American tribes who were his lobbying clients. He spent $69,000 for a family vacation and $232,000 on personal travel, mostly aboard charter jets. He bought a BMW for $134,000, paid $69,000 for a driver, ran up $103,000 in credit card charges, and contributed $28,000 to lawmakers. He leased four skyboxes at arenas and stadiums for $1 million a year. He flew government officials on golfing trips to Scotland and Saipan. For charitable work, he started a Jewish school for boys. He gave jobs to former congressional staffers and paid money to lawmakers' wives. He started a high-end restaurant across from the National Archives, called it Signatures, and gave free meals to lawmakers and their aides.

Abramoff's method: From his days as a College Republican, Abramoff was close to top Republican operatives such as Ralph Reed and Grover Norquist. He was friendly with Tom DeLay, Bob Ney, and other congressional leaders, and with Bush aides such as Karl Rove, who hired Abramoff's former assistant to work for him in the White House. He was a Pioneer, one of President Bush's top fund-raisers. And he used these contacts to make himself fabulously wealthy.

In just four years, various firms in which he had an interest hauled in more than $82 million, mostly from unsuspecting tribes who had plenty of gambling money and wanted to make sure their casinos were protected in Washington. Along the way, he worked out kickbacks for himself by creating schemes with playful names such as Gimme Five.

Unfortunately for Abramoff, he didn't get much done for his Native American clients, whom he described in e-mails as "morons" and "troglodytes" and "knuckleheads." And other lobbyists, losing their Native American clients to Abramoff, began to grumble. In 2004, the *Washington Post* ran a story about the accusations. Within two years, Abramoff pleaded guilty to fraud, tax evasion, and conspiring to bribe public officials, accepting a decade in prison and restitution of more than $26 million.

Perhaps most damaging to Abramoff as a Potomac Man was the release by government investigators of his e-mails.

On racquetball: "I'm a fat pig so you should whoop me."

On prospective clients: "I'd love to get our mitts on that moolah."

On his clients: "I have to meet with the monkeys from the Choctaw."

On his business: "We need that moolah. . . . We need to get some $ from those monkeys!! . . . We really need mo money."

And so Abramoff found himself on a January day in 2006 in the federal courthouse three blocks from Signatures, which had closed and had been converted into an Italian seafood restaurant. Abramoff arrived at court in his best gangster attire: black fedora and raincoat.

"I just want to say words will not ever be able to express my sorrow and my profound regret for all my actions and mistakes," Abramoff, slouched over the defense table, said quickly and softly into the microphone. "For all of my remaining days, I will feel tremendous sadness and regret for my conduct and for what I have done. I only hope that I can merit forgiveness from the Almighty and from those I have wronged or caused to suffer."

The once-athletic lobbyist was now overweight and stuffed into his double-breasted suit. He accepted soothing pats on the back from his lawyer, Abbe Lowell, before a pack of one hundred journalists chased the pair to their car.

Abramoff was back in court the next day, this time in Florida and wearing a baseball cap, to plead guilty to fraud and conspiracy over his purchase of casino boats with a counterfeit document. The company went bankrupt and its previous owner was killed in a gangland-style hit; two associates of Abramoff's partner in the venture were charged with the killing.

Even then many a Potomac Man asked another whether Abramoff

had done anything different from thousands of other Potomac Men in the lobbying trade. A congressman wrote to the judge for leniency. So did a local physician, who recalled Abramoff "trying to find a lost hamster on a Friday night." Abramoff's former clients from the Northern Mariana Islands wrote in his defense. A rabbi wrote to say that Abramoff was not your "average criminal." So did a Washington lawyer, praising Abramoff for opening the kosher deli "at great personal sacrifice." He made no mention of the kosher pigs.

There was rather less sympathy the further one got from Washington and the realm of Potomac Man. Accepting a Golden Globe award, actor George Clooney used his brief national audience to muse, "Who would name their kid Jack with the last words 'off' at the end of your last name? No wonder that guy is screwed up."

This drew a rebuke from Frank Abramoff, Jack's seventy-eight-year-old dad, who published a letter to Clooney in the Palm Springs newspaper scolding Clooney for his "glib and ridiculous attack," which drove "my sweet twelve-year-old granddaughter" to tears.

"You can't really respond for your kid," replied Nick Clooney, seventy-two, responding for his.

ART AND ARTIFACTS

Because Potomac Man's economic model is so primitive and his markets so inefficient, both officeholders and Big Men have trouble determining just how much must be paid in the form of *moka,* or campaign contributions, to get the Big Man the desired amount of federal money for a business project.

To simplify the process, Randy "Duke" Cunningham, a California Republican congressman, worked with defense contractor Mitchell Wade to determine list prices for various official acts. They devised a list, written on one of Cunningham's congressional notecards:

16 BT 140
17 50
18 50

19 50
20 50
21 25
22 25
23 25
24 25
25 25

What this meant is that in order for his company to receive a $16 million defense contract, Wade would have to give Cunningham a yacht (BT, or "buoy toy") worth $140,000. For each additional million dollars, Wade would give Cunningham $50,000. If the contract went above $20 million, Cunningham charged Wade a reduced rate of $25,000 per million dollars.

Prosecutors later described this as a "bribery menu" and said Cunningham had put a "For Sale sign upon our nation's capital." But in fact, Wade and Cunningham had merely developed a more efficient variation of what is routinely done by Potomac Man: giving lawmakers campaign cash and receiving huge government grants in return.

Between 1994 and 2004, the number of earmarks, congressional funds for pet projects, has grown from 4,155 to 14,211, worth nearly $53 billion. And the House Appropriations Committee—on which Cunningham had a seat—is the main vehicle for these awards. In 2005, the Appropriations Committee received ten thousand earmark requests on just one spending bill. Even after the House passed a transparency rule to discourage earmarking, the military spending bill passed in 2006 contained 2,800 earmarks worth $11 billion.

A dozen members of the Appropriations Committee have recruited lobbyists with business before the committee to be their campaign fund-raising chiefs. Wade merely took one step out of the process: instead of giving Cunningham just campaign cash in exchange for contracts, he gave him actual cash.

In November 2001, Wade spent $12,000 buying the lawmaker three nightstands, a leaded-glass cabinet, a washstand, a buffet, and four armoires. Cunningham, in return, promised to make Wade "somebody." Over the next year, Wade gave Cunningham $50,000 in cash, $6,600 for a leather sofa and sleigh bed, $7,200 for a Louis Phillipe period commode (circa 1850) and a Restoration period commode (circa 1830), $31,000 to buy and repair a used Rolls-Royce, use of the $140,000 "buoy toy" yacht on Cunningham's menu (the congressman renamed the forty-two-foot boat *Duke-stir*), and $25,000 for boat repairs and yacht club fees.

Then things started to get out of hand. In 2003, Wade sold the congressman a GMC Suburban for half its market value. He paid $4,600 for Cunningham's trip to the Greenbrier resort and jewelry purchased there. Wade bought his congressman a laser shooting simulator; spent tens of thousands more on antiques and entertainment; and, finally, bought Cunningham's home—worth under $1 million—for $1,675,000. He, along with other contractors, retired Cunningham's mortgage on the new mansion he bought. No need was overlooked: In May 2004, Wade paid $2,100 for a graduation party for Cunningham's daughter. That same year, Wade walked into the Caucus Room, a Washington steakhouse started by lobbyists, and handed Cunningham an envelope with $6,500 in cash.

Wade favored other lawmakers, too. He arranged for $46,000 in phony "straw contributions" to Representative Virgil Goode, a Virginia Republican, and $32,000 for Representative Katherine Harris, a Florida Republican. He also spent $2,800 taking Harris to dinner at Citronelle in Georgetown and offered to host a fund-raiser for her. In all, Wade himself gave more than $300,000 in campaign contributions. Cunningham got a large share of it.

In return? Goode got Wade's company a $9 million contract. Harris struck out on a $10 million project Wade wanted. But Cunningham was the real mother lode. He helped Wade's business, MZM Inc., grow from revenues below a million a year to tens of millions a year. From no federal contacts in fiscal year 2002, he got $170 million worth over the next three years.

The exchanges were perfectly transparent. The month after MZM got a $140,000 contract for computer programming in the White House, Wade paid $140,000 for the buoy toy. Soon after that, Wade got a five-year blanket purchase agreement allowing MZM to get up to $225 million in Pentagon contracts—without competitive bidding.

Wade pleaded guilty to paying Cunningham bribes of more than $1 million. Cunningham's guilty plea said he took $2.4 million in total. Then there was "co-conspirator number 1," Wade's mentor, fellow defense contractor Brent Wilkes. Wilkes gave Cunningham more than $600,000 in bribes and gifts, according to prosecutors. The FBI is examining Wade's charge that his old friend provided Cunningham with prostitutes as part of some wild poker parties Wilkes hosted in his hospitality suites in the Watergate Hotel. Among those alleged to have attended: the third-ranking official at the CIA, Wilkes's college roommate Dusty Foggo; and Foggo's boss, CIA director Porter Goss. The rumors were denied, but both men soon stepped down, and the CIA's inspector general launched an investigation of Foggo's activities.

In February 2007, Foggo and Wilkes were both indicted on bribery charges, and federal authorities provided an impressive list of *moka* to accompany the indictments. Among the gifts Wilkes and subordinates gave Cunningham: two Sea-Doo Speedster watercraft, catered dinners on the yacht, an inflatable dock, a computer, tickets to the Super Bowl and a Jimmy Buffett concert, a $4,000 meal in Las Vegas, golf equipment, a "fully automatic machine gun shooting session" in Idaho, and various trips and vacations such as a $6,600-per-night suite in Hawaii, including the services of two prostitutes. Foggo demanded relatively little for his efforts to get Wilkes CIA contracts: trips to Scotland and Hawaii, a job offer, and a cigar humidor.

Duke enjoyed one measure of revenge, when the White House arranged for his prosecutor to be fired. But that was too late for Cunningham, who had nobody but his fellow inmates to regale with tales about his time as a Navy pilot in Vietnam, which, he has said, inspired parts of the movie *Top Gun*. He shot down five MiGs and became the first ace of the war. Once in Congress, he was still on war footing. "I have flown an F-14 over this Capitol with a twenty-millimeter gun that could shoot six thousand rounds a minute," he boasted in one debate. "I could disintegrate this hall in a half-second burst." He said Democrats who would cut defense spending were the same ones "who would put homos in the military." He proposed that House Democratic leaders should be "lined up and shot." He engaged in a shoving match with Jim Moran, a Democrat from Virginia, when they disagreed about sending troops to the Balkans. At one speech to constituents in 1998, he flipped his middle finger at a constituent and announced that a rectal exam he had received was "just not natural, unless maybe you're Barney Frank."

It was a different Duke who, outside a San Diego courthouse in 2005, wept as he read a statement about his guilty plea. "In my life," he said, "I have had great joy and great sorrow, and now I know great shame."

MOKA PARTNERS

As Wilkes and Wade demonstrated, the Potomac Big Man has an impressive menu of *moka* available to win an official's following—and no shortage of public officials happy to accept the gifts. There was, for example, Congressman John Doolittle, a California Republican on the House Appropriations Committee, who helped Wilkes get $37 million worth of government contracts; Wilkes and people tied to him gave $118,000 to Doolittle's political action committee, and about 15 percent of that was skimmed off in the form of consulting fees—to Doolittle's wife. In April 2007, the FBI searched the home office of Julie Doolittle. Investigators are also examining the committee's former chairman, Jerry Lewis, and the hundreds of thousands of dollars raised for him by lobbyist Bill Lowery. Lowery gave fat paychecks to former Lewis aides, while Lewis directed millions of government dollars to Lowery's clients.

Abramoff was arguably the most creative in his *moka* giving. One White House staffer asked Abramoff for four floor tickets, worth $1,300, to a Washington Wizards basketball game. "You got 'em," Abramoff replied. An aide to former House majority leader Tom DeLay, Tony Rudy, received use of a skybox for a bachelor party at a Redskins game and tickets to football games, a NASCAR race, hockey playoffs, and the U.S. Open golf tournament. He also got to hop around the country on a private jet and secured nearly $100,000 for his wife's consulting firm. Also receiving Abramoff's gifts were Representative Bob Ney, an Ohio Republican, and one of his aides,

Neil Volz. There were trips to Scotland; New Orleans; Lake George; and Tempe, Arizona. There were tickets to the Fiesta Bowl and to Abramoff's skyboxes at Washington's MCI Center and Baltimore's Camden Yards.

In return for the *moka,* Ney was dubbed a "champion" by Abramoff and his team: He met with Abramoff clients, got one of them a contract, sponsored legislation, and put comments into the *Congressional Record.* These transactions also got Rudy, Volz, and Ney prime seats in a federal courthouse where, like Abramoff, they entered guilty pleas for their activities.

For every Big Man who falls from power, there is another available to take his place. In 2007, the *Wall Street Journal* reported a series of e-mails written by software entrepreneur Warren Trepp as he and his wife were about to go on a Caribbean cruise with Congressman Jim Gibbons, a Republican who is now governor of Nevada, and his wife. "Please don't forget to bring the money you promised Jim and Dawn," Trepp's wife wrote to him. He responded, "Don't you ever send this kind of message to me! Erase this message from your computer right now!" In addition to the gifts, Trepp, who has several government software contracts, and his relatives gave more than $30,000 to the Gibbonses in campaign contributions. Gibbons must have been under a great deal of stress after taking such gifts; in October 2006, a Las Vegas cocktail waitress accused him of shoving her against the wall of a parking garage and threatening her because she rejected his sexual advances.

Fortunately for the aspiring Big Man, there are plenty of office-holders in Potomac Land willing to do favors in exchange for gifts. This is true even in the executive branch, where the officials are appointed and therefore not in need of campaign contributions. For these officials, the *moka* comes in the form of luxury gifts and offers of future employment.

David Safavian got both. As chief of staff of the General Services Administration, which administers the government's vast real estate holdings, he was in a position to help Abramoff get two pieces of land he was seeking. Safavian tipped off Abramoff about the government's plans for the properties and arranged for him to have access to the relevant people at GSA. In exchange, Abramoff dangled the prospect of a lucrative lobbying career to Safavian, who had worked previously for Abramoff. The lobbyist also treated the official to endless rounds of golf, including a lavish golfing trip to Scotland's St. Andrews.

Federal prosecutors released a thick stack of e-mails detailing their exploits on the greens.

"Can't pull weekday golf until I'm a bit more ensconced as chief of staff," Safavian writes.

"Loser!" Abramoff replies. "I told you to come with me and not the gov!! You'd be playing golf non-stop."

"Do you want me to see if [GSA chief] Steve Perry wants to join you?" Safavian wants to know.

Abramoff sends Safavian a blank e-mail with the subject line "Golf Friday? Golf Monday? Golf Sunday? Golf golf golf!!!"

Finally, the men are ready for a change. "Want to go to the Redskins game on Sunday?" Abramoff offers. Safavian counters with a racquetball-and-lunch proposal.

The winter comes and Abramoff makes Safavian another offer. "I'll be in Florida for the Nickles tournament. (Join me?)"

"I am a hard-working civil servant," Safavian replies, "and I have the people's business to do."

For all the people's business Safavian did, a federal jury found him guilty of lying and obstructing justice as part of the government's Abramoff probe. The offenses carried up to twenty years in jail and $1 million in fines.

A few months before Safavian's troubles became public, the *Federal Times* asked Safavian for the "best career advancement advice you ever got."

"The best advice I've gotten," he replied, "was from my grandfather, and that advice is, you've got to have ethics and integrity in everything you do. Especially here in D.C. It's such a small town that if you gain a reputation as someone who does not play by the rules, that does not do things with integrity, your career is ended."

Fore!

THE BIG MAN AND THE SEA

It is important to remember that being a Big Man requires neither noble birth nor innate intelligence; it merely requires the ability to deliver the *moka*. Consider this exchange between Abramoff and his partner, Michael Scanlon:

Abramoff: The f'ing troglodytes didn't vote on you today. Dammit.

Scanlon: What's a troglodyte?

Abramoff: What am I—a dictionary? :) it's a lower form of existence basically.

But it didn't take great smarts for Scanlon, a former lifeguard who became a spokesman for congressional boss Tom DeLay, to learn that he could turn his connections into millions of dollars. All he had to do was get his friend Abramoff to direct the tribes' money his way and secretly send half back to Abramoff. The two had a compatible business style.

"Fire up the jet, baby—we're going to El Paso!!" Abramoff said to Scanlon about a new tribal client in Texas.

"I want all their MONEY!!!" said Scanlon.

"Yawzah!" replied Abramoff.

Before long, Scanlon had bought a mansion on the Delaware coast, property in St. Barts, and a pad at the Ritz-Carlton in Washington. And he even had the generosity to bring his old lifeguard friend from Rehoboth Beach, Delaware, into the *moka* transaction. Unfortunately for the lifeguard, David Grosh, all he got was $2,500, tickets to a hockey game, and a demand that he appear before a Senate committee probing Abramoff.

"I'm embarrassed and disgusted to be a part of this whole thing," said Grosh, who had switched from lifeguarding to excavation work and tending bar. "The Lakota Indians have a word, *wasichu,* which aptly describes all of us right now."

Grosh didn't say what *wasichu* means—literally, "he who steals the fat"—but it was apt. He and a friend, a yoga instructor, agreed to run a think tank out of a Rehoboth beach house. The think tank advertised itself as "bringing great minds together from all over the globe" under the "high-power directorship" of the two.

Grosh told the committee he got a call from Scanlon one day. "Do you want to be head of an international corporation?" his friend asked.

That, Grosh added, was "a hard one to turn down." He added: "I asked him what I had to do, and he said 'Nothing.' So that sounded pretty good to me."

The committee chairman, John McCain, asked if there were any board meetings.

"I recall one," Grosh replied.

"And how long did that last?"

"Fifteen minutes," Grosh estimated.

"Do you recall any business that was discussed?"

"Off the top of my head, no."

Grosh said he "got out of it when I found out it involved the federal government, Indian tribes, and gambling. I knew that it was headed down the wrong way."

Why did he join the Big Men in the first place? "It was wintertime in Rehoboth," he said. "You need to make rent money."

Now Scanlon does, too. At the tender age of thirty-five, he pleaded guilty to conspiring to bribe public officials and agreed to repay $19 million. While out on bail, he went over to Johns Hopkins University to defend his master's thesis—on the history of the House ethics process.

How the Big Man "Humps"

Though Potomac Man nominally embraces Christianity, he rejects one of its most fundamental tenets: "Ye cannot serve God and mammon." That quaint admonition has no relevance to modern Potomac Man, who serves mammon—or *moka*—alone. Even the practice of Christianity in Potomac Land is frequently a means to amass power and wealth.

The exemplar in this category is Ralph Reed, who, while still in his early thirties, built the Christian Coalition into the most powerful voice of the religious right. Reed was the director of the College Republicans in the mid-1980s, when he underwent a "faith commitment" to Christianity, in part influenced by Sabbath dinners at the home of Abramoff, an orthodox Jew.

Reed's discovery of evangelical Christianity proved to be a brilliant career move. He built Pat Robertson's Christian Coalition into a major political force with an annual budget of $26 million and political figures begging for his blessing. He appeared on the cover of *Time* in 1995 with the headline "The Right Hand of God."

Then, with the group at its peak of power, Reed cashed out to become a Big Man. Starting out as a political consultant in 1997, he quickly made millions from politicians and interest groups seeking to claim support from Christian conservatives. Verizon, Microsoft, and Ken Lay's Enron all signed up for his help. Powerful political friends directed business his way; after Rove recommended Reed to Enron, Reed wrote to the soon-to-be-disgraced company: "In public policy, it matters less who has the best arguments and more who gets heard—and by whom." And Reed could be heard by anybody. He became chairman of Georgia's Republican Party and a top fund-raiser and adviser for Bush. He went on a European golf junket with government officials and lobbyists.

Using his good reputation among millions of evangelicals, Reed delivered for his clients—including some sent to him by his old friend Abramoff. In 1999, Reed's company sent a mailing to Christians in Alabama asking them to tell their congressmen to vote against legislation subjecting the Northern Mariana Islands to federal wage and worker safety laws. The legislation, Reed's group wrote, would block an influx to the Marianas of Chinese workers who, while on the islands, "are converted to the Christian faith and return to China with Bibles in hand."

Never mind that a U.S. government report found that Chinese women on the islands were subject to forced abortions and that Chinese women and children were pushed into the sex tourism trade. Reed's client didn't want stronger labor protections, and Reed found a way to turn it into a Christian cause.

Likewise, Reed's company accepted more than $4 million to mobilize Christians against Indian casinos that were competing with Abramoff's Indian casino clients. Reed stirred up Christian opposition to proposed Indian gambling in Texas and Louisiana. But he didn't tell the antigambling Christians that he was being funded by rival tribes, who were trying to protect their own casinos from competition.

When the arrangement became public in 2004, Reed said he had "no direct knowledge" that the clients backing the campaign were tribes with their own casinos to protect. But in 2005 Senate investigators released a 1999 e-mail from Abramoff to Reed saying exactly who the client was. Investigators also found that antitax activist Grover Norquist served as a "pass through" providing an indirect conduit for Abramoff's tribal money to get to Reed.

Investigators also released some rather un-Christian e-mails Reed wrote.

He told Abramoff that "I need to start humping in corporate accounts! . . . I'm counting on you to help me with some contacts."

He wrote about how he got "our pastors all riled up" to close one tribal casino. In one e-mail requesting an additional $300,000, he wrote: "We are opening the bomb bays and holding nothing back."

Even Abramoff, writing to Scanlon, was surprised by the big bills. "He is a bad version of us!" Abramoff wrote. "No more money for him."

Some of his fellow Christian conservatives began to complain. Marvin Olasky, a magazine editor, wrote that Reed has confirmed "for some the stereotype that evangelicals are easily manipulated and that evangelical leaders use moral issues to line their own pockets."

Such complaints helped sink Ralph Reed's hopes to become lieutenant governor; he lost in a Republican primary in 2006. But for the former Christian Coalition chief, there were still plenty of corporations to be humped.

SURVIVAL IN EXILE

The officeholder who loses his job in Potomac Land faces a bleak future indeed. Once he is out of power, his influence is no longer sought by Big Men. This is a virtual death sentence in the Potomac economy: The former officeholder, in losing the Big Man's *moka*, loses his main source of livelihood. In that sense, Potomac Man is not unlike the

Pacific tribesmen who would put an exile in a canoe full of holes. The out-of-power officeholder's choices: go into exile or become a Big Man himself.

Al Gore was in desperate shape when he conceded defeat in the 2000 presidential race. His assets had been listed to be possibly as low as $800,000—a pittance by Potomac Man standards. And he was a Democrat in a town suddenly owned by Republicans.

"As for what I'll do next, I don't know the answer to that one yet," he said in his concession speech.

He suggested he might pursue a career in landscaping. "I know I'll spend time in Tennessee and mend some fences, literally and figuratively," he said.

Pretty soon he had lined up some jobs as a teacher. He signed on at the Columbia Journalism School to teach a seminar called "Covering National Affairs in the Information Age." It wasn't sexy, but it was enough to make ends meet.

Over time, however, Gore was able to prove that it is possible for a Democrat to subsist when his party was out of power—as long as the Democrat is willing to leave the Potomac Men and go into exile in what people in Washington patronizingly call "the heartland."

First, in 2001, he agreed to be a part-time adviser to Google. Then, in 2003, he joined the board of Apple. In 2004, he started a cable network called Current TV and formed a "green" investment management firm with former Goldman Sachs executive David Blood; they called it Generation Investment Management rather than going for the quick laugh with Blood & Gore Inc. In 2006, Gore's book and movie about global warming, *An Inconvenient Truth,* hit bookstores and theaters. And then there are his speeches, which earn him up to $150,000 a pop.

Forbes, moved to write an article called "Gore Inc.," said his holdings, particularly the undisclosed amount from Google, could qualify as "an immense sum."

But what does an out-of-power Potomac Man do if he does not have the visibility of Al Gore and isn't willing to leave Washington? Alan Mollohan, a Democratic congressman from West Virginia, has one possible answer: He tries to become a Big Man himself.

As a member of Congress, Mollohan earned $165,000—three times the income of an ordinary person but still modest by Potomac Man standards. But between 2000 and 2004, Mollahan found a way to increase his assets from no more than $565,000 to at least $6.3 million.

His method was strikingly innovative, one that most Democrats had assumed was beyond their abilities. Using his seat on the House Appropriations Committee, he won more than $150 million for some nonprofit groups. One group, as luck would have it, was headed by a former aide who, along with Mollohan, invested in $2 million worth of property in North Carolina. Another recipient of Mollohan's taxpayer-funded largesse, Dale McBride, bought a three-hundred-acre farm with Mollohan along the aptly named Cheat River in West Virginia. By dedicating the funds, Mollohan was able to enrich his business partners, who then had more pocket change for their ventures with Mollohan.

Mollohan says his activities in bringing hundreds of millions of dollars to his district are "squeaky clean." He said he just got lucky on some highly leveraged real-estate purchases. But, all the same, he and his colleagues decided after news of his business dealings broke that it might be a good idea for him to quit his position as vice chairman of the House Ethics Committee. He also thought it wise to correct "inadvertent errors" he had made on disclosure statements misstating the values of his transactions.

The FBI launched an investigation. And, in the 2006 campaign, people loitered outside Mollohan's campaign office with signs saying MAN OF STEAL and BE MY CELLMATE. No matter: Mollohan was returned to Congress with 64 percent of the vote.

ICED MOKA

It doesn't take long after an officeholder arrives in Potomac Land for him to realize that he is not a Big Man and therefore is not as powerful as he had supposed. For some, this produces risky behavior: Rather than waiting for the Big Man to come to him and attempt to influence him with *moka,* the lawmaker will attempt to solicit *moka*—openly offering his services to the Big Man.

This behavior was in evidence one morning in July 2005, when Representative William Jefferson, a Louisiana Democrat, met his business partner Lori Mody in the parking lot of the Ritz-Carlton in Pentagon City. There, Jefferson reached into Mody's car trunk and pulled out a reddish-brown leather briefcase that held $100,000 in $100 bills.

Had he done his homework, Jefferson would have had reason to be suspicious about the location. The complex was where Monica Lewinsky was stung by Linda Tripp and the FBI, and where Pentagon official Larry Franklin was exposed for leaking secrets to Israeli interests.

And, sure enough, it turned out poor Jefferson's friend Mody was wearing an FBI wire, and his acceptance of the briefcase was "videotaped by the FBI from several vantage points," according to an affidavit. They filmed him putting the money in his own Lincoln Town Car and leaving the lot.

Jefferson had told Mody that he needed the money to give it to Nigerian vice president Atiku Abubakar as a "motivating factor" to make sure they obtained contracts in Nigeria for businesses affiliated with Mody and Jefferson. But raiding Jefferson's home in northeast Washington on August 3, FBI agents found $90,000 of the $100,000—wrapped in aluminum foil in $10,000 increments, stuffed in frozen food containers and stuck in the lawmaker's freezer.

Earlier, Jefferson had been taped by the FBI demanding that, for his troubles, his stake in the Nigerian company be increased from 7 percent to 30 percent but put in the name of his five daughters. "I make a deal for my children," the family man explained. Total payments he took were put at $400,000.

Jefferson knew that this was risky behavior. At one point, dining at a restaurant with Mody and scribbling notes about kickbacks, he joked about "all these damn notes we're writing to each other as if we're talking as if the FBI is watching." Mody's recording device picked that up.

Jefferson argued that he was merely passing along money to corrupt people. "If he's got to pay Minister X, we don't want to know. . . . That's all, you know, international fraud crap." Or it would have been if Jefferson hadn't kept the money.

Just before the freezer raid, Mody asked Jefferson what had become of the "package."

"Um, I apologize, but, um, all I want to know is, did you deliver it?" Mody asked.

"Ah," Jefferson replied, "I gave him the African art that you gave me, and he was very pleased."

Even after the freezer raid, Jefferson refused to cooperate, leading FBI agents in 2006 to raid his congressional office. It was the first such raid of a congressman's office and sent the capital into a brief constitutional crisis as even Republicans protested the FBI's heavy hand. Bribery is one thing, lawmakers argued, but interfering with congressional prerogatives is a far more serious matter. "We need to protect the division of powers in the Constitution of the United States," proclaimed House Speaker Denny Hastert.

Despite all the footage of his bribe receipt and the cold cash in the freezer, Jefferson retained the Potomac Man's characteristic sense of righteous indignation. "There are two sides to every story," he said in a Capitol Hill news conference. "There are certainly two sides to this story."

Jefferson perspired as he talked and rubbed his fingers together anxiously, but he said he would continue his bid for reelection because he had "been extraordinarily effective."

Ultimately, Jefferson lost his challenge to the FBI raid of his office, and his Democratic colleagues kicked him off the powerful Ways and Means Committee. But he retained the cool of a man who keeps his cash in the freezer.

A PBS reporter asked Jefferson if he would "concede that it does not look good."

"I can't talk about the facts of the matter with respect to whether things look good or don't look good," Jefferson replied.

Fox News tried a different tack: "If you did not take a $100,000 bribe, why not just say it now?"

"I simply will decline to answer," he said.

And, in fact, he did not have to. Voters reelected Jefferson in 2006, months before his inevitable indictment on charges that could send him to prison for 235 years.

THE FATHER PROTECTOR

Jefferson's instinct, "I make a deal for my children," is a common instinct among Potomac Men. The powerful realize that it appears unseemly to profit financially from one's government position, but they assume that it would not carry the same taint if they're directing a Big Man's *moka* to a spouse or a child. The assumption is as pervasive as it is flawed.

Congressman Curt Weldon, a longtime Republican representative from Pennsylvania, thought nothing of rounding up thirty of his lawmaker colleagues to attend a dinner honoring Igor Makarov, the head of Russia's Itera International Energy Corporation. U.S. trade authorities, suspicious about the company, had rescinded a grant to Itera, but Weldon, on the House floor, called the company's actions "absolutely refreshing."

He felt it unnecessary to mention that, just days before the dinner and floor speech, Itera had given a $500,000 contract to a company run by Weldon's daughter, Karen, to do public relations work. She got $170,000 up front.

Weldon may have thought it unnecessary to mention that arrangement because there were so many others like it—about $1 million worth, in fact. Russia's Saratov Aviation paid his daughter's firm $20,000 a month after father and daughter took a trip to Russia together; around the same time, Weldon began to champion an aerial drone made by Saratov. Reports indicated both Saratov and Itera agreed to make "reward payments" to Ms. Weldon if they got federal contracts.

If Weldon didn't think it such a big deal, that's no surprise for a Potomac Man. *USA Today* found that in 2005 alone, lawmakers approved $750 million for projects sought by lobbyists who employed their relatives. The thirty relatives of lawmakers earned millions of dollars in fees.

Senator Byron Dorgan, a North Dakota Democrat, fought for keeping the estate tax while his wife was lobbying for the same purpose. Senator Elizabeth Dole, a North Carolina Republican, defended a Dubai ports operator while her husband was lobbying for the company. When Democrats in the House vowed to take up railroad-safety laws, the railroad industry hired the father of one congressman and the father and brother of the railroad subcommittee's staff director.

WAR SPOILS AND TRIBUTE

A constant state of warfare has vastly increased Potomac Man's use of *moka* transactions. By increasing the government's outlay by hundreds of billions of dollars of "emergency" spending, Potomac Man has greatly expanded the amount of government contracts that can be won by and for Big Men. The system is not unlike ancient civilizations' demand for war spoils from the various conquered regions. In Potomac Man's system, however, the greatest opportunity for wealth is to be found in the government contracts meant to aid the conquered adversary.

Joe M. Allbaugh is an inscrutable man—and not only because he insists on using a middle initial even though his first name is a nickname. He is six feet four inches tall, weighs nearly three hundred pounds, and has a military crew cut. As Bush's campaign manager in 2000, he instilled fear in his staff. After Bush won, he opted for a fairly low-profile job as head of the disaster agency FEMA. Though it made little sense at the time, Allbaugh's choice of assignment became clear when, just days before Bush launched his invasion of Iraq, Allbaugh left the government. He wanted to use his connections and know-how to make money from a new disaster: Iraq.

Allbaugh, along with Republican lobbyist Ed Rogers, formed New Bridge Strategies, a group describing itself as a collection of former high government officials "particularly well suited" to help clients win government business. He also started Diligence-Iraq, a security firm. Explained one of Allbaugh's partners to *Fortune* magazine: "In a gold rush, you can make money by selling picks and shovels." Another partner described Iraq to the *Washington Post* as a potential "gold mine" and predicted that "a Wal-Mart could take over the country."

The versatile Allbaugh also formed Allbaugh Company, a lobbying group helping clients in the disaster relief business. Among Allbaugh's many paying customers: Halliburton, the oil-services company once run by Vice President Cheney. His firm's Web site invoked the September 11 attacks and said Allbaugh is "dedicated to helping private industry meet the homeland security challenge." This put Allbaugh into direct competition with his FEMA predecessor during the Clinton administration, James Lee Witt, whose firm advertises: "Being able to arrange an audience with influential decision makers at the highest levels is the stock-in-trade in Washington and a privilege James Lee Witt and his team are proud to have and one not taken for granted."

Indeed not. In the early days after Hurricane Katrina, more than $1 billion in government contracts was given with little or no bidding. Two of the big winners were Halliburton and Shaw Group—both represented by Allbaugh. Shaw, relatively unknown, snagged a $200 million no-bid contract. The lobbyist argued that he did not help his clients win federal contracts, leaving open the unsettling possibility he was advising them on hairstyles.

Four

MYTHOLOGY AND
FOLKLORE

According to classical mythology, the walls of Troy were built not by man but by the gods. Poseidon and Apollo, forced by Zeus to labor among mortals, built the city walls for Laomedon, king of Troy and son of its founder (who wound up defaulting on the payment). This type of mythology has come to be known as the prestige myth, used to elevate a hero, city, or nation.

Potomac Land, like every culture, depends on mythology to justify itself and its institutions; to explain natural phenomena; and, usually, to put itself at the center of the universe. Here, as elsewhere, ritual myths justify religious practices, cult myths explain festivals, origin myths explain creation, and eschatological myths portray the apocalypse. But Homo politicus is particularly dependent on prestige mythology, which makes Potomac Land the most important place on earth. Selected by and named for the nation's founding hero, Potomac Land is described by its inhabitants without self-consciousness as "the most powerful city in the world" or "the capital of the free world." A letter writer to the *Washington Post,* complaining about animals' conditions at the zoo, harumphs: "We are talking about the National Zoo of the most powerful city of the most powerful nation." Even orang-utans should be treated with respect in George Washington's city.

This prestige mythology extends through most aspects of Potomac life and has left Potomac Man singularly impervious to reason, nuance, and scientific truth. The most incidental of policy disagreements inevitably becomes a clash between good and evil. War is justified merely by saying that "we love freedom" and the enemies "hate freedom." Each lawmaker, regardless of the position he or she takes, invariably professes to be acting in "the national interest" and conducting "the people's business." Walking in the marble corridors of the classical temples of Potomac Land, Potomac Man holds a firm belief that his town, like Troy, was built by the hands of gods.

THE CLIMATE GODS MUST BE ANGRY

In Australia, some aboriginals believe that the moon was a man who, instead of dying, threw his bones into the sea, then rose into the sky. The lunar cycle comes from the man regaining his mass by eating lotus roots. The rising and setting of the sun, similarly, is explained by the actions of the sun goddess, who carries a torch across the sky, dipping it in the water in the west and using the embers to find her way under the earth back to her starting point in the east. Dawn and dusk are attributed to her body paints.

Potomac Land has many such myths to explain natural phenomena, too. These folktales are so powerful that no scientific advancement or discovery can sway the faithful from their belief in the mythology.

One such adherent is Jim Inhofe, who served as chairman of the Senate Environment and Public Works Committee. No quantity of scientific evidence could sway the Republican from oil-rich Oklahoma from the central myth of his existence: that global warming was bunk. "With all the hysteria, all the fear, all the phony science," he said in 2003, "could it be that man-made global warming is the greatest hoax ever perpetrated on the American people? It sure sounds like it."

Among scientists, this position was about as credible as Holocaust denial or flat-earth theory. The National Academy of Sciences concluded: "In the judgment of most climate scientists, earth's warming in recent decades has been caused primarily by human activities that have increased the amount of greenhouse gases in the atmosphere." The rising temperatures caused by heat-trapping carbon dioxide, it concluded, will cause rising sea levels, severe storms, and disruptions to water supplies and living things. The United Nations, the American Meteorological Society, and the American Geophysical Union have arrived at similar conclusions. Even the Bush administration, a skeptic on global warming, said it was "likely due mostly to human activities."

But this means nothing to the man from Oklahoma, who drives a Hummer to work to show his view on conservation. On the Senate floor in September 2006, he proclaimed that global warming was "the most media-hyped environmental issue of all time." He denounced "an unprecedented parade of environmental alarmism," which he said was refuted by even a cursory review of "the Medieval Warm Period from about 900 A.D. to 1300 A.D. and the Little Ice Age from about 1500 to 1850. . . . Earth was warmer than today during the Medieval Warm Period, when the Vikings grew crops in Greenland."

This non sequitur led Inhofe to affirm to the Senate that global warming was a natural phenomenon that had nothing to do with mankind. "My skeptical views on man-made catastrophic global warming have only strengthened as new science comes in," he said. "In fact, after years of hearing about the computer-generated scary scenarios about the future of our planet, I now believe that the greatest climate threat we face may be coming from alarmist computer models."

He blamed global warming on the spirit world. "God's still up there, and we still have the cycles every fifteen hundred years or so," he told senators.

The midterm elections of 2006, which put the global-warming alarmists in control of the Senate, unnerved Inhofe. He called a press conference to attack a children's book on global warming produced by the United Nations. "The book is about a young boy named Tore who lives in an Arctic village," Inhofe announced. "Tore loses a dog sled race because he crashes through the thinning ice allegedly caused by man-made greenhouse gas emissions." Inhofe railed against this "un-precedented attempt" to "instill fear in young, impressionable minds." Later, speaking to a conservative group in March 2007, he quarreled with a Bush administration proposal to list polar bears as a threatened species. "They're overpopulated," he declared. "Don't worry about it: The polar bear is fine." His staff handed out a paper that included the claim that "MARS HAS GLOBAL WARMING DESPITE ABSENCE OF SUVS."

Even Inhofe's fellow Republicans have found words such as "ridiculous" to describe his beliefs. But that is of little concern to Inhofe, who has dubbed the Environmental Protection Agency a "gestapo bureaucracy" and likened its administrator to Tokyo Rose. He said the Kyoto global warming treaty "would deal a powerful blow on the whole humanity similar to the one humanity experienced when Nazism and communism flourished."

"I have been called—my kids are all aware of this—dumb, crazy man, science abuser, Holocaust denier, villain of the month, hate-filled, warmonger, Neanderthal, Genghis Khan, and Attila the Hun," he announced, "and I can just tell you that I wear some of those titles proudly."

His private life is equally exciting. An airplane pilot, he has twice had crash landings, once when a propeller broke and again when a rudder malfunctioned on a plane built by his son. As for his family, he boasted that their "recorded history" has not documented "any kind of homosexual relationship." But even that is tame compared to Inhofe's most fervent belief: the need to end global warming worries, or, as Inhofe calls it, "climate porn."

POTOMAC MAN'S FOLKLORIC NARRATIVE

Each culture has its folklore—its demons and fairies, its omens and amulets—and Potomac Land is no different. In fact, the fantastic has such a priority here that the keeper of the folkloric narrative in modern-day Potomac Land is among the highest ranking: Vice President Dick Cheney. He is something of a mythic figure himself: impossibly dour, his lips sagging in one corner, emerging occasionally

to speak about the imminent demise of humanity, the absolute cor-
rectness of the Bush administration, or both. His very existence is
something of a mystery: A pacemaker, bypass surgery, and cardiac
catheterization and stent have kept his failing heart pumping after
four heart attacks.

In the days after the September 11 attacks, he went from bunker
to hunting trip to bunker, only occasionally emerging from his "secure, undisclosed location." Eventually, *Saturday Night Live* turned it
into a skit, revealing that Cheney's secret location was Kandahar,
Afghanistan.

"I'm a one-man Afghani wrecking crew," growled the Cheney impersonator in combat gear. "I got me a bionic ticker. This thing regu-
lates my heartbeat, gives me night vision, and renders me completely
invisible to radar. Check this out. I brew my own Sanka. . . . Thanks
to this baby, I can achieve a top speed of up to seventy miles an hour."

Cheney enjoyed the image. Emerging at an awards dinner in
New York, he told the crowd, "The Waldorf is a lot nicer than our
cave." Cheney relished the mystery so much that the White House
continued to list his location as "undisclosed" even when any by-
stander could see his motorcade screaming up Massachusetts Avenue
at 6:30 P.M. each day to his official residence near the Naval Obser-
vatory.

When not stalking the Taliban, he shot game with abandon. On a
single morning in Pennsylvania he shot 70 pheasants and a number of
ducks, just some of the 417 farm-raised birds his party bagged; then,
of course, there was the time he famously shot his friend Harry
Whittington on a Texas quail hunt. The Cheney mouth was similarly
dangerous. On the floor of the Senate, he told the top Democrat on
the Judiciary Committee to "fuck yourself"—reminiscent of his agreement when Bush called a *New York Times* reporter a "major-league
asshole."

"Big-time," Cheney concurred.

Cheney set about to create folktales wherever he went, whatever
the subject, leading up to his description of the Iraqi insurgency on
Larry King Live on May 30, 2005: "I think they're in the last throes, if

you will, of the insurgency." The insurgency promptly spiraled into civil war.

He spoke of the U.S. terrorism prison in Guantanamo Bay, Cuba, as a resort. "They got a brand-new facility," he told CNN's Wolf Blitzer. "We spent a lot of money to build it. They're very well treated down there. They're living in the tropics. They're well fed. They've got everything they could possibly want."

The prospect that his tales might be proven false did not deter the vice president. At a vice presidential debate in Cleveland in October 2004, he looked Democratic nominee John Edwards in the eye and said, "The first time I ever met you was when you walked on the stage tonight." It didn't take long for videotape to surface of the prayer breakfast where Cheney sat next to Edwards—one of three prior meetings between the two.

In 2002, Vice President Cheney told Treasury Secretary Paul O'Neill not to worry about the federal deficit, according to a book O'Neill helped produce. "Reagan proved deficits don't matter," O'Neill recalled Cheney saying. In 2001, the White House scrambled to repair Bush's "green" credentials after the vice president mocked conservation as "a sign of personal virtue" but not an energy policy.

Even after President Bush abandoned his public claims that illegal weapons would be found in Iraq, Cheney contradicted him and said the search would continue. He told National Public Radio that the discovery of trailers in Iraq offered "conclusive evidence" that Saddam Hussein "did in fact have programs for weapons of mass destruction." The CIA said the trailers were likely facilities used to make hydrogen for weather balloons.

Likewise, he continued to implicate Saddam Hussein in the September 11 attacks long after Bush said, "We've had no evidence that Saddam Hussein was involved with September the 11th." As evidence of an Iraq/al-Qaeda link, he pointed reporters to a Defense Department report the Pentagon itself labeled "inaccurate."

As time went on, Cheney's tales grew taller. His office, facing demand for records from the National Archives, decided that the vice president was not "an entity within the executive branch"—and tried to abolish the office seeking the records.

Cheney adored the telling of folktales and the spreading of myths. Of course, his opponents in the rival tribe, and scribes in the media, quickly pointed out that what Cheney was saying was demonstrably false. But Cheney had a way to deal with this, too. He made many of his most fantastic pronouncements on *Meet the Press*, the top-rated Sunday politics show. That way he could beam his mythology directly to more than five million viewers. Even under the questioning of Tim Russert, perhaps the most respected interviewer in Potomac Land, Cheney found he could make his tall tales part of the folklore long before media truth squads caught up with him.

In the 2007 trial of Cheney's former chief of staff, Scooter Libby, Cheney aide Cathie Martin testified about the vice president's belief that he "controlled" Russert. Flashed on the courtroom computer screens were her notes from 2004 about how Cheney could respond to allegations that the Bush administration had misrepresented evidence of Iraq's nuclear ambitions. Option 1: "MTP-VP," she wrote, then listed the pros and cons of a vice presidential appearance on the Sunday show. Under "pro," she wrote: "control message."

"I suggested we put the vice president on *Meet the Press*, which was a tactic we often used," Martin testified. "It's our best format."

At two of their early *Meet the Press* encounters, in July and August 2000, Cheney said that "I have had no health problems" and the "doctors have vouched for me." If he thought he would have more heart trouble, "I wouldn't be here today," Cheney said. One hundred days later he suffered his fourth heart attack. Bush went out and told the world, incorrectly, that Cheney "had no heart attack." Unfailingly optimistic, Cheney returned to Russert after the heart attack to say, "I'm stronger and healthier now than I was six months ago."

Cheney also used the NBC show to spin a folktale about his connections to Halliburton, the oil services company he led. "We'll resolve any conflict before I'm sworn in," he vowed to Russert in 2000. In 2003, he returned to the show to say, "I've severed all my ties with the company, gotten rid of all my financial interests. I have no financial interest in Halliburton of any kind and haven't had now for over three years."

What viewers didn't hear was that Cheney still owned 433,000

Halliburton stock options as he said those words. He was also receiving deferred compensation from Halliburton worth hundreds of thousands of dollars. A report by the Congressional Research Service said
such an arrangement would be considered a "continuing financial interest" under federal law, regardless of Cheney's explanation that he
intended to give proceeds from the stock options to charity.

The September 11 attacks redoubled Cheney's dedication to folklore. Five days after the attacks, Russert visited him near Camp David.
Cheney explained that Bush's hopscotching around the country on the
day of the attack was not a sign of indecision, as much of the country
supposed, but a reasonable response to a real threat. "The president
was on Air Force One," Cheney recounted. "We received a threat to
Air Force One—came through the Secret Service."

"A credible threat to Air Force One?" Russert asked. "You're convinced of that?"

"I'm convinced of that," Cheney said.

In fact, it was not credible. The credibility was based on the belief
that the person calling in the threat had used a secret code for Air
Force One, "angel." But, in fact, the Secret Service, not the crank
caller, had translated the word to code.

The terrorist attacks made Cheney, always gloomy, turn toward a
dark and vengeful mythology. The onetime pragmatist adopted the
hard-line folklore of the neocon movement. His longtime associate
Brent Scowcroft would later tell the *New Yorker*: "Dick Cheney I don't
know anymore."

The unknown Cheney returned to *Meet the Press* three months after the attack, to give an update. He had changed his mind, and now
he was quite sure Iraq was, after all, involved in September 11. He
said he was pretty sure Mohamed Atta, ringleader of the attacks, had
met in Prague with an Iraqi intelligence official.

"Well, what we now have that's developed since you and I last
talked, Tim, of course, was that report that—it's been pretty well confirmed that he did go to Prague and he did meet with a senior official
of the Iraqi intelligence service in Czechoslovakia last April," the vice
president said. "That's clearly an avenue that we want to pursue."

What Cheney didn't say, but certainly knew, was that the CIA doubted any such meeting had occurred. Eventually, it became obvious that no such meeting had. An FBI probe concluded Atta was likely in Florida at the time of the alleged meeting, while the Czech authorities who made the claim backed away from it.

But that was of no significance to Cheney. His assertions helped to establish in Potomac folklore that Saddam Hussein was behind the 9/11 attacks. In the fall of 2003, seven in ten Americans thought so. When, in 2004, Gloria Borger asked Cheney on CNBC why he had said the meeting was "pretty well confirmed," the vice president was indignant. "I never said that," Cheney answered. "I never said that. Absolutely not."

Cheney was back on *Meet the Press* in May 2002. The midterm elections were approaching, and it was time to get everybody good and worried. Russert asked Cheney about intercepts "hinting at a new attack" on the United States. "We don't know if it's going to be tomorrow or next week or next year," Cheney replied, "but the prospect of another attack against the United States is very, very real." The vice president said the indications were similar to those that preceded the 9/11 attack.

The vice president said, repeatedly, that the administration made no mistakes in the time before the attacks, but in terms of getting to the bottom of what happened on that day, Cheney was reticent. He said there should be no commission investigating the attacks. "I think there's a trade-off here, frankly, between safeguarding the national interest, which is very much at stake here, and satisfying what sometimes becomes a search for headlines on Capitol Hill."

The bigger worry was that the commission, and the resulting headlines, would produce a counter to Cheney's folkloric narrative. This is exactly what happened when the commission unearthed an August 6, 2001, CIA briefing for Bush titled "Bin Laden determined to attack inside the U.S." and specifically cited "preparations for hijackings."

Returning for another tête-à-tête with Russert just before the election in 2002, Cheney turned his attention to Iraq. He had no doubt that Hussein was "actively and aggressively seeking to acquire nuclear weapons." If allies didn't share that view, it was because "we're better than anybody else, generally, in this area." The evidence, he said, was "very clear."

"We do know, with absolute certainty, that he is using his procurement system to acquire the equipment he needs in order to enrich uranium to build a nuclear weapon," Cheney said. Over and over, he repeated that Hussein was "working actively to improve his biological weapons program and his nuclear weapons program."

He again hinted at a Hussein link to 9/11, then warned, "The danger of an attack against the United States by someone with the weapons that Saddam Hussein now possesses, or is acquiring, is far more costly than what it would cost for us to go deal with this problem." Cheney said he expected the rest of the Arab world to remain stable.

Republicans gained seats in the 2002 midterm elections, as Americans accepted the Cheney narrative and prepared for imminent war. Days before the U.S. invasion of Iraq, in March 2003, Cheney returned to the *Meet the Press* set. As a purveyor of folklore, it was Cheney's best-ever performance.

On the reception American troops would get in Iraq: "My belief is we will, in fact, be greeted as liberators."

On the United Nations' doubts that Hussein had a nuclear program: "We believe he has, in fact, reconstituted nuclear weapons."

On the need for "several hundred thousand troops" in Iraq: "I disagree."

On the rationale for war: "To ensure that we don't get hit with a devastating attack when the terrorists' organization gets married up with a rogue state that's willing to provide it with the kinds of deadly capabilities that Saddam Hussein has developed and used over the years."

Wrong, wrong, wrong, and wrong. Cheney, in fact, already knew that the fourth statement was dubious when he uttered it. CIA chief George Tenet told Congress and the administration that Hussein would not give weapons of mass destruction to terrorists—unless attacked. But, again, the facts didn't matter. The narrative mattered, and the United States went to war on Cheney's tale.

In September 2003, Cheney returned to Russert's show for a victory lap. Though the insurgency was just starting, Cheney's narrative was about success: "Fairly significant success in terms of putting Iraq back together again . . . [nothing] to suggest or think that the strategy is flawed or needs to be changed. . . . The fact is that most of Iraq today is relatively stable and quiet. . . . We've had major success, major progress."

The emboldened Cheney offered his most expansive version of the myth linking Hussein to the September 11 attacks. In Iraq, he said, "We will have struck a major blow right at the heart of the base, if you will, the geographic base of the terrorists who have had us under assault now for many years but most especially on 9/11."

It was the last time Cheney would appear on Russert's show for three years. Reality gradually caught up with Cheney's folklore, as Americans became aware of a competing narrative of bloodshed and civil war in Iraq. Finally, with the 2006 midterm elections approaching, the great myth teller agreed to visit the *Meet the Press* set once more.

"I can't believe it!" Russert said after booking Cheney. It was indeed a strange decision: Instead of spinning new folklore, the vice president spent the hour answering for his past yarns.

Russert cited a poll showing Americans, by 54 percent to 15 percent, thought wars in Iraq and Afghanistan were creating more terrorists rather than eliminating them.

"I—I—I can't buy that," Cheney stammered.

Russert cited a *Washington Post* story that quoted intelligence officials saying the trail of bin Laden had gone "stone cold."

"I—I—I haven't read the article," the myth maker replied.

Russert pointed out that most Americans said Iraq was not part of the war on terrorism.

"I beg to differ," Cheney differed.

In the exchanges that followed, Cheney tried to explain his previous certainty that Iraq had weapons of mass destruction and his belief that Atta met with the Iraqis. "We've never been able to confirm any connection between Iraq and 9/11," he confessed.

Russert read Cheney's 2005 quote about the Iraq insurgency being in its "last throes."

"Hmm," Cheney answered. When Russert pointed out that 1,656 American soldiers had died in Iraq since then, Cheney acknowledged the insurgency was "more difficult than I had anticipated," before saying, "It was the right thing to do and if we had it to do over again, we'd do exactly the same thing."

"Exactly the same thing?" Russert asked.

"Yes, sir," the vice president said. He went on to justify his prediction that Americans would be viewed as "liberators," the Supreme Court's rejection of the administration's treatment of terrorism prisoners, and Cheney's earlier attacks on the United Nations nuclear experts, who turned out to be correct.

Then it was time for some new folktales.

"What happens if the Democrats win the House of Representatives?" Russert asked.

"I don't think it'll happen," Cheney replied. "I don't expect that Nancy Pelosi will be Speaker. I think we're doing very well out there."

"You're fully confident you'll maintain control of both houses?" the surprised Russert pressed.

"I think we will, I really do," Cheney said. "I can bet you a dinner that we hold both houses." Russert unwisely declined the wager.

COMING OF AGE AT NASA

Among surviving civilizations, none works as hard as Potomac Man to protect his tribal mythology from the intrusions of science and discovery. The Bush administration, for example, in 2004 told scientists at its Department of Health and Human Services that they could not consult with the World Health Organization unless they agreed to advocate only official policy. In 2006, the House passed legislation making it more difficult to make legal challenges to jurisdictions that chose to teach the neo-creationist theory of intelligent design as an alternative to evolution.

That same year, the National Oceanic and Atmospheric Administration ordered that any media questions about endangered salmon must be handled by one of three political appointees in agency headquarters, not by scientists. At the Food and Drug Administration, experts voted 23 to 4 in favor of the Plan B contraceptive, but the agency's political leadership overruled the decision and stalled the approval for months. And though the National Academy of Sciences joined the scientific community's assessment that there was no such thing as Gulf War syndrome, Congress, yielding to the pressure of veterans' groups, in 2006 offered $75 million to a scientist who believed otherwise.

For those people of science who challenge Potomac Land mythology, the punishment can be severe. Nikki Tinsley, the inspector general at the Environmental Protection Agency, issued a report in 2005 that the agency ignored scientific evidence and ordered its experts to set limits on mercury pollution that would be consistent with Bush's already-announced program. That forced scientists to work backward, justifying a predetermined outcome and allowing power plants to pump out far more of the toxic metal.

The energy industry and the EPA leadership reacted with equal fury. Jeffrey Holmstead, the assistant administrator, condemned "several inaccuracies and flaws" in the inspector's report. Republicans in Congress threatened to investigate the investigator for a political bias, saying her "politicized office is not fit to evaluate the quality of policies."

Within a year, Tinsley announced that she was bringing her thirty-five-year career as a government auditor to an end. To replace her, the Bush administration tapped Alex Beehler, a former top official with Koch Industries—a petroleum refining and chemical company.

If there were a face behind Potomac Land's efforts to preserve tribal myth against the encroachments of science, it would be that of George Deutsch, a twenty-four-year-old NASA political appointee who, after a stint in the Bush campaign's war room in 2004, labored mightily to gag NASA scientists in 2005 and 2006.

After James Hansen, director of NASA's Goddard Institute, gave a lecture calling for rapid action to reduce global warming, Deutsch, four decades Hansen's junior, ordered that all Hansen's lectures and interview requests be vetted for any inconsistencies with official Bush policy. If he continued to say that 2005 was the warmest year in a century, he would face "dire consequences," headquarters said. Deutsch blocked him from granting an interview to National Public Radio, calling it too "liberal." One of Hansen's colleagues told the *New York*

Times that Deutsch justified the Hansen muzzling by saying his job was "to make the president look good."

The *Times* also got hold of a Deutsch e-mail directing a Web designer to add the word "theory" to every mention of the Big Bang on NASA's Web site. The Big Bang is "not proven fact; it is opinion," he wrote in a 2005 e-mail. "It is not NASA's place, nor should it be, to make a declaration such as this about the existence of the universe that discounts intelligent design by a creator." Deutsch argued that "This is more than a science issue, it is a religious issue. And I would hate to think that young people would only be getting one half of this debate from NASA."

The *Times* stories put Internet sleuths on the case of Deutsch. Nick Anthis, who writes a blog called the Scientific Activist, discovered that Deutsch did not have the bachelor's degree in journalism he claimed to have received from Texas A&M. Turns out, Deutsch left school to work on the Bush campaign in 2004, then never returned. The extent of this high school graduate's scientific knowledge was authorship of a few articles about video games.

George Carlton Deutsch III was quickly ousted in an episode that said as much about Potomac Land as it did about him: While he survived the accusation that he muzzled senior government scientists to make Bush "look good," he couldn't survive the revelation that he lied on his résumé. After a four-month probe, NASA concluded that Deutsch acted "contrary to NASA policy," leading the agency and the Commerce Department to begin larger investigations. Deutsch, for his part, apologized for the résumé problem but not for silencing the scientists. "I have never been told to censor science, to squelch anything, or to insert religion into any issue," he told a Texas radio station. Of course, he didn't need to be told; for a Potomac Man, the need to defend myth against science was obvious.

DEFYING THE ANIMAL TOTEMS

In Celtic tradition, as in many cultures, animals have totemic, or spiritual, qualities that make them sacred and earn them status as power animals. In early Ireland, the great Ulster hero Cuchulain belonged to a clan that had the dog as its family totem. There was therefore a geis, or prohibition, against his consuming dog meat. When three half-blind hags tricked him into eating dog roasted on a spit, the great warrior immediately lost the strength in his fighting arm and quickly died.

For years, Potomac Men shared this reverence for animals. The 1973 Endangered Species Act allowed the federal government to preserve vast tracts of land from development and so prevent the extinction of rare types of animals. But in recent years, some in Potomac Land have attempted to defy these power animals—and this has produced bad omens for those who have challenged the totems.

There was the case of Richard Pombo, a California rancher who won election to Congress promising to rewrite the Endangered Species Act so that fewer animals would be protected and more land open to development.

He worked his way up to chairman of the House Resources Committee, where he repeatedly wrote bills that would restrict species' protections. He held hearings packed with critics of the law. But while he occasionally got the legislation through the House, it never cleared the Senate. "It's the sacred cow," Pombo told a home state reporter, inadvertently using the language of animal totems.

Pombo was not subtle in his efforts. One of his aides responded to an editorial in a Connecticut newspaper opposed to oil drilling by saying: "Connecticut should have its statehood taken away from it." The aide wrote in an e-mail, intercepted by *Roll Call*: "The foolishness of its pampered residents should be demonstrated to others by a government program to bulldoze the entire state, salt the land and construct a windfarm to supply NYC with electricity. And its residents should be relocated to Guantanamo Bay where they can take a number behind the 3 who hung themselves this weekend, since they seem so intent on suicide."

This effort to place himself above the animals did not play well for Pombo. Nor did it help that he received gobs of Jack Abramoff money. Environmental groups spent lavishly on the campaign of a wind-energy expert running against Pombo. In one of the surprises of 2006, Chairman Pombo went the way of Cuchulain after eating the dog.

Pombo's abrupt departure from Potomac Land left Julie MacDonald as Potomac Land's leading protector of humans against encroaching animals. The deputy assistant secretary of the interior for fish and wildlife and parks repeatedly rejected recommendations from agency scientists to protect endangered animals and plants.

There was, for example, the case of the white-tailed prairie dog. Government scientists informed MacDonald in 2004 of a "general consensus" that the animal was in "substantial" trouble because of oil and gas drilling, among other things, and that an additional, ninety-day review was warranted. But an answer came back to the scientists that "Julie McD and the Department want to go with a not warranted ninety-day finding." MacDonald then distributed an official notice "with the finding changed from substantial to not substantial per Julie's instructions."

Likewise, in 2006, when agency biologists concluded that the Gunnison sage-grouse merited protection under the Endangered Species Act, MacDonald ordered the scientists to rewrite their proposal and then rejected their findings. In another incident, she ordered scientists to downgrade the protection for the Santa Barbara and Sonoma salamanders even though the scientists reached the opposite conclusion.

When scientists said a proposed road might limit the greater sage-grouse's habitat, MacDonald replied that their judgment "has nothing to do with sage-grouse. This belongs in a treatise on 'Why roads are bad?'"

When the *Washington Post*'s Juliet Eilperin asked MacDonald about her flip treatment of the issue, she offered more of the same. "Mea culpa," she said. "I shouldn't be flippant." Meanwhile, she managed to slow down listings of new endangered species by 80 percent.

But animal totems can be flouted only so long, even in Potomac Land. As part of the Democrats' takeover of Congress in 2006, Pombo's replacement at the House Natural Resources Committee, Nick Rahall, said he would hold hearings into MacDonald's behavior.

BORROWING KABUKI ART FORMS

Potomac Land—because of the presence of foreign diplomats, traders, tourists, and journalists—borrows art forms from many cultures. The most popular folk-art form borrowed by Potomac Man is the Japanese drama known as Kabuki. Developed in seventeenth-century Japan during the Edo period, it is a highly stylized and sometimes bawdy art form designed to appeal to the common man rather than merely the higher classes. Its themes are relatively simple and predictable, but the actors' voices, movements, and makeup are exaggerated. So elaborate is Kabuki that it is sometimes difficult to distinguish the acting from dancing.

In Potomac Land, Kabuki is most commonly performed in Congress, but it is also staged routinely at the White House and even at the Supreme Court. By far the most expert Kabuki show in recent years was the confirmation of John Roberts as chief justice of the Supreme Court, performed in five days of hearings before the Senate Judiciary Committee.

Supreme Court confirmations follow a common plot device. The fight is all about abortion, and everybody knows the nominee's position (opposed to legal abortion if nominated by a Republican, in favor of legal abortion if a Democratic nominee). But the nominee must go through the entire process without providing his views on the subject. In fact, it helps if the nominee has no paper trail revealing what he felt about abortion in the past.

Roberts was ideal in this regard. Nobody doubted he would vote to outlaw abortion, but they could find little evidence of this in his writings. In fact, they found little about anything in his writings, other than a deep dislike for Michael Jackson. Among the thousands of pages of documents released by the government from Roberts's days working as an administration lawyer in the 1980s were several memos in which Roberts opposed any effort by the Reagan White House to honor Michael Jackson.

"The office of presidential correspondence is not yet an adjunct of Michael Jackson's PR firm," Roberts wrote in June 22, 1984, opposing a request by the singer's publicist for a presidential letter praising the star's work against drunken driving.

Three months later, Jackson's personal manager made a new request, this one for a letter from Ronald Reagan to thank Jackson for performing in Washington and for providing four hundred tickets for "needy youngsters." Wrote Roberts: "I hate to sound like one of Mr. Jackson's records, constantly repeating the same refrain, but I recommend that we not approve this letter. . . . Frankly, I find the obsequious attitude of some members of the White House staff toward Mr. Jackson's attendants, and the fawning posture they would have the president of the United States adopt, more than a little embarrassing." Obsessed, Roberts noted "reports that some youngsters were turning away from Mr. Jackson in favor of a newcomer who goes by the name 'Prince,' and is apparently planning a Washington concert. Will he receive a presidential letter?"

It was long before Jackson ran into trouble over accusations of his nocturnal behavior with boys, but Roberts was already wary of the pop star. "If one wants the youth of America and the world sashaying around in garish sequined costumes, hair dripping with pomade, body shot full of female hormones to prevent voice change, mono-gloved, well, then, I suppose 'Michael,' as he is affectionately known in the trade, is in fact a good example. Quite apart from the problem of appearing to endorse Jackson's androgynous lifestyle, a presidential award would be perceived as a shallow effort by the president to share in the constant publicity surrounding Jackson. . . . The whole episode would, in my view, be demeaning to the president."

Roberts's confirmation was assured even before his hearings began. He was good-looking and had cute kids. Democrats judged that he was a good man because he lived in Chevy Chase, Maryland, a liberal enclave. He further won over the country, and the Senate, when he filled his opening remarks at his hearing with baseball references. He argued that "judges are like umpires" and "it's my job to call balls and strikes and not to pitch or bat." The vote could have been held right then, but there were four days of Kabuki still to be performed.

Republican senators played their part by directing the nominee not to answer questions. "Don't take the bait," suggested John Cornyn of

Texas. Orrin Hatch of Utah said it is "patently false" that Roberts must provide answers. Jon Kyl thought it could even be "unethical."

Democratic senators, in turn, played the well-rehearsed role of being frustrated that Roberts wasn't answering questions. "Your failure to answer questions is confounding me," New York's Chuck Schumer fumed. "It's as if I asked you: 'What kind of movies do you like? Tell me two or three good movies.' And you say, 'I like movies with good acting.' Then I ask you if you like *Casablanca,* and you respond by saying, 'Lots of people like *Casablanca.*' You tell me, 'It's widely settled that *Casablanca* is one of the great movies.'"

The chairman moved to call a recess, but Roberts asked if he could reply to Schumer. "*Dr. Zhivago* and *North by Northwest,*" he replied. But whenever a sensitive issue came up, the nominee demurred, saying the topic might "come before the court."

Having ruled out any possibility of a legal discussion, the senators and nominee chose to expand on Roberts's judge-as-umpire metaphor, producing a fielder's choice of baseball allusions.

"You hit a home run yesterday," said Democrat Joe Biden, but "the founders never set a strike zone." Biden said questioning Roberts was "like pitching to Ken Griffey" but added gamely, "Let's play baseball."

Fellow Democrat Herb Kohl, owner of the Milwaukee Bucks basketball team, picked up the ball. "As all of us with any involvement in sports know, no two umpires or no two referees have the same strike zone or call the same kind of a basketball game," he said.

Cornyn ruled those balls foul. "Yesterday we were talking about baseball, but today we're talking about dodgeball," he said.

Roberts, for his part, had moved on—to tennis. When a senator quizzed him about eminent domain and a recent Supreme Court case, the nominee replied, "That leaves the ball in the court of the legislature."

Roberts easily won confirmation and, to nobody's surprise, became a deeply conservative judge. In his first term he voted with Antonin Scalia 86 percent of the time. He voted to limit the Clean Air Act, ban assisted suicide, and expand police powers. Fortunately for Michael Jackson, his legal troubles were resolved before they reached the Supreme Court.

FOLK LAW, ACTUAL LAW

There are two types of law in Potomac Land. One is the actual law: the statutes passed by Congress, signed by the president, and enforced by the Justice Department. The other form of law is folk law, formed by whoever is in power using whatever mythological legal theory he enjoys. Under this system, the president enjoys near complete power: He can do anything he wants, regardless of whether it appears to violate the Constitution or statutory law, until some other body such as Congress or the Supreme Court forces him to stop. In theory, Congress or the courts could move quickly to stop the president; in practice, they almost never do. As a result, all the president needs to do to create any law he wishes is to hire a few good folklore specialists in the White House counsel's office and the Justice Department's Office of Legal Counsel.

President Bush found such folk lawyers in the forms of John Yoo and Jay Bybee, who worked at the Justice Department in the months after the September 11 attacks. U.S. law, and the country's signing of the Geneva Conventions, meant that prisoners of war could not be tortured. But in a pair of memos in 2002, these lawyers rewrote those laws so that prisoners of war would no longer be called prisoners of war and torture would no longer be torture.

In January 2002, Bybee wrote a memo to the White House that, despite appearances to the contrary, the Geneva Conventions and American laws of war do not apply to the enemy of the moment: al-Qaeda and the Taliban. "The president has the constitutional authority to temporarily suspend our treaty obligations to Afghanistan under the Geneva Conventions," Bybee decreed. Then came an August memo, signed by Bybee but written largely by Yoo, redefining "torture."

Abuses of prisoners "must be of an extreme nature to rise to the level of torture," they concluded. "Physical pain amounting to torture must be equivalent in intensity to the pain accompanying serious physical injury, such as organ failure, impairment of bodily function, or even death."

Given such advice, the attorney general wrote to President Bush that the terrorism war "renders quaint" some aspects of the Geneva Conventions, and Bush issued an order giving himself authority to suspend compliance with international agreements. These lawyers and others, including Cheney's chief of staff, David Addington, went on to argue that the administration could unilaterally create a new justice system to try terrorism prisoners and that it could perform telephone wiretaps without a warrant. As this was going on, photos emerged from the U.S.-run Abu Ghraib prison in Iraq showing naked prisoners piled on the floor and being threatened with dogs and electrocution. And for a couple of years, the president operated under a form of folk law that said he had "inherent authority" to disregard actual laws on the books.

Gradually, the actual law caught up with the president's folk law. In 2004, the Supreme Court ruled that the president could not deny constitutional protections to prisoners merely by changing their name to "enemy combatants." Two years later, the court decided that the "military commissions" the administration invented violated U.S. military law and the Geneva Conventions. Still, this was but a minor setback for an administration operating under folk law; by then, it had perfected a technique known as the signing statement, in which the president, while signing a law passed by Congress, reinterprets the law in whichever way he prefers.

Yoo, meanwhile, went to teach at Berkeley and continued to spin tales of unrestricted presidential power. He said Congress's warmaking powers, assigned by the Constitution, were in fact a figment of the "popular imagination." He also said it was the president's "choice," not obligation, to follow national security law passed by Congress. As Yoo made these points in a lecture at the Heritage Foundation in Washington, a follower of Lyndon LaRouche started heckling him. "That was Hitler's argument!" the LaRouchie cried. It was a risky act: Under actual law, the heckling qualified as free speech; under folk law, the LaRouche follower could be declared an enemy combatant.

Five

NORMS AND DEVIANCY

Potomac Land is extraordinarily tolerant of behaviors that other cultures would immediately attribute to psychiatric disorders. Here, people who are thought by the outside world to be utterly mad are commonly embraced as respected members of the community. This is all the more strange because Homo politicus, in his public utterances, hews to the straight and narrow, pronouncing his fealty to "heartland values" or "traditional values."

The happy result of this calculation is that Potomac Land has long encouraged eccentricity. There was Helen Chenoweth, a Republican congresswoman from Idaho, who held "endangered salmon bakes" and sounded an alarm that federal "black helicopters" were threatening the freedom-loving people of her state. There was "B-1 Bob" Dornan, Republican from California, also known as the "Mouth of the House" for such lines as "Every lesbian spear chucker is hoping I get defeated" and "the coke-snorting, wife-swapping, baby-born-out-of-wedlock radical Hollywood left." And there was James Traficant, Democrat of Ohio, who ended his speeches with "Beam me up, Mr. Speaker," and, pursued by the Justice Department for corruption, said

Attorney General Janet Reno was being blackmailed by somebody with a video of her and a prostitute.

Only in Potomac Land would the chairman of a powerful committee in the House, Dan Burton, shoot a pumpkin in his backyard as part of his official research; the Indiana Republican was investigating the death of Clinton White House official Vince Foster. But his colleagues were merely amused (Democrats distributed photos of a gourd with the plea "Don't Shoot Me"), as they were in 2005 when Burton skipped a crucial vote on the International Relations Committee on United Nations Reform—to play golf with lobbyists. Likewise, Georgia congressman Bob Barr gained fame for once licking whipped cream off a buxom woman's breasts (he said it was for charity). This licking history caused snickers when the thrice-married Barr, speaking for the Defense of Marriage Act, proclaimed: "the flames of self-centered morality are licking at the very foundations of our society." During a Republican Senate primary in 2002, Barr accidentally fired a .38 pistol through a glass door at a fund-raising reception.

The toleration of this Potomac madness can be explained by what psychiatrists and anthropologists call a culture-bound syndrome: any condition that is fairly common in one culture but virtually unknown in others, and there is no medical explanation for the phenomenon. In Southeast Asia, for example, *koro,* the belief that their penises are retracting into their abdomens, afflicts many men. Similarly, people in Southeast Asia sometimes suffer from a *latah*—a trancelike state in which they may mimic the speech of people around them—caused by being startled. To outsiders, this is bizarre. To those in the culture, it is an accepted medical condition.

As with nearly everything in Potomac Land, this culture-bound acceptance of madness can be explained by party allegiance. Because party has primacy, Democrats and Republicans alike will tolerate almost any oddity in a person's character as long as that person contributes to the strength of the party. Before banishing a person for deviancy, fellow partisans ask themselves who would replace the person. If it is decided that a seat in Congress might be lost, or a crucial constituency offended, the deviant is retained—at least until public embarrassment caused by the individual outweighs his benefit to the party. In the case of the Mark Foley scandal, for example, Republican leaders knew of his affections for teenage boys but, fearing the loss of his seat in Congress, did nothing about it until public disclosures of Foley's actions forced them to act.

In recent years, the rough parity between the two parties has further encouraged Potomac Man's embrace of eccentrics. Eager to hold every possible seat and constituency, Potomac Man welcomes deviancy long past the point that other cultures would cast out the eccentric. Democrats kept the late Henry Gonzalez as chairman of the House Banking Committee long after the aged lawmaker was universally suspected of senility. After Senator Jim Jeffords of Vermont quit the Republican Party in 2001, Democrats were happy to overlook his declining condition for years until he acknowledged he was "a little bit in the Alzheimer's area." Republicans, meanwhile, clung to the warm body of Senator Strom Thurmond of South Carolina long after his mind failed him.

The most extreme case of Potomac Land's embrace of the eccentric in recent years is that of Rudy Giuliani. The former New York mayor had an impressive list of demerits: He was repeatedly photographed dressing as a woman; rented himself out as a motivational speaker for $100,000 per speech; was thrice married; and, after one divorce, lived with gay men while his estranged wife performed in *The Vagina Monologues*. But at the start of the 2008 presidential race, Giuliani was by far the most popular Republican in opinion polls; desperate for a victory—and frightened of a Hillary Clinton candidacy—Republicans were willing to avert their gaze when it came to Giuliani's oddities.

EMBRACING THE PARANOID

Potomac Man admirably tolerates those of deviant character even at substantial personal risk. For example, Potomac Republicans openly welcomed Katherine Harris as a congresswoman from Florida even though there were voluminous signs of trouble in her mental state.

This resulted in a particularly embarrassing episode on an August day in 2006 when she held a campaign rally in Orlando.

Harris, heroine of the 2000 Florida recount before getting elected to Congress in 2002, was battling for the Republican Senate nomination. She sent out flyers announcing the airport rally and included the names of nine prominent state officials who would endorse her candidacy. But when the event came, none of the nine was in attendance. Worse, there were only forty people in the cavernous hangar for the rally—and most of those were reporters or campaign workers. The best known official was a state representative who had been out of office for four years. When she finished her speech, red, white, and blue balloons fell, political convention style, on a completely empty stage.

Evidently embarrassed by all the no-shows, she announced that so few of her supporters were there because, at the last minute, a tree had fallen on the hangar where the event was supposed to be held. "There was a last-minute change in location," she announced. But there was a problem with that explanation: Airport officials said none of its hangars had been damaged by a fallen tree, and the hangar used was the one that was originally reserved. Then the *Orlando Sentinel* discovered that one of the nine officials listed on the Harris flyer was actually supporting one of her opponents.

The *Sentinel* unkindly pointed out that Harris had previously claimed the endorsements of four U.S. representatives, the Florida GOP chairwoman, and Governor Jeb Bush. But none of them had backed her and some had actively discouraged her from running.

This began to explain why Harris's chief strategist, who like most of her staff quit the campaign, told the *Washington Post* that working for Harris was like "being in insanity camp." The first of the three campaign managers to quit set his cell phone to play *The Exorcist* theme when Harris called.

And yet Harris, a two-term congresswoman, had become a prominent figure in Potomac Land. President Bush praised her legislative work, Vice President Cheney heralded her "long record of public service," and both men stumped for her election to the Senate. She was occasionally mentioned as a vice presidential possibility in 2008.

How did somebody so loony rise so high? The answer is found in Potomac Man's legendary tolerance.

Six years earlier, Harris had been introduced to the nation as a caricature. The *Washington Post*'s fashion critic Robin Givhan, in a critique that became known as the "Mascara Smear," described her this way: "Her lips were overdrawn with berry-red lipstick—the creamy sort that smears all over a coffee cup and leaves smudges on shirt collars. Her skin had been plastered and powdered to the texture of prewar walls in need of a skim coat. And her eyes, rimmed in liner and frosted with blue shadow, bore the telltale homogenous spikes of false eyelashes. Caterpillars seemed to rise and fall with every bat of her eyelids, with every downward glance. . . . They were cartoon lashes. Lashes destined for a *Saturday Night Live* skit!"

Givhan proceeded to observe that Harris "seems to have applied her makeup with a trowel"—presciently predicting that she might not be the delicate touch needed to resolve the disputed election results satisfactorily.

It quickly turned out that Harris's problems weren't just skin deep. Though Florida's secretary of state, she had spent almost no time before the election working on electoral issues, leaving understaffed and ill-equipped underlings to devise the ballot format that would cause the election-day chaos. Harris's office left each of Florida's counties running their elections with different, and in some cases conflicting, standards.

But Harris, by her performance in November and December 2000, won a place in the hearts of hard-core conservatives across America. Republicans in Potomac Land privately acknowledged she was a bit odd but dared not question her rise so as not to offend the conservatives who adored her. Running for Congress in 2002, she directed those introducing her to read a text. "It is my pleasure to introduce, in my opinion, an American heroine," the script said, adding that during the recount, "she stood her ground with grace and courage."

The conservatives loved her, and her election was preordained. "She's going to be the next congresswoman from this area, like it or not," the managing editor of the *Sarasota Herald-Tribune* wrote to a reader complaining about the lack of coverage of her Democratic opponents. "I blame our culture for craving as its public figures, women like Katherine who are very pretty, hard-working, and without original ideas that I can find." The editor quit before she could be fired. But her prediction was correct about Harris's easy victory.

Harris, though a darling of conservative bloggers and talk show hosts, proved unremarkable as a legislator in Potomac Land. Months after arriving, she drew attention to herself when she was trying to parallel park her SUV and smashed another car's taillight; she got out of the car in a white tae kwon do outfit, and the incident was written up in *Roll Call*. One of her most noteworthy acts was attempting to get a $10 million grant for the felonious military contractor Mitchell Wade after he took her to a $2,800 dinner and arranged for $32,000 in illegal contributions to her campaigns. Harris at first insisted she paid her share of the dinner, then confessed that Wade had. Three months after submitting the spending request, she told the *Tampa Tribune* she knew little about the project.

Harris's true trademark: erratic behavior. In 2004, at a rally for President Bush, she announced that a Middle Eastern man had been arrested in Carmel, Indiana, with hundreds of pounds of explosives. "He had plans to blow up the area's entire power grid," she said. Asked later for details, she said she had already "said too much." Indeed, she had. Federal and local officials pronounced themselves "dumbfounded" and said no such plot had been foiled.

Things got worse when Harris started her run for the Senate in 2005. When party officials were trying to talk former congressman Joe Scarborough into running, she insinuated that he had killed one of his employees, whispering about "that dead girl." (The staffer had died of natural causes.) She later declared that voters were "legislating sin" if they didn't elect Christians like herself.

Harris's aides grew worried when she told them that God wanted her to be elected to the Senate. They grew more worried when she started ignoring their advice and turning instead for strategic guidance from a "spiritual adviser," a woman who founded the Biblical Heritage Institute in Florida. They tried and failed to convince her that her clothes were too revealing for a senator. Her paranoid rants drove out three campaign managers, her media consultant, her strategist, her field director, and her political director—two dozen in all, some en masse. This only made her more paranoid.

"I didn't know I was going to get the knives in my back from my own party, and I'll be honest, it's infiltrated my campaign staff," she told one campaign crowd. She changed the locks at one of her campaign offices. She spread, then retracted, an account of a longtime aide leaking a damaging story about her. She announced new staffers who apparently didn't exist. She switched to the first-person plural. "Come November 7, God willing, we'll be the next senator," she said.

One Florida paper decided it was watching a "freak show." Sometime during the show, Florida's GOP governor Jeb Bush reached the obvious conclusion that Harris "can't win." But the governor's brother knew better than to alienate the constituency of passionate conservatives who still backed Harris. He and the vice president both flew to Florida.

"She has our support," Cheney told a Republican rally.

"I, too, encourage you to vote for Katherine Harris for the United States Senate," the president said.

Far from Potomac Land, the voters of Florida had a different view. She lost by 22 percentage points to a plain-vanilla Democrat named Bill Nelson. But she will always be welcome among Potomac Men.

Mainstreaming of the Eccentric

In January 2004, former Vermont governor Howard Dean, a physician by training, suffered what was perhaps the most public emotional collapse any culture has ever seen. The front-runner in the race for the Democratic presidential nomination, he had just suffered a surprise defeat in the Iowa caucuses. Coming out to greet his supporters, he skipped the concession speech that such occasions usually demand and instead began a growly diatribe that would within hours become known as the "I Have a Scream Speech."

"We're going to South Carolina and Oklahoma and Arizona," Dean hollered into the microphone in Des Moines, referring to the subsequent primaries. "And North Dakota. And New Mexico. And we're going to California and Texas and New York. And we're going to South Dakota and Oregon and Washington and Michigan. And then we're going to Washington, D.C., to take back the White House!"

To this day, people have not settled on how to spell the sound that came out of Dean's mouth next, but it sounded something like this: "Yeeeeaaaaaaagggggghhhhhhhhh!!!"

The crowd cheered, as it was duty bound to do, but to millions watching on television, a thought occurred: This man is nuts.

Within hours, the Scream was everywhere. Web sites with names such as DeanGoesNuts.com were remixing it into rap songs. TV weathermen imitated it while giving the report. Screaming Howard Dean dolls appeared. David Letterman advised Dean to "cut back on the Red Bull." A bookshop on Capitol Hill gave discounted Howard Dean bobbleheads to customers who gave their renditions of the Scream.

Dean's presidential campaign quickly collapsed as people whispered about his temper and his stability. The party went instead with John Kerry, who proved himself fully capable of losing quietly, without any of the outbursts Dean was known for.

In other cultures, Dean would have been marginalized, perhaps institutionalized. But in Potomac Land, wiser Democrats knew they could not merely dismiss Dean as a screamer. Thousands of young voters who called themselves Deaniacs remained fanatically faithful to the man who claimed to represent the "Democratic wing of the Democratic Party." Worried that Dean and his Deaniacs might flee the party the way Ralph Nader and the Naderites went to the Green Party in 2000, sinking Al Gore, Democrats looked for a way to keep Dean in the fold while reducing the chance that he would embarrass the party again by running for president in 2008.

They hatched a win-win solution: In exchange for a promise from Dean not to run for president in 2008, several Potomac Land Democrats agreed to back him as chairman of the Democratic National Committee. Harold Ickes, the inside favorite for the job, threw his support to Dean, and fifty DNC delegates immediately lined up with Dean. And so, a year after the Scream, Dean was at the

DNC's meeting in New York, once again the seemingly inevitable frontrunner—and once again, the man with the biggest mouth.

"I hate the Republicans and everything they stand for," he pronounced.

In their speeches and answers to questions at the meeting here, the other candidates tried to position themselves as anti-Deans.

"We need a chair who doesn't only represent the Democratic wing of the Democratic Party," former representative Tim Roemer of Indiana told a quiet crowd.

Ex–Denver mayor Wellington Webb called for a candidate who has an appeal "not only in the northeastern part of the United States."

Nonsense, said Dean. Democrats can "change the way we talk" about issues, he said, but they should not be changing their views. "We need to dance with the people who brought us," he declared. Potomac Democrats agreed. They overwhelmingly elected Dean, calculating that the energy he brought into the party would outweigh his erratic pronouncements.

It was a bold calculation, and, for some time, it appeared to be a mistake.

In October 2005, Dean went on *Hardball with Chris Matthews* to talk about the short-lived nomination of Harriet Miers to the Supreme Court and whether Bush could refuse to give the Senate her writings from when she was White House counsel.

"Do you believe that the president can claim executive privilege?" Matthews asked.

"I think with a lifetime appointment to the Supreme Court, you can't play, you know, hide the salami, or whatever it's called," Dean said. Matthews looked stunned and even Dean seemed to recognize that he had just employed a crude reference to sexual intercourse.

Dean had already caused indigestion among Potomac Democrats for two pronouncements regarding the GOP: "They all look the same" and "The truth is they are a white, Christian party." At a hotel meeting with the Democratic Black Caucus, Dean wondered aloud: "You think the Republican National Committee could get this many people of color in a single room? Only if they had the hotel staff in here."

"He's accustomed to thinking that anything he has to say, he should say," Senator Joe Biden, a Delaware Democrat with his own history of verbal problems, judged after meeting with Dean. "I think in the future we will see him become a little more careful in how he phrases things."

Biden thought wrong. Dean refused to admit he'd goofed. "This is exactly what the Republicans want, and that's a diversion," he replied. He continued the hysteria. "All we ask is that we not turn into a country like Iran where the president can do anything he wants," Dean proposed on *Good Morning America*; elsewhere he called his opponents "the ayatollahs of the right wing." He drew extended condemnation for his defeatist (if truthful) observation to a radio show that "the idea that the United States is going to win the war in Iraq is just plain wrong."

The anti-Republican epithets flowed unimpeded. He called them "evil" and, in the middle over the fight about the fate of Terri Schiavo, "brain-dead." "These guys are bad for democracy. . . . Republicans are not very friendly. . . . They are not nice people. . . . This administration is beginning to erode the core of our democracy. . . . A lot of them have never made an honest living in their lives." As for his own supporters, Dean was quoted by the *Atlantic* saying: "They may have fucked up Iowa, but they sure changed America."

Meantime, Potomac Democrats were grumbling that Dean didn't bring in the energy—and money—they had hoped for. A year into Dean's tenure, *Roll Call,* the Capitol Hill newspaper, reported that Democrats were "furious" to learn that the DNC had just $5.5 million on hand, versus $34 million for the Republicans. Democrats in Potomac Land were "bringing him to Jesus," the newspaper reported, but Dean "doesn't need them. He's his own power center." Dean entered into a semipublic dispute with Senator Chuck Schumer of New York and Representative Rahm Emanuel of Illinois, who were in charge of the House and Senate Democratic campaigns.

But in the months that followed, something strange happened. Democrats began to creep up in opinion polls, forecasters began to predict big Democratic gains in the midterm elections, and the money began pouring in. It may have had nothing to do with Howard Dean, but that didn't matter. Democrats in Potomac Land suddenly loved their eccentric chairman—even his mouth.

They winced, but did not complain, when Dean, on the morning after the election, started screaming again. In a morning news conference at the National Press Club, he stood with hands in his pants pockets and used the word "extraordinary" nine times and "huge" twelve times to explain the triumph: "Huge night!" "Huge achievement!" "Huge step forward!" "Huge mark!" "Huge piece!" "Huge breakthrough!"

"Yeeeeaaaaaaagggggghhhhhhhhh!!!"

A TOLERANCE FOR VERBAL TICS

Among the most intriguing characters in Potomac Land is Harry Reid, the Senate majority leader. He is intriguing because he has attained his high stature despite being afflicted with what can be best described as Potomac-variant Tourette's syndrome: Without any warning, he will blurt out the most shocking of epithets. This is a particularly frightening experience for his aides and a thrilling possibility for the journalists who follow Reid. Reid has survived this affliction largely because his epithets are invariably hurled at the other political party.

At first glance, Reid is slight and soft-spoken. He is a small-town Mormon and, for the most part, a man of modest appetites. His affliction may have resulted from brain injury during his earlier career as a boxer, although it is generally agreed that the onset occurred at about the time Reid ascended to Senate leadership.

There was, for example, the appearance on CNN in 2005 when Reid was asked about Federal Reserve chairman Alan Greenspan, a man held in universally high regard for his stewardship of the economy. "I think he's one of the biggest political hacks we have in Washington," said Reid.

Weeks after that, Reid was talking with high school students when the subject of President Bush came up. "I think this guy is a loser," he said.

The tics began to pile up. A Supreme Court justice was dubbed an "embarrassment," Bush was branded a "liar" who "betrayed the country," and Republicans' "amateur leadership" was said to be "drunk with power" and passing "racist" laws. The chairman of the Joint Chiefs of Staff was "incompetent." He challenged his opponents to "go behind the pool hall" to settle a dispute over filibusters. Of his own Democrats, he said it would take a "miracle" for them to recapture the Senate. The miracle happened, only for Reid to hand Republicans a rhetorical gift by announcing that "this war is lost" in Iraq.

Republicans started a publication to keep track of the tics and called it *Reid All About It*. But Reid was not about to apologize for his outbursts—and most Potomac Men were unwilling to condemn him for a trait so many of them shared.

When reporters outside the Senate chamber asked Reid why he called the president of the United States a "loser," Reid went into a new, extended tirade. He blamed Bush for "a fictitious crisis on Social Security," "deficits that are absolutely unbelievable," "an intractable war in Iraq," "destroying public education," "attempting to change the very basis of this country," paying "no attention" to the uninsured and leaving people "begging for prescription drugs."

"So maybe my choice of words was improper," Reid allows, "but I want everyone here, I repeat, to know I'm going to continue to call things the way that I see them. And I think this administration has done a very, very bad job for this nation and the world."

Reid walked away. "Tell us what you really feel," one of the reporters called after him.

AN ACCEPTANCE OF SCHIZOPHRENIC TENDENCIES

As Republicans learned in the case of Katherine Harris and Democrats discovered in Howard Dean, Potomac Man's readiness to embrace erratic personalities can turn against him unpredictably. But perhaps no Potomac Man has proven as volatile as Walter B. Jones. His genius for political theater was immense—but so was his capacity for changing his mind. Thus did Jones become both a leading proponent of the war in Iraq and one of its leading critics.

In March 2003, days before the American invasion of Iraq, Jones, a Republican congressman from coastal North Carolina, happened upon a restaurant in his state that had taken a stand against France for its refusal to authorize the U.S.-led war. The restaurant, Cubbie's, had changed its menu to remove any trace of France; French fries became freedom fries, French toast became freedom toast, and French bread became freedom bread. Jones drafted a letter to the director of House food services asking that congressional cafeterias do the same. The House administration committee got word of Jones's request and ordered the changes.

Signs were put up at cash registers: UPDATE. NOW SERVING IN ALL HOUSE OFFICE BUILDINGS, FREEDOM FRIES. Overseas, the incident became an example of American boorishness. The French embassy reminded callers that French fries are in fact Belgian. But Jones's gastronomical plan became a rallying cry for supporters of the Iraq war—and Jones became known as the "freedom fries guy."

Two years later, Jones was ready for his next act of political theater. Richard Perle, the neoconservative godfather who championed the war in Iraq, was appearing before the House Armed Services Committee, and it was Jones's turn to question him. He wasn't happy that none of the promised "weapons of mass destruction" had been found in Iraq—a fact Perle blamed on misinformation from Iraqi double agents.

"I'm just amazed with that kind of statement," the congressman told Perle. He then dove, without warning, into the realm of conspiracy theories about the Iraq war's origins. "In 1996 did you and others, and the others eventually became part of the Bush administration, did you all meet with the newly elected [Israeli] Prime Minister [Benjamin] Netanyahu, and try to encourage him to go in and remove Saddam Hussein?"

"The answer is no," Perle said.

Jones moved to another antiwar theory. "Were you aware or involved with the Policy Counter Terrorism Evaluation Group headed by David Wurmser . . . under the office of Douglas Feith?"

"No, I was not," Perle said, but he recognized the theory. "Let me just say that it's clear from the line of questioning that you have been reading substantially incorrect accounts of the way in which intelligence analysis was done within the Department of Defense."

Jones was not entirely satisfied. "I will tell you that it is just amazing to me how we as a Congress were told that we had to remove" Saddam Hussein, he said. Becoming angry and near tears, he continued: "But the reason we were given was not accurate information. And when you make a decision as a member of Congress and you know that decision is going to lead to the death of American boys and girls some of us take that pretty seriously and it's very heavy on our heart."

Those in the audience began to murmur. "I've taken it upon myself to write letters to every family in America that's lost a loved one, and I sign them, by the way, myself," Jones said, alluding to the machine-signed condolence letters sent by Defense Secretary Donald Rumsfeld. "I have signed over nine hundred letters," he said, then again ridiculed Perle's explanation for the missing weapons. "I am just incensed with this statement and I cannot believe that this statement, that you would even allow that to be printed to be honest with you," the gentleman from freedom fries said.

"Forgive me," Perle said mildly. "I don't understand the source of your anger."

The source was Jones's attendance at a funeral for a young Marine sergeant at Camp Lejeune in his home district, soon after the war started. Jones, looking at the Marine's wife and three young children, underwent a personal conversion. He started writing the letters to the parents of the dead. He grew angrier when the weapons failed to turn up.

And, eventually, he turned with ferocity against the war. Outside his office, he hung posters with photographs of the dead soldiers from Iraq. When House officials acting on orders from the Speaker told Jones to take the posters down, he replied, "As long as they're serving and as long as they're dying, I will never take them down." He began dabbling in some far-out conspiracy literature. He met with anti-Bush activist Cindy Sheehan, the mother of a dead soldier. He crossed the Capitol to attend an antiwar meeting of the Democratic Policy Committee in the Senate, where he quoted Rudyard Kipling: "If any question why we died / Tell them, because our fathers lied."

Finally, a few months after his showdown with Perle, Jones joined a Democratic colleague and an antiwar libertarian in introducing legislation calling for an Iraq withdrawal plan. The legislation, as Jones proposed it, went nowhere. But, just as his freedom fries earned him the adoration of Republicans in Potomac Land, his new campaign earned their animosity. When Bush went to an event near Jones's home, the congressman wasn't invited. His home state senator, Republican Elizabeth Dole, took a shot at him by saying his antiwar proposal "emboldens the terrorists."

Still, Potomac Republicans were inclined to indulge Jones's idiosyncrasies. He was still a Republican, and was still a reliable vote on important issues, as when the party took up legislation banning horsemeat. Jones went to the House floor and proclaimed, in typical fashion, "The horses are part of the history of this nation, and the West would never have been settled if it weren't for the horses."

TENDENCY TOWARD MEGALOMANIA

It is well-known that Potomac Man is inclined toward a grand sense of his own importance. But it is not as well-known that this tendency toward megalomania is less a sign of mental trouble than a rational reaction to life in Potomac Land. Congress frequently exempts itself from the laws it passes that apply to others. The president frequently invokes the amorphous "executive privilege" to block the sort of inquiries and prosecutions that ordinary citizens encounter. And officials throughout Potomac Land are permitted to hire large staffs whose salaries are paid by the taxpayer; these staffs serve at the whim and pleasure of the official, and the surest way to protect employment is to praise and flatter the boss. The result of all this, plus the lavish affections of lobbyists, causes Potomac Man to believe he is, in fact, master of all he surveys.

The lawmaker with the keenest sense of entitlement is John Conyers, who is the top Democrat on the Judiciary Committee and the second most senior member of the House, having been elected in 1965. He helped himself to a wife from his staff. In 1990, at the age of sixty-one, he married a twenty-five-year-old woman who had worked for him in Washington; a month later, the young lady gave birth to the first of their two sons. He enjoyed having staff so much that he hired too many, even putting Rosa Parks on his payroll at one point. Twice, he had to fire aides and cut the pay of others because he far exceeded his taxpayer-funded budget and was being pursued by creditors. His staffers have doubled as babysitters, toting around the Conyers children.

His aides learned to indulge his little eccentricities, as when, in the middle of a conversation, he sometimes walks away without warning. Though a natty dresser, he would sometimes neglect to put on socks. When I saw Conyers, a Baptist, help himself to communion at a Catholic Church, an aide patiently explained that the lawmaker thought it his duty to sample the local ethnic cuisine. Other traits seemed more ominous. During the Clinton impeachment, Conyers twice went missing on one crucial day for an hour at a time. The *Washington Post*'s Kevin Merida, writing about Conyers for *Emerge*, reported that his chief of staff eventually tracked him down at the House barbershop. There, Conyers grabbed a mirror and looked at himself, then spoke to the barber: "I don't think I need anything, do you?"

Conyers has treated the House floor as his legislative playground. He authored a resolution affirming that jazz is a "rare and valuable American national treasure." A similar resolution touted tap dancing. He has pushed for a depopulation of the nation's prisons, a thirty-two-hour workweek, and reparations for descendants of slaves. He introduces his legislation as "HR 40" each time, recalling "forty acres and a mule." He was a champion of Nixon's impeachment—before Watergate.

Conyers's charm tends to wear off the farther he gets from his district. He twice ran for mayor of Detroit, getting 4 percent of the vote and then 3 percent. But in his district, it's the rare election where he doesn't get some 80 percent of the vote—and this adds to his well-honed sense of entitlement.

Even the punishment of being in the minority didn't dampen Conyers's sense of importance. When the House wasn't taking sufficient action to investigate a British memo alleging the Bush administration decided on war in Iraq regardless of the intelligence, Conyers decided to hold his own hearings in June 2005.

He booked a conference room in the Capitol basement that he and other Democrats then pretended was the Judiciary Committee hearing room. They draped white cloths over folding tables to make them look like witness tables and brought in cardboard name tags and extra flags to make the event look official.

Conyers, presiding, banged a large wooden gavel and got the other lawmakers to call him "Mr. Chairman." He liked that so much that he started calling himself the chairman and produced other chairmanly phrases, such as "unanimous consent" and "without objection so ordered."

Conyers was having so much fun at the rump session that he ignored aides' entreaties to end the session after a couple of hours. "At the next hearing," he told his colleagues, "we could use a little subpoena power." Even Conyers's firm hand on the gavel could not prevent something of a free-for-all; at one point, a former State Department worker rose from the audience to propose criminal charges against Bush officials. Early in the hearing, somebody accidentally turned off the lights; later, a witness knocked down a flag. Matters were even worse at Democratic headquarters, which handled the overflow crowd. When the C-SPAN feed ended after just an hour, activists groaned and one shouted, "Conspiracy!"

As frequently happens to Potomac Men, Conyers's delight with the perks of power got him into some trouble. In 2003 and 2006, several former aides filed complaints with the House Ethics Committee and the Justice Department that Conyers violated House rules by making them his personal gofers. And they had proof, in the form of e-mails, notes, and memos they shared with the Capitol Hill publication *The Hill*.

Two former aides, Deanna Maher and Sydney Rooks, charged that the lawmaker's Washington aides were sent to Detroit to help Conyers's wife's losing campaign for the state Senate, as well as other officials' city and county races. More demeaning, Conyers made them care for his two young boys, John and Carl. Rooks had to tutor Little John during her work hours. A different staffer picked the boy up from school, made him a snack, and helped him with homework. Conyers prevailed on another aide to use his truck to chauffer members of the lawmaker's family. The *Detroit Free Press,* in 2003, found separate incidents of Conyers having staffers do campaign work on taxpayer time and using government equipment.

In the most egregious case, Conyers had Maher live at his house and care for his boys for six weeks while the lawmaker was in Washington and Monica Conyers was taking law classes in Oklahoma. Maher cleaned the house, did laundry, drove the children to and from school, cooked them meals, and put them to bed. She was in effect a full-time nanny funded by Conyers's congressional payroll. Lawyers on Conyers's staff, meanwhile, were assigned to tutor Monica in her legal studies.

All of this, if proven, would be a violation of House rules, if not federal law. But Conyers has little to worry about. Because the House Ethics Committee is so backlogged with other lawmakers' problems, it may never get to those of Conyers, who has since assumed the chairmanship of the House Judiciary Committee—and ushered a new ethics bill through the House.

Normalizing the Bizarre in Potomac Land

Tolerance of deviance is so high in Potomac Land that eccentrics tend to flourish here. Indeed, it is often difficult to distinguish the truly psychopathic (a small but significant minority) from the merely odd (pretty much everybody).

Clearly, some of Potomac Man's eccentricity is harmless. There is, for example, the example of Senator Orrin Hatch, a Utah Republican known for his devout Mormonism and his highly peculiar fashion sense. First he wore enormous collars that covered his entire neck. Then he donned Save the Children novelty ties. In 2000, he ran a presidential campaign in the Iowa caucuses based improbably, his advisers said, on mobilizing both Mormons and chiropractors.

Hatch, though a Potomac Man of long standing, continues to see himself as a tourist in Potomac Land. In hearings, he lobs theatrical softballs at Bush administration witnesses, drawing embarrassed grins from his fellow Republicans. At the Senate Judiciary Committee hearing in 2005 to vote on the nomination of John Roberts to be chief justice of the Supreme Court, Hatch decided to record the moment for posterity.

It started around the time Patrick Leahy, a Vermont Democrat, observed that the "hearings were dignified." Hatch whipped out his camera phone and snapped a photo of Leahy. Charles Grassley, an Iowa Republican, complained about Democrats' "loyalty to their ideological and single-interest groups." Hatch took a picture. Ted Kennedy asked if Roberts would "lead us on the path of continued equality." Hatch snapped a photo. Joe Biden announced that he had "serious doubts" about Roberts. Hatch pointed and shot. Mike DeWine of Ohio countered that Roberts "bears no ill will." Hatch closed his right eye to line up the picture. Hatch's enthusiasm was contagious. Biden took out his own camera phone and shot a candid of Leahy and Chairman Arlen Specter.

Other types of strange behavior are less easy to laugh off. There was, for example, Democratic congressman Jim Moran's meeting in 2003 when he blamed the war in Iraq on Jews—allegedly adding an epithet for good measure. The Virginian had already earned a reputation as a street brawler, roughing up an eight-year-old boy in an Alexandria parking lot (he said the boy was pretending to have a gun) and getting into fisticuffs with Duke Cunningham on the House floor; he had earlier challenged Dan Burton and Washington mayor Marion Berry to fights. His political career survived even though he received loans from a drug company lobbyist and a credit card company whose interests he had aided. It even survived his wife—Moran is on his third now—calling the police in 1999 claiming the congressman grabbed her. The subsequent divorce proceedings showed that he was broke from trading losses.

Among the most powerful eccentrics in Potomac Land in recent years was House Speaker Newt Gingrich. His reign was a series of odd props and inappropriate emotions. For a while, he carried an ice bucket with him to demonstrate that Republicans had removed ice privileges from congressional offices. He kept a model of a dinosaur in his office to show man's insignificance. Later, he carried a vacuum tube and a computer chip to each speech. "This is a vacuum tube," he would proclaim, then lift the other prop. "This is Intel's Pentium chip. This is three million vacuum tubes." He led off his speech to the 1996 GOP convention with a history of beach volleyball. He tried to pet a squealing pig on the *Tonight Show*.

When Gingrich rose to power, reporters assumed it was harmless eccentricity of the Hatch variety. At one "issues conference," they found doodles Gingrich had written: crisscrosses, lines and squares, a smiley face, and the words "clean, cheap service." But over time, Potomac Man took a more somber view of Gingrich's oddities, particularly after he got in trouble with the House Ethics Committee over a book deal. His once loyal lieutenants gossiped to the *New Republic*. "Emotionally, he's still holding it together," one said, but another wondered if a "good dose of antidepressants might not help," or perhaps swimming laps. "He has been told to smile more and use the phrase 'fun,'" one Republican lobbyist reported.

But Gingrich wasn't having fun. Returning on Air Force One from Israeli prime minister Yitzhak Rabin's funeral, the Speaker was given a seat toward the back of the plane. He had a public tantrum about the slight. Joked David Letterman: "It was just to balance the weight." Clinton aides offered him presidential M&Ms as a consolation prize. It was all downhill from there. Gingrich, having an affair with an aide during the Clinton impeachment, eventually married the young lady. On their wedding registry was a $198 Waterford ice bucket.

ATTEMPTS AT ANGER MANAGEMENT

If Gingrich's idiosyncrasies exceed Potomac Man's tolerance but Hatch's are happily accepted, how should Potomac Land treat Tom Tancredo? The Republican congressman from Colorado represents a crucial constituency: the angry anti-immigrant right.

Or perhaps just the angry. In 2005, he went on a Florida talk radio show and asked what the response should be if terrorists were to launch a nuclear attack on the United States.

"If this happens in the United States, and we determine that it is the result of extremists, fundamentalist Muslims, you know, you could take out their holy sites," the congressman proposed.

"You're talking about bombing Mecca?" the incredulous host asked.

"Yes," Tancredo answered.

Tancredo later said he was merely "throwing out some ideas"—but he declined to apologize even after the State Department said he had gone too far.

In addition to Muslim-baiting, Tancredo has become so consumed by the anti-immigrant cause that he also flirts with racist and white-supremacist groups. This presents a difficult situation for fellow Republicans, who want the support of Tancredo's constituency but worry about Tancredo himself. I pondered this trade-off as I watched Tancredo, in February 2006, giving a speech on the Capitol grounds to the Minutemen, a vigilante group devoted to stalking illegal immigrants. "The president doesn't want secure borders!" Tancredo shouted to the Minutemen, condemning his fellow Republican for being insufficiently anti-immigrant. "He has the resources to do so, but the unfortunate, dirty truth of the matter is he has no desire to do so."

While the Minutemen rallied, they were approached by two men dressed in brown and wearing swastikas. The pair goose-stepped toward the Minutemen and gave a Nazi salute. The men, straight out of *The Producers,* handed out flyers encouraging the Minutemen to "end your alliance with the Republicans!!!"—and join the American Nazi Party.

"Nazis, go home!" cried Minuteman Project founder Jim Gilchrist. It was assumed at first that these were actors trying to sabotage the event, but further investigation revealed they were genuine white supremacists. They wanted to join Tancredo's cause. And while Republicans were happy to harness the anger of Tancredo's anti-immigration voters, they didn't want Nazis.

Tancredo argued, plausibly, that he wasn't endorsing the groups that were praising him, such as U.S. Immigration Reform PAC and the Council of Conservative Citizens. But this became a difficult line of argument when, in September 2006, he gave a speech sponsored by the South Carolina League of the South, which favors Southern secession and opposes equal rights. The racist group announced that Tancredo was its guest. He spoke from a podium draped in the Confederate flag in a room full of Confederate relics, the *Denver Post* reported.

What to do? Potomac Republicans pondered their options—and decided to stick with Tancredo. A month after Tancredo's Confederate speech, a Democratic congressman from Colorado, John Salazar, accused Tancredo of "race-baiting" on another issue. Republicans immediately jumped to Tancredo's defense. He cruised to reelection with 59 percent of the vote—and promptly announced his candidacy for president.

Six

SHAMANISM

The Arunta, an aboriginal tribe from central Australia, believe that life and death are determined by sorcerers who bestow or dispel evil spirits. As a result, an Arunta man finds it to his benefit to have his own personal medicine man, or shaman, who can break the evil spells cast by hostile shamans—and, in turn, cast evil spells on the Arunta man's enemies. To cast a spell on an enemy, the sorcerer must point a sharp bone or stone at the victim and recite a curse. To reverse this curse, a friendly shaman, in the presence of the victim, casts his own magic spells over a number of magical objects such as stones, crystals, and snail shells. If the victim dies, the shaman will use his pointer to direct a curse at the suspected villain, who is certain to die unless his own shaman has a countercurse.

The situation is much the same in Potomac Land, less the bones and snail shells. Potomac Land spirituality is primitive and pagan. Though professing monotheistic belief, Homo politicus in fact worships the gods of public sentiment. Those who gauge public sentiment—the pollsters—and those who attempt to alter it—the consultants and certain lawmakers—are the medicine men, or shamans, of Potomac Land. Using focus groups and randomized surveys as his magical objects, the Potomac shaman devotes himself to healing his clients and colleagues, and casting curses on those of the rival tribe. He does this both by predicting which actions a political leader can take to increase the blessings of public sentiment for himself and, more likely, to decrease the blessings for his opponent.

Potomac shamans have long relied on animal totems. These power animals are at the core of Potomac spirituality: the elephant or the donkey, the hawk or the dove, the lapdog, pit bull, and Hill rat all have special roles in Potomac culture. The shaman also depends on ancestral spirits: According to popular myth, all Democrats descend from either Thomas Jefferson or Andrew Jackson, while all Republicans trace their lineage to Abraham Lincoln; rival festivals, called Jefferson-Jackson and Lincoln Day Dinners, honor the mythic ancestors. But however primitive this system sounds to outsiders, Potomac Man is deadly serious about his magic. If a shaman proves himself to be successful in multiple elections, an ecclesiastical cult forms about him and his services become valued in the millions of dollars.

SHAMANIC HEALING

In his personal life, Potomac Man is a firm believer in modern medicine. At the first sign of a health scare, he will book himself an appointment with the finest specialist, using connections if he has them to persuade a doctor at Johns Hopkins in Baltimore to take his case. In public, however, Potomac Man trusts himself to witchcraft. In making medical decisions, a Potomac Man cares less about science than whether a witch doctor's prescription is consistent with the policy position the Potomac Man has taken. In that sense, he is not unlike the tribes of the Andaman Islands in the Bay of Bengal. Even recently, their sole method of treating illness was to wrap victims in bark and cover them in turtle fat, honey, and ocher pigments.

One such shamanic healer in Potomac Land was Bill Frist. Before coming to the Senate in 1994 as a Republican from Tennessee, he was a heart surgeon who had performed more than 150 heart-lung transplants. In his 1980 book, *Transplant,* he wrote about how, during medical school, "I visited the various animal shelters in the Boston suburbs, collecting cats, taking them home, treating them as pets for a few days, then carting them off to the lab to die in the interests of science."

Once in the Senate, the former cat killer made great efforts to remind everybody of his medical credentials. The sign on his office door in the Capitol said WILLIAM H. FRIST, M.D.—as if he had hung out a shingle and was expecting patients. He signed letters "Bill Frist, M.D." and kept a doctor's bag in his office. When he became Senate majority leader in 2002, ABC News gave him the cheeky title "Dr./Leader/Sen. Frist." Speaking at his alma mater, Princeton, he said: "William H. Frist, majority leader, M.D., can be merged together. But at the end of the day, it allows me to address things with a perspective that's just different."

Just how "different" became apparent in 2005, when Congress decided to intervene in the case of Terri Schiavo. The woman had been in a persistent vegetative state for fifteen years, and Florida courts, citing voluminous medical evidence, sided with her husband's wishes to have her feeding tube removed. Enter Bill Frist, M.D. He went to the Senate floor to back a plan calling for federal courts to take over. "Speaking more as a physician than as a United States senator," the good doctor reminded everybody that "I've been in a situation such as this many, many times before as a transplant surgeon."

His diagnosis? There was "insufficient information to conclude that Terri Schiavo is in a persistent vegetative state." How did he know this? By reviewing a videotape. "I question it based on a review of the video footage which I spent an hour or so looking at last night in my office here in the Capitol," he said, "and that footage, to me, depicts something very different than persistent vegetative state."

The doctor quoted from page 1,625 of a medical textbook. Besides, he added, "Terri's brother told me that Terri laughs, smiles, and tries to speak. Doesn't sound like a woman in a persistent vegetative state."

This struck Frist's classmates from Harvard Medical School as witchcraft, not medicine; thirty-one of them sent him a letter complaining about the quackery. A liberal group distributed e-mail addresses for

Frist's staffers and encouraged them to send photographs of bunions and other ailments and ask for a long-distance diagnosis from Frist. Then, after Schiavo died, an autopsy report found—to the surprise of few people other than Frist—that Schiavo was blind and unaware of her surroundings. Her severely damaged brain was half the normal size and the pathologist concluded that "no amount of treatment or rehabilitation would have reversed the massive loss of neurons."

So much for Frist's diagnosis. Asked about this embarrassing situation, Frist later told NBC News: "I never, never, on the floor of the Senate made a diagnosis."

At the start of his political career, Frist had retained some of his medical sensibilities. When a gunman killed two Capitol police officers in 1998, Frist rushed to the scene and was credited with saving the gunman's life (he only discovered it was the shooter while riding in the ambulance with him). On recess, he flew to Africa and Southeast Asia to volunteer his medical services. But presidential ambitions, and his role as majority leader, pulled Frist toward witchcraft. In December 2004, ABC News's George Stephanopoulos asked him about a government-funded abstinence program that put out the false claim that tears and sweat can transmit AIDS.

"Now, you're a doctor," the interviewer said. "Do you believe that tears and sweat can transmit HIV?"

"I don't know," Frist replied.

"You don't know?" the surprised Stephanopoulos said. "You believe that tears and sweat might be able to transmit AIDS?" When Stephanopoulos continued to press, all Frist would grant is that "it would be very hard" to get AIDS from tears and sweat.

To those watching at home, far from Potomac Land, that sounded absurd. But in Potomac Land, witch doctors were flourishing. There was Phil Gingrey, a Georgia congressman and a gynecologist by training, who contended that Schiavo "responds to the people around her" and "with proper treatment . . . can improve." And there was Dave Weldon, a Florida congressman who advised PBS: "She follows commands, she smiles." He said he saw Schiavo, later confirmed to be blind, "developing a look of recognition on her face and smiling and then trying to vocalize."

And, most notably, there was Tom Coburn, a family practitioner who made it to the Senate from Oklahoma after surviving charges that he sterilized an underage woman without her consent while operating on her for an ectopic pregnancy (he said the consent was oral). Coburn had already developed a reputation as a ferocious religious conservative; shortly after he was elected to the House, he sent out an e-mail to fellow lawmakers saying, "The verse for today is 'Behold I am the Lord, the God of all flesh—Is anything to difficult for me?' " (The Lord left the second "o" off "too.") A congressional colleague of Coburn's complained to the daily *Oklahoman*. Coburn also became known for hosting an annual pizza lunch at which lawmakers and their staffers watched a slide show about venereal disease.

During the Schiavo episode, Coburn argued that the woman was functioning, then, without performing the examination himself, challenged the findings of the autopsy "based on what I have on my desk in Washington." Coburn reached even higher levels of shamanic healing during the John Roberts Supreme Court confirmation hearings. In front of the Judiciary Committee and a televised audience, he became a human polygraph test.

"As you have been before our committee, I've tried to use my medical skills of observation of body language to ascertain your uncomfortableness and ill at ease with questions and responses," the senator-doctor told the witness. "And I will tell you that I am very pleased, both in my observational capabilities as a physician to know that your answers have been honest and forthright as I watch the rest of your body respond to the stress that you're under."

Frist, for his part, had moved on to new realms of science. He began operating on gorillas at the National Zoo. He submitted to a profile by the *Washington Post*'s Laura Blumenfeld, who turned a number of phrases likely to be unhelpful to Frist in the presidential race he was planning: that he once "cut out a dog's heart and held it in his palm," and that "the stink of ape sweat and gorilla testosterone soaked his hair and clothes." Frist said of his patient, a gorilla named Kuja: "He's on my side." But, as it happened, Kuja was not registered to vote in the New Hampshire primary, and Frist, noticing a distinct lack of support, decided not to run for president.

DIVINATION

Potomac Man's sense of his own importance extends to his relationship with God. Like other American and Western cultures, he is monotheistic. But unlike similar cultures, Potomac Man believes he has a direct pipeline to the Almighty. Years ago in Potomac Land, the common view was, as President Kennedy put it, "here on earth God's work must truly be our own." Potomac theology has shifted enormously in the forty-five years since then, and Potomac Man now believes that God plays an active and even decisive role in Potomac Land's daily affairs.

In Florida, Katherine Harris told aides that God wanted her to be a senator. The Lord did not prevail in that race, but He did in two others, also in 2006. At an event for Ed Rendell in Pennsylvania, a minister introduced the governor by saying, "The God of Israel said, 'One more term.'" And at a Florida gubernatorial event, another minister introduced candidate Charlie Crist by saying, "The Lord Jesus spoke to me, and he said . . . 'Charlie Crist will be the next governor of the state of Florida.'"

To understand the will of God, Potomac Man requires the assistance of several Old Testament–style prophets who discuss political affairs with the Heavenly Father and then convey his predictions and wishes back to Potomac Land. There are many such prophets, but the most famous by far is the Reverend Pat Robertson, a former presidential candidate who formed the Christian Coalition and other organizations for religious conservatives.

At the start of each year, Robertson has a one-on-one conversation with God, then delivers a summary on his television show, *The 700 Club*. In 2005, Robertson announced: "The Lord had some very encouraging news for George Bush. . . . What I heard was that Bush is now positioned to have victory after victory and that his second term is going to be one of triumph, which is pretty strong stuff." Indeed. Showing remarkable attention to specifics, God told Robertson that Bush will "have Social Security reform passed, that he'll have tax reform passed, that he'll have conservative judges on the courts."

Further, God told Robertson, "I will remove judges from the Supreme Court quickly and their successors will refuse to sanction the attacks on religious faith." On the downside, God indicated that the Second Coming would not occur in calendar year 2005.

Skeptics might point out that nothing turned out quite that way. Either Robertson was wrong about God's views, or Potomac Man's God is not as all-powerful as he assumes. Still, God, through Robertson, correctly predicted the winner of the 2004 presidential race, even if not by the margin He promised. ("I'm hearing from the Lord it's going to be like a blowout," Robertson had said.)

Because of his personal relationship with God, Robertson has, in recent years, gone further afield with his prophecies. After Israeli prime minister Ariel Sharon suffered a massive stroke, Robertson attributed it to divine retribution for pulling out of the Gaza Strip, and "woe unto any prime minister of Israel who takes a similar course." When a Pennsylvania town, in late 2005, voted out school board members who favored Christian intelligent design theory over evolution, God's messenger warned, "If there is a disaster in your area, don't turn to God."

The Pennsylvania prophecy followed Robertson's call for the assassination of Venezuelan President Hugo Chávez and his earlier warning that Orlando invited "earthquakes, tornadoes, and possibly a meteor" for displaying gay-pride flags. In 2003, he said of Colin Powell's State Department: "If I could just get a nuclear device inside of Foggy Bottom, I think that's the answer." He had earlier proposed "a very small nuke thrown off on Foggy Bottom to shake things up."

Chávez, Orlando, Pennsylvania, and the State Department survived the prophecies, but Robertson kept delivering what his supporters called "messages from God." "If I heard the Lord right," Robertson announced in 2006, "the coasts of America will be lashed by storms. There well may be something as bad as a tsunami in the Pacific Northwest." He also received a divine promise that a liberal justice would retire from the Supreme Court—but Justice John Paul Stevens, celebrating his eighty-sixth birthday, evidently didn't get the same message.

CHARMS AND MAGIC

Though Potomac Man is avowedly monotheistic, he retains a number of pagan tendencies. These pagan inclinations center around elections, which are Potomac Land's holiest days and which shape the fate of almost every Potomac Man. When it comes to this biennial festival—the one day in 730 when people outside Potomac Land have a say in Potomac culture—Potomac Man is highly superstitious. He studies historical patterns. He anxiously awaits each public opinion poll as if it were a divine judgment. And he turns for prophecies to the oracle at Watergate—a figure as important to Potomac Man as the pharaoh was to Joseph and the oracle at Delphi was to the Greeks.

The oracle at Watergate is an unassuming figure who goes by the everyman name of Charlie Cook. Working out of the modest, five-person offices of the *Cook Political Report* in the Watergate complex, he is chubby, wears big glasses, and talks with a soft Louisiana accent. His boyish haircut causes constant speculation about a hairpiece. And, luckily for Potomac Man, he is not shy about his prophecies.

Two weeks before the 2006 midterm elections, I followed the oracle around Potomac Land for a day and watched as he saw the future.

The Seer of Future Congresses was asked how many seats the Democrats would gain in the House. "Twenty to thirty-five," he answered.

The oracle was asked to consult his crystal ball about Democratic gains in the Senate. "At least four," he answered without hesitation. "Most likely five or six."

Two weeks later, the results were in. The Democrats gained twenty-eight seats in the House, six in the Senate.

Mere mortals pay handsomely for such vision—$5,000 up to $20,000 for a Cook speech. I caught him in between speeches to the American Beverage Association in Las Vegas, American Express and a hedge fund in New York, the paper industry in Georgia, a law firm and an automobile group in Washington, and a corporate housing group in Boston.

At each stop, Cook read the candidates' life lines and the parties' tea leaves. "Senators Santorum in Pennsylvania and Mike DeWine in Ohio are pretty much done," he told a law firm's audience at the Willard hotel. Including Senators Conrad Burns and Lincoln Chafee, Cook added, "I'd be surprised if any of those four can survive." Correct, correct, correct, and correct.

The law firm's guests at the Willard were profuse in their praise for the oracle. "A renowned expert . . . one of the best political handicappers . . . the Picasso of election analysis. . . . He's hot."

"Hot" is not the first description that comes to mind for Cook, who entered the ballroom lugging an overstuffed canvas bag, a torn padded envelope, and an overflowing blue file folder. He had the tail of his tie tucked into his shirt and carried a Starbucks venti latte. But this modest oracle created an industry of election prognostication, commissioning his own polls, writing a column, appearing almost daily on television during election season, and answering every reporter's phone call.

There are other seers and diviners in Potomac Land. Stuart Rothenberg started handicapping elections even before Cook did. And others have tried to take market share from Cook, using the same terms—"toss-up," "lean Democratic," "likely Republican"—to call races. The day I wrote about Cook, I got an e-mail from Quin Hillyer of the *American Spectator*. "I beat Cook at predicting, always," Hillyer wrote.

But on Election Day, Rothenberg, predicting thirty-four to forty House seats for Democrats, proved too high. Hillyer, forecasting a gain of only two seats for Democrats, was way too low. Cook was just right. "The oracle is happy," he wrote in an e-mail after the election. "I have NEVER stuck my fat ass (or when it was skinny) out this far before." In Potomac Land, these are the words of a prophet.

SORCERY AND THE OCCULT

Potomac Man is obsessed with black magic. It is quite fashionable for a Potomac Man to proclaim that the political trade is evil, and, while believing in his own virtuousness, he supposes that he alone is good in a land of bad people. This belief that politics is a black art is somewhat self-fulfilling. Because he believes that politics is evil and voters are motivated by base sentiments, he has in recent years converted campaigning into a round-the-clock effort to defile and degrade the political opposition. And he has a healthy regard for those in either party who have demonstrated their ability to destroy others' reputations.

In that sense, the most widely admired shaman in all of Potomac Land is Karl Rove. Officially, he was the chief strategist for President Bush; but unofficially, he is the man who created President Bush, known alternately as "co-president," "Rasputin," "the Architect," or "Bush's Brain." After Republican victories in 2000, 2002, and 2004, he gained a place among the greatest shamans Potomac Land has ever seen: Lee Atwater, James Carville, Dick Morris, Michael Deaver. In each case, these men had a mystical sense for what the voters' sentiment would be on Election Day, and was able to position his candidate to match that sentiment.

Rove first practiced his black magic in 1970 when he stole letterhead from a Democratic candidate for Illinois state treasurer. He sent out thousands of invitations to a supposed opening of the candidate's campaign headquarters with the promise of "free beer, free food, girls, and a good time for nothing." In 1973, with the College Republicans, he was accused of "dirty tricks" such as going through opponents' garbage. In 1986, he wrote a memo advising a candidate for governor in Texas: "Attack, attack, attack." During that same race, a listening device was found in Rove's office, causing a scandal about the opposition but apparently planted by Rove himself.

Rove got better and better at the occult. In 1990, he made an ad for a candidate for Texas agriculture commissioner alleging a month before the race that the Democratic opponent's aides would soon be indicted; this was followed by claims that Rove himself had ordered the investigations. Finally, in 1994, he was the brains behind the George W. Bush defeat of Texas governor Ann Richards—a campaign that included a whisper campaign suggesting that the Democrat was a lesbian. When Bush won that race, Rove began grooming him for the presidency, assigning him books to read and recruiting experts such as Condoleezza Rice to tutor Bush on policy. Rove likened himself to Mark Hanna, the strategist behind the election of President William McKinley at the end of the nineteenth century and three decades of Republican dominance.

In the 2000 presidential campaign, Rove was suspected of having great powers of sorcery. He was tagged with a smear campaign before the South Carolina primary suggesting that opponent John McCain was unstable because of his years as a prisoner of war in Hanoi. Bush triumphed in the state. Joining Bush in the White House, Rove became a celebrated shaman. When a Democratic Senate aide found a disk near the White House containing a PowerPoint presentation Rove had authored (a Rove intern had dropped it), Potomac Land reacted as if the Dead Sea Scrolls had been discovered.

Rove's presentation, "The Strategic Landscape," and one by his deputy, predicted, accurately, that two Republican senators would not win reelection. It also spoke of Bush's difficulty in relating to black and Hispanic voters, suburban women, and Catholics. *The New Yorker* wondered whether it was "the Rosetta stone to the mind of Karl Rove or a piece of deliberate disinformation designed to throw the Democrats off the scent."

Evidently, it was the former. In a sweeping victory for Republicans in 2002, Democratic senator Max Cleland, a triple amputee from the Vietnam War, lost his seat after his patriotism was questioned and a GOP ad linked him to Osama bin Laden. Likewise, before the Republican wins in 2004, ads by an outside group called Swift Boat Veterans for Truth questioned Bush opponent John Kerry's patriotism and military service. Eyes again turned to Rove. "This town is built on myths, and I've become a convenient myth," he said on Fox News. But he enjoyed his mythic position: After left-wingers in 2004 accused Bush of using a hidden radio receiver during a debate, Rove pretended to dictate lines to Bush during a stump speech.

The mythology was enhanced by his eerily accurate forecasts. True, he had forecast a big win for Bush in Florida in 2000. But just days before the 2004 election, he said the gods had told him that Bush was ahead in eight of ten battleground states. On the eve of the election, he predicted a three-point win for Bush—more accurate than the exit polls. Rove's magic powers had never been higher; in early 2005, he was given authority not just over White House political operations but over policy as well.

Rove was in position to lead Republicans to another election win in 2006—and perhaps a McKinleyesque Republican majority for years to come. But then, perhaps convinced of his own invincibility, the shaman stumbled. He got wrapped up in the Valerie Plame scandal. Though White House spokesman Scott McClellan had sworn to Rove's innocence, the prosecutor learned not only that Rove leaked the identity of the CIA operative but that he lied about it when asked by a grand jury. Rove employed the "foggy-memory defense," suggesting that he just forgot about his role. This was hard to believe coming from Bush's brain, and Rove was forced to return three more times to the grand jury, the last time for four and a half hours as prosecutors weighed an indictment and demonstrators outside distributed "Karl Rove brand" condoms ("Some things should never leak").

"Karl," the Associated Press's Pete Yost called as Rove entered the courthouse, "if it came down to a root canal or a couple of hours with [Prosecutor] Fitzgerald, what would you do?" Rove only turned and stared.

Rove ultimately escaped indictment, but his magic was fading. In the White House, he was stripped of his newly acquired policy duties. And his crystal ball grew cloudy. Two weeks before the election, he went on National Public Radio to announce that his predictions "add up to a Republican Senate and Republican House. You may end up with a different math, but you're entitled to your math, I'm entitled to *the* math." The Republicans soon lost both chambers, and the day after the election, Bush held a press conference and said Rove spent too much of the fall reading books. "I obviously was working harder on the campaign than he was," the president said. Rove gave a sheepish grin and stared at his lap.

CULT OF NINO

Antonin Scalia occupies a crucial position in Potomac Land. A Supreme Court justice for two decades, he is the leading originalist, which means that he rules on cases according to what he believes the framers had in mind when they wrote the Constitution, Potomac Man's most sacred text. But because those who wrote the Constitution have been deceased for the better part of two centuries, "Nino" Scalia finds himself in the heady position of being the sole arbiter of the Constitution's meaning.

This has, understandably, produced a certain degree of arrogance. For one, he objects to the production of graven images: He forbids cameras in the Supreme Court chambers, and even when giving a speech outside the Court in 2005, he cried out, "Could we stop the cameras? . . . click, click, click, click, click." Same thing for audio likenesses: In 2004, federal marshals confiscated the recorders of reporters who dared to tape a speech Scalia was giving to high school students about constitutional protections. When he went on a hunting trip with Vice President Cheney shortly before ruling on a case against Cheney, he wrote a two-page memo explaining why there was no reason to recuse himself. Leaving church in 2006, he made an obscene gesture when asked about those who question his impartiality on matters of church and state.

As the Court's sole arbiter of constitutional meaning, Scalia offers legal views that are equally intemperate. On a death penalty case, he remarked, "Mere factual innocence is no reason not to carry out a death sentence properly reached." Disagreeing with the Court's decision against a juvenile death penalty, he said his colleagues had engaged in "sophistry," wondering, "By what conceivable warrant can nine lawyers presume to be the authoritative conscience of the nation?" He has also accused his peers of ruling on the "flimsiest of grounds." When he disagreed with the majority on executing the mentally retarded, he awarded his colleagues "the prize for the Court's Most Feeble Effort to fabricate 'national consensus.'"

He has particular contempt for justices who believe the Constitution is a "living" document that must be interpreted according to contemporary views; this interferes with Scalia's status as the lone interpreter of the Constitution's meaning. He scolds those who think the Constitution reflects "the evolving standards of decency that mark the progress of a maturing society—if that is what you think it is, then why in the world would you have it interpreted by nine lawyers? What do I know about the evolving standards of decency of American society?" Before gaining a conservative majority on the Court, Scalia assorted: "My most important function on the Supreme Court is to tell the majority to take a walk."

Scalia believes he carries a heavy burden being the only person who can know the framers' minds. He complains that he is often asked, " 'When did you first become an originalist?' like it's a weird affliction that seizes people, like 'When did you start eating human flesh?' " And his fealty to the framers' wishes sometimes overrules even his own. "Though I'm a law-and-order type, I cannot do all of the mean, conservative things I'd like to do to the society," he laments.

Cult of the Neocon

Just as Scalia is the guru of domestic affairs, Potomac Man entrusts his relations with foreigners almost entirely to one man, the prince of darkness, Richard Perle. Virtually all decisions in foreign policy, from the anti-Soviet hard line to the war in Iraq, have origins in Perle's brain. Like many of the most powerful figures in Potomac Land, Perle holds no prominent office; his highest rank was assistant defense secretary in the Reagan administration. But as godfather of the hawkish neoconservative movement—a movement that has dominated in recent years—Perle is viewed as the intellectual firepower behind such important pawns as Cheney and Donald Rumsfeld.

"Of course I'm pulling all the strings," Perle said with a laugh when asked about this in 2002. "I've been doing this for years!" He also tried some modesty: "My so-called pawns inside are all smarter than I am." But then came the Iraq war, when administration officials followed his prophecies as if they had been delivered by a burning bush.

A year before the invasion, Perle descended from the mountaintop to announce that the war "isn't going to be over in twenty-four hours, but it isn't going to be months, either." He forecast that Iraq could "finance, largely finance, the reconstruction of their own country, and I have no doubt that they will." When UN weapons inspectors failed to turn up contraband munitions, the prince knew that they were "being seriously deceived . . . the way the Nazis hoodwinked Red Cross officials." He delivered the good news to a Senate committee that "we need not send substantial ground forces into Iraq"—no more than forty thousand. Days before the war, which he had been advocating for years, Perle divined that the war would last three weeks at most, "and there is a good chance that it will be less than that."

Days after the invasion, Perle had more visions. He proclaimed that "the war has demonstrated a really quite remarkable ability of the United States to operate more or less independently." Further, he boasted, "the predictions of those who opposed this war can be discarded like spent cartridges. You remember them? We will kill hundreds of thousands. We will create thousands of new terrorists. The Arab world will rise up and set the region aflame. Tony Blair and George Bush knew better."

Or did they? Ultimately, each one of Perle's portents turned out to be wrong. By 2006, he was widely seen as a false prophet. But the prince of darkness rose up to defend his earlier visions. In October, he told a writer for *Vanity Fair* that his prophecies had been true but that he had cast his pearls before swine. His followers, he charged, were "dysfunctional."

"Huge mistakes were made, and I want to be very clear on this: They were not made by neoconservatives, who had almost no voice in what happened, and certainly almost no voice in what happened after the downfall of the regime in Baghdad," Perle unloaded. "I'm getting damn tired of being described as an architect of the war. I was in favor of bringing down Saddam. Nobody said, 'Go design the campaign to do that.' I had no responsibility for that."

Who was to blame? "At the end of the day, you have to hold the president responsible," the dark prince said of his most important disciple. "I don't think he realized the extent of the opposition within his own administration, and the disloyalty." Then he said something truly astounding: "I think if I had been delphic, and had seen where we are today, and people had said, 'Should we go into Iraq?' I think now I probably would have said no."

Richard Perle, not delphic? It was as astonishing an admission as ever had been heard in Potomac Land.

CULT OF THE COMMISSIONERS

Because Potomac Man organizes his life by partisanship, it is difficult for him to find anything approaching objective truth. Pseudoacademic institutions known as think tanks align with one party or the other. Journalists are presumed to be Democrats unless they are from a smaller group of explicitly conservative outlets. Residents of McLean, Virginia, are presumed to be Republican. Federal bureaucrats are presumed to be Democrats. Since the Bush versus Gore decision in the 2000 presidential election, the Supreme Court is judged to be as partisan as the Republican National Committee.

In this tribal atmosphere, the demand for a truly neutral authority is intense. One such authority, Norman Ornstein of the American Enterprise Institute, is quoted more than one hundred times a month on average by Potomac Land news outlets. Thomas Mann, an equivalent authority at the Brookings Institution, rates some seventy quotes per month. Obviously, Ornstein and Mann cannot keep up with all of Potomac Land's problems, so Potomac Man has developed a system that attempts to override partisanship when a problem proves too vexing for normal channels: the blue-ribbon commission. In practice, the commissions rarely solve problems; they merely allow elected representatives to postpone decisions and deflect responsibility. Recent commissions—on Social Security, tax reform, election reform, intelligence capabilities, the September 11 attacks, and the Iraq war—have generally led in the same direction: inaction.

Yet the proliferation of these commissions has created a new kind of Potomac shaman: the permanent commissioner. There are perhaps three dozen such people, retired lawmakers, cabinet officals, and judges, who move from commission to commission, mulling the nation's problems and drafting reports full of recommendations and executive summaries. These professional commissioners, because they do not answer to voters, are relatively free to give honest advice—though too much honesty could jeopardize an appointment to a future commission.

Among the permanent commissioners is Warren Rudman, the former senator who sat on an intelligence commission, a Gulf War commission, an Energy Department commission, a Mideast commission, and a national security commission. Then there's Brent Scowcroft, the former national security adviser who has sat on a foreign intelligence board, the Iran-Contra commission, a defense management commission, an arms control committee, and a strategic forces commission. Senator Daniel Patrick Moynihan, a commissioner of great renown, died while sitting on a Social Security commission. (Nothing happened with that commission's recommendations, and the president announced plans to form a new one.)

Surveying the Iraq Commission in 2006, commentator Michael Kinsley wondered: "Where is Dick Holbrooke? Does Sandra Day O'Connor's new availability mean that Madeleine Albright is out of luck from now on? Are they sure that Larry Eagleburger is still alive? But Vernon Jordan is there, along with Ed Meese and Alan Simpson and Lee Hamilton. This is one torch that has not been passed to a new generation, although former Virginia senator and presidential son-in-law Charles Robb (age sixty-seven) is a fresh face in the pool of Washington Wise Men. Welcome, Chuck."

Actually, Robb was no newbie: He had just served on the commission looking into intelligence failures. Still, Robb couldn't come close to the commission-sitting prowess of Lee Hamilton, the former Democratic congressman from Indiana who replaced Henry Kissinger as the preeminent commissioner in Potomac Land. In Congress, he was an energetic panelist, serving on the International Relations Committee, the Joint Economic Committee, the Permanent Select Committee on Intelligence, the Joint Committee on the Organization of Congress, something called the October Surprise Task Force, the Select Committee to Investigate Covert Arms Transactions with Iran, and the Standards of Official Conduct Committee. This prepared him for nonstop commissioning when he quit the Capitol in 1999: the Hart-Rudman Commission on national security, the Baker-Hamilton

Commission on Los Alamos security, the Homeland Security Advisory Council, the 9/11 Commission, the Independent Task Force on Immigration and America's Future, the Carter-Baker Commission on Federal Election Reform, and the Foreign Intelligence Advisory Board.

Few of Hamilton's recommendations were acted upon, of course, but Hamilton himself gained special powers as an independent authority. During the 2004 presidential campaign, John Kerry argued that "Lee Hamilton, the co-chairman of the 9/11 Commission, has said this administration is not moving with the urgency necessary to respond to our needs." The Bush administration also used Hamilton to make its case. When the *New York Times* was threatening to publish a sensitive article about terrorist financing, the White House had Hamilton argue to *Times* editors that publication could harm the program.

Hamilton jealously guarded his status as an independent authority. For years, he praised the integrity of Tom Kean, chairman of the 9/11 Commission. But when Kean, a Republican former governor of New Jersey, crossed the partisan line in 2006 and helped to produce a docudrama that put disproportionate blame for September 11 on Bill Clinton, Hamilton sandbagged his friend in a joint appearance at the National Press Club. "I do not think that that is good for the country," Hamilton said of his friend's film, "because an event of this consequence is very hard to understand, and to distort it or not to present it factually in this kind of a presentation, I think, does not serve the country well." Kean stood at Hamilton's side, his hands clasped in front of him, grinning awkwardly. He tried to distance himself from his efforts. "I was not the producer or director or the author or the writer or whatever else," said Kean, who was, in fact, the co–executive producer.

Score that one for Hamilton. Still, even a highly professional commission sitter like Hamilton can be manipulated by a savvy Potomac Man. Hamilton let that happen to himself on his next commission gig: the Iraq Commission, which he cochaired with Jim Baker, the Republican former secretary of state who led the Bush forces in the Florida recount. Like Hamilton, Baker was a veteran commission sitter; unlike Hamilton, he retained fierce partisanship. So when Baker, seeking to protect Republicans in the 2006 midterm elections, insisted that the commission present none of its ideas about Iraq before the election, Hamilton agreed—even though Iraq violence was increasing by the day.

The two men called a news conference to give a progress report—only to announce to the dozen television cameras and scores of reporters that they could not say anything at all. "We're not going to speculate with you today about recommendations," Baker announced. Can the war in Iraq be won? "We're not going to make any assessments today about what we think the status of the situation is in Iraq," said Hamilton. Could they at least explain their definitions of success and failure in Iraq? "We're not going to get into that today," Baker replied. After more such probing, Hamilton became categorical. "We've made no judgment of any kind at this point about any aspect of policy with regard to Iraq."

It was a grievous blow to shaman Hamilton's credibility. On the one hand, he said that "the next three months are critical" and that "the people of Iraq have the right to expect immediate action." On the other hand, he agreed to a three-month delay out of respect for Baker's political agenda. By the time the two commissioners finished their press conference, reporters were laughing aloud at them. "This," one of the cameramen contributed, "is pitiful."

Actually, the pitiful part was just beginning. While Iraqis were being slaughtered by the thousands and American troop deaths were reaching three thousand, Hamilton and Baker agreed to pose for an Annie Leibovitz photo shoot for *Men's Vogue* (commissioner Sandra Day O'Connor judiciously killed a plan to involve all ten panelists).

By the time Hamilton and Baker released their findings in December, Hamilton pronounced a "grave and deteriorating" situation. "Our ship of state has hit rough waters," the shaman told the cameras. Hamilton, on the other hand, was doing quite well, thank you. Escorted to the Capitol in a motorcade with the other commissioners, he took a cell phone call in the Capitol basement and bragged to reporters that it was Bill Clinton on the line. At a news conference, he boasted that "I think we have fifteen or twenty invitations to testify."

But not, alas for the shaman, much impact. Bush received the report without asking a single question—and proceeded to ignore virtually everything in it as he took Iraq policy in the opposite direction.

SHAPE-SHIFTING

One of the most fascinating aspects of Potomac spirituality is the ability of a very small number of Potomac Men to escape the party framework that imprisons all others. While it is quite common for ordinary Potomac Men to shift their shapes from time to time—Bill Clinton looked like a Republican when he condemned rapper Sister Souljah, and George Bush looked like a Democrat when he criticized "leave us alone" conservatives—almost nobody can criticize people in his own party for an extended period of time and yet survive in Potomac Land.

The most notable exception to the partisan dichotomy in recent years has been John McCain, a Republican senator from Arizona who was able to shift his form into that of a Democrat on a regular basis. He drew his extraparty strength from his time as a Navy pilot; his family's long history of military service; and, particularly, his years as a prisoner of war in Hanoi. This left him with extraordinary powers in Potomac Land: the only member of the Keating Five to survive the savings-and-loan scandal of the 1980s and arguably the leading deal maker in the Senate.

This power came despite—or perhaps because of—his incessant and almost fratricidal criticism of his fellow Republican Bush. This began when he challenged Bush in the 2000 GOP primaries and said, among other things: "Bush wants to give 38 percent of his tax cut to the wealthiest 1 percent of Americans"; "Governor Bush is one of the great polluters in history"; and "Bush's plan has not one penny for Social Security, not one penny for Medicare, and not one penny for paying down the national debt." Later he criticized Bush's policies on global warming, prescription drugs, and veterans. He objected to a Bush campaign ad in 2003, and in 2004 defended Democrat John Kerry against attacks on his military record and accused his fellow

Republicans of "spend[ing] our nation into bankruptcy while our soldiers risk their lives."

Then, in 2006, he ridiculed the happy talk Bush administration officials used to describe the war in Iraq. " 'Stuff happens,' 'mission accomplished,' 'last throes,' 'a few dead-enders': I'm just more familiar with those statements than anyone else because it grieves me so much that we had not told the American people how tough and difficult this task would be. . . . They were led to believe this would be some kind of day at the beach."

With an eye on another presidential run, McCain shifted back to Republican form at critical times. He voted for the Bush tax cuts. He championed the war in Iraq. He gave a warm speech at the 2004 Republican convention celebrating Bush's leadership.

This created some awkwardness. McCain, for example, was on the record as stating both that Bush has "earned our trust" on national security and that he (McCain) had "no confidence" in Bush.

Such shape-shifting alienated Republican primary voters as McCain sought the party's 2008 presidential nomination; he quickly fell from front-runner to nearly bankrupt. But in Potomac Land, this flexibility allows figures in both parties to see McCain in any shape they wish. At a Senate hearing on torture techniques, for example, lawmakers in both parties hid behind McCain's skirts. Asked for an opening statement, Senator Mark Dayton, a Minnesota Democrat, said only, "I just wanted to salute Senator McCain for his comments." Added Lindsey Graham, Republican of South Carolina, "I'd also like to associate myself with Senator McCain."

Things become tricky for McCain, however, when he tangles with another politician who has shape-shifting powers. This happened early in 2006, when McCain attacked Senator Barack Obama, a black Democrat from Illinois and prospective presidential candidate who was developing a following for his crossover appeal to Republicans. It began when Obama, after a meeting in McCain's office, sent him a letter—a press release, really—about proposed lobbying reforms.

"Dear John," the freshman senator wrote, "I know you have expressed an interest in creating a task force to further study and discuss these matters, but I and others in the Democratic Caucus believe the more effective and timely course is to allow the committees of jurisdiction to roll up their sleeves and get to work on writing ethics and lobbying reform legislation that a majority of the Senate can support."

McCain replied with some of the most caustic language ever heard in Potomac Land.

"Dear Senator Obama," he began. "I would like to apologize to you for assuming that your private assurances to me regarding your desire to cooperate in our efforts to negotiate bipartisan lobbying reform legislation were sincere. . . . Thank you for disabusing me of such notions. . . . I'm embarrassed to admit that after all these years in politics I failed to interpret your previous assurances as typical rhetorical gloss routinely used in politics to make self-interested partisan posturing appear more noble. . . . I have been around long enough to appreciate that in politics the public interest isn't always a priority for every one of us."

Obama, wisely, responded mildly. "Dear John," he wrote. "I confess that I have no idea what has prompted your response. . . . The fact that you have now questioned my sincerity and my desire to put aside politics for the public interest is regrettable but does not in any way diminish my deep respect for you nor my willingness to find a bipartisan solution to this problem."

McCain quickly realized he had erred. He wasn't attacking the president, after all. He was attacking a fellow shape-shifter. "We're still friends," McCain announced after patching things up with Obama by phone, not letter. Obama said McCain is "an American hero" who is entitled "to get cranky once in a while."

At a hearing a few days later, McCain and Obama posed jointly for the cameras. "Senator Obama and I are moving on and will continue to work together, and I value his input," McCain recanted. Contrition was an unusual form for the senator to assume.

Seven

AGGRESSION

In medieval Iceland, the fiercest of all Viking warriors were known as the berserkers. They prepared themselves for battle by donning animal skins, drinking the blood of bears and wolves, biting their shields, and howling. Reaching a frenzy, they fought without regard for their own survival and managed to ignore the pain of even severe wounds until the battle ended. They worshipped the god Odin and, like him, were believed to be able to change forms to that of a wolf or bear. Berserker bands were common throughout Scandinavia until the twelfth century. In those times, the warriors' rage was believed to come from animal spirits, while recent theories attribute the frenzy to alcohol or psychoactive mushrooms. Occasionally, a berserker would kill members of his own tribe, but this was regarded as an acceptable price to pay.

Contemporary Homo politicus frowns on the consumption of wolf and bear blood, but his is one of the few cultures that continues the berserker ethos to this day. Indeed, Potomac Men are fierce warriors, and almost every aggressive tradition is represented in Potomac Land. These traditions range from the berserker to counting coup, the stylized battle practice of the Native American tribes of the Great Plains.

In this form of aggression, as much game as warfare, the warrior would touch an enemy with his coup stick without harming him, then run away. The tribes believed this entitled the warrior to some of his victim's spiritual powers, and the coup counter kept score by cutting notches in his coup stick. Extra coup points were awarded for striking an enemy's tepee or stealing a horse. But it was not all fun and games: If the warrior was in the mood, he could also score points by killing and scalping the enemy in the traditional way.

Potomac Land provides plenty of opportunity for the warrior to practice his art, thanks to the perpetual blood feud between Democratic and Republican tribes. Aggression may begin with simple competition, then progress to threat gestures and end in outright fighting. But in any form there can be no doubt that Potomac Man enjoys claiming scalps. In domestic policy matters, winning is the most important thing, even if a party's triumph—say, the blocking of any effort to improve Social Security's finances—is not good for the country. Fights with other civilizations—Iraq, Afghanistan, Muslim extremists—are of grave importance to much of the world but are viewed in Potomac Land primarily as opportunities for party advantage.

THE HEADHUNTER

With the possible exception of Potomac Man, the Jivaro Indians of the jungles of southern Ecuador are arguably the people most dedicated to perpetuating grudges. In the morning, a Jivaro father recites to his sons a list of those he believes have insulted him or killed his kin. Every few years, a Jivaro man goes to a *kakaram*—a cross between a guide and a hit man, essentially—and organizes a hunting party that will locate the hut of the man's enemy, kill him, and cut off his head, separating the skin from the skull. Over the next week, the scalp is boiled and shrunk with hot stones and sand until the resulting *tsanta*, or shrunken head the size of a fist, can be worn as jewelry. To prevent himself from becoming a *tsanta*, the sensible Jivaro man surrounds his own hut with traps and poison-tipped spikes.

Potomac Man does not pursue a collection of shrunken heads, but he is as avid a headhunter as the Jivaro, and each tribe in Potomac Land has his own *kakarams* to advise members on the kill. By far the most prominent *kakaram* in Potomac Land in recent years has been Tom DeLay, who was a pest exterminator in Texas before joining the House of Representatives.

DeLay was originally called "Hot Tub Tom" because of his hard partying, but he became a devout Christian and rose to become House majority leader and, along the way, earned the nickname "the Hammer" for his bullying ways with colleagues. He kept two bull-whips in his Capitol office. He championed the impeachment of Bill Clinton, once telling the *Washington Post* that it's "hard for me not to hate Bill Clinton." He threatened judges with violence during the Terri Schiavo right-to-die case, saying, "The time will come for the men responsible for this to answer for their behavior." He attacked the news media as "blow-dried Napoleons."

DeLay called for his followers to "march forward with a biblical worldview" to counter the "cultural coup d'état" staged by his opponents. He argued that the United States should be governed by fundamentalist Christian beliefs, comparing those who disagreed to the killers of Jesus. "The truth hurts," he told the *Washington Post*. "People hate the messenger. That's why they killed Christ."

In his role as headhunter, DeLay went after the Electronics Industries Alliance for hiring a Democrat as its president—and then, as punishment, holding up action on legislation the group favored. The House Ethics Committee rebuked him for "badgering a lobbying organization." He earned another rebuke from the ethics panel for telling Republican congressman Nick Smith of Michigan that if Smith would vote DeLay's way on Medicare legislation, DeLay would support the congressional candidacy of Smith's son. DeLay kept the ethics panel busy: He also earned its wrath for holding a golf fundraiser with energy company Westar while the House was working on an energy bill. Westar had paid $25,000 for the chance to talk with DeLay about the bill.

Meanwhile, former DeLay aides Tony Rudy and Michael Scanlon pleaded guilty in the lobbying scandal of Jack Abramoff, who was also close with DeLay and arranged three foreign junkets for the congressman. All these activities earned DeLay the dubious status of "most-admonished" of the 435 members of the House. But DeLay believed that he was not subject to the rules that governed his colleagues. Though House rules generally limit roll-call votes to fifteen minutes, DeLay didn't hesitate to keep a vote open for an hour or two if that's how much time it took for him to twist arms.

The Hammer's biggest headhunting expedition—and the one that ultimately cost him his own scalp—was his effort to oust five Texas Democrats from their congressional seats in 2004. DeLay rolled out his plan in 2002: He would start a campaign to have an unprecedented mid-decade redistricting plan in Texas, whereby the GOP state legislature could redraw the map in a way that would give the Republicans five to seven more seats in Congress. DeLay's justification: "I'm the majority leader and we want more seats." He had even set up a group, Texans for a Republican Majority, to fund the effort.

Democrats, outnumbered in the Texas legislature, hatched a plan: If enough of them were out of the state, the legislature could not reach the quorum needed to implement the new districts. And so a group of Texas Democratic legislators fled to Ardmore, Oklahoma. DeLay was determined to stop them. One of his aides called the Federal Aviation Administration and reported that "over fifty Texas legislators were in hiding and that the governor of Texas had issued a warrant for their apprehension." The DeLay aide requested the FAA's help in locating a plane belonging to Democratic state representative Pete Laney.

Some thirteen FAA people worked on DeLay's requests for eight hours, and one of them later protested that he "felt used" when he learned the reason for the request. DeLay also asked the Justice Department, unsuccessfully, to put the FBI and U.S. marshals on the case. This got DeLay another spanking from the now-familiar ethics committee.

DeLay ultimately got his redistricting, and five more Republican seats in the House—but it was a fleeting victory at enormous cost. A year after the 2004 win, DeLay was preparing to face trial on money laundering and conspiracy. Two grand jury indictments charged that he conspired with two political aides to use illegal corporate contributions in the 2002 state elections that gave Republicans their majority in the state legislature. DeLay, the indictments said, laundered $190,000 in Texas corporate contributions through the Republican Party in Washington and then sent the money back to Texas legislative candidates. Under indictment, he had to give up his permit to carry his concealed handgun.

DeLay surrendered to authorities in Austin and, in a last bit of political showmanship, grinned broadly for his mug shot so it couldn't be used against him in political ads. He became the first member of House leadership to be indicted in at least half a century. Republicans had tried and failed to rewrite a rule requiring indicted leaders to resign their posts, so DeLay had no choice but to go. Even old friends, following Potomac Land custom, backed away. The White House proclaimed that "we need to let the legal system work." Even Speaker Denny Hastert, DeLay's front man, joined in. "The conference has to go on," he said.

Fortunately, DeLay still had the shoulders of conservative talk show hosts to cry on. "They say a clever prosecutor can indict a ham sandwich if he gets the right grand jury," Pat Robertson told him.

"This is a ham sandwich with no ham," DeLay replied.

Another host, Mike Gallagher, read a quotation from Ann Coulter that "the party that's now celebrating and popping champagne corks over Tom DeLay's indictment . . . worships at the altar of the president who was getting oral sex in the Oval Office on Easter Sunday."

"Ha-ha," DeLay answered.

Gallagher predicted, "You're going to make it, my friend."

That was not so. When DeLay's trial preparations dragged on, Republicans elected new leaders. DeLay eventually quit his seat in Congress, too.

His political kin honored him as a Christian martyr. "I believe the most damaging thing that Tom DeLay has done in his life is take his faith seriously into public office, which made him a target for all those who despise the cause of Christ," Rick Scarborough, convener of a conference called The War on Christians, declared with DeLay in the audience. Scarborough reminded DeLay: "God always does his best work right after a crucifixion."

DeLay tried on the martyr mantle and decided he liked it. "Sides are being chosen, and the future of man hangs in the balance!" he warned the crowd. "The enemies of virtue may be on the march, but they have not won, and if we put our trust in Christ, they never will. . . . It is for us then to do as our heroes have always done and put our faith in the perfect redeeming love of Jesus Christ."

"Keep your eyes on Jesus," Scarborough called after DeLay as he departed the stage.

On June 8, 2006, DeLay gave his farewell speech on the House floor, celebrating partisanship and decrying those who sought consensus. "It is not the principled partisan, however obnoxious he may seem to his opponents, who degrades our public debate but the preening, self-styled statesman who elevates compromise to a first principle," the martyr said. "For the true statesman, Mr. Speaker, we are not defined by what they compromise but by what they don't."

DeLay was out of power, but he still was a warrior. And so he devoted his considerable talent to getting country singer Sara Evans declared the winner of the *Dancing with the Stars* television show. "One of her opponents on the show is ultraliberal talk show host Jerry Springer," DeLay wrote to his supporters in September 2006. "We need to send a message to Hollywood and the media that smut has no place on television by supporting good people like Sara Evans." Evans, whom DeLay said represented "good American values," made it to the final six couples but then pulled out of the show, saying she had filed for a divorce from her husband.

Pugilism as a Lifestyle

Like the samurai of thirteenth-century Japan, the Potomac warrior lives by a code. The samurai's Bushido warrior code required the fighter to show absolute loyalty to his master, self-discipline, and respectful behavior. The warrior code for Potomac Man is nearly identical, except for the last bit about respectful behavior.

Donald Rumsfeld was the very model of a modern secretary of defense. When a terrorist-piloted plane struck the Pentagon on

September 11, Rummy, as he is known, felt the building shake and then ran toward the smoke, helping to evacuate the injured. On television, his extreme self-confidence, his smart-alecky responses to questions, and his exceptional vigor for a septuagenarian made him the most celebrated of Potomac Land warriors.

"Do you like this image?" Larry King asked him one night on CNN. "You now have this new image called sex symbol."

"For the AARP," Rumsfeld protested modestly.

As the public face of a successful war to depose the Taliban in Afghanistan, Rumsfeld watched his stature soar. But, as with the Nordic berserker, Rumsfeld's war frenzy at times became indiscriminate, and he cut down friend and foe alike—particularly as things started to go wrong in his second war, in Iraq.

Before the Iraq war, he confidently predicted that the campaign "certainly isn't going to last any longer" than five months.

Turning on European allies who refused to back the war, he scoffed: "You're thinking of Europe as Germany and France. I don't. I think that's old Europe."

When Americans failed to find the promised weapons of mass destruction in Iraq, he breezily asserted: "We know where they are. They're in the area around Tikrit and Baghdad and east, west, south, and north somewhat."

When the anti-American insurgency began in Iraq, Rumsfeld blew off the attackers as "dead enders."

When looters ransacked Baghdad, he was unimpressed. "Stuff happens," he said. "Freedom's untidy."

Finally, he even turned on his own troops. Answering soldiers' complaints, he parried, "You go to war with the army you have, not the army you might want or wish to have at a later time."

Unsurprisingly, Rumsfeld's rage earned him a great number of antagonists, who were only angered further by his pedantic responses. Explaining the nature of terrorist threats, he once lectured: "There are no knowns. There are things we know that we know. There are known unknowns. That is to say there are things that we now know we don't know. But there are also unknown unknowns. There are things we do not know we don't know."

Rumsfeld the warrior turned his spear on all in his path. In early 2005, lawmakers were anxious about the hundreds of billions of dollars going to Iraq and the Abu Ghraib torture scandal. But Rumsfeld, coming to Congress to testify, was not about to play nice. At a hearing of the House Armed Services Committee in February, two dozen lawmakers had not yet had their turn to question Rumsfeld when he decided he had had enough.

At 12:54, he announced that at 1 P.M. he would be taking a break and then going to another hearing in the Senate. "We're going to have to get out and get lunch and get over there," he said. When the questioning continued for four more minutes, Rumsfeld picked up his briefcase and began to pack up his papers.

The chairman, California Republican Duncan Hunter, apologized to his colleagues for a rather "unusual" situation.

Not that Rumsfeld was answering their questions anyway. Did he care to voice an opinion on efforts by U.S. pilots to seek damages from their imprisonment in Iraq? "I don't." Could he comment on what basing agreements he might seek in Iraq? "I can't." How about the widely publicized cuts to programs for veterans? "I'm not familiar with the cuts you're referring to." How long will the war last? "There's never been a war that was predictable as to length, casualty, or cost in the history of mankind."

Rumsfeld seemed to be spoiling for a fight from the start, when in his opening statement he implicitly chided Congress for "an increasingly casual regard for the protection of classified documents and information."

When the ranking Democrat on the House Armed Services Committee, Ike Skelton of Missouri, asked about the number of insurgents in Iraq, the secretary said, "I am not going to give you a number for it because it's not my business to do intelligent work." (He presumably meant to say "intelligence.") Ultimately, Rumsfeld admitted he had estimates at his fingertips. "I've got two in front of me," he said.

"Could you share those with us?" Skelton inquired.

Not just now, Rumsfeld said. "They're classified."

Even death did not stop the Rumsfeld rage. When a predecessor at the Pentagon, Caspar Weinberger, died in 2006, Rumsfeld eulogized Weinberger as a fellow warrior, noting a favorite Churchill phrase, "Never give in—never, never, never, never—in nothing, great or small, large or petty, never give in." Rumsfeld left out the qualifying part of the phrase: "except to convictions of honor and good sense."

And when he did not like a question he was asked, he merely asked himself a different one. Pressed by a reporter about strains on the army, Rumsfeld replied: "Now, does the force still need more rebalancing? You bet. . . . Do we have too big an institutional army, as opposed to a war-fighting army? You bet. And is that what we've been doing for five years, fixing that? You bet."

Rumsfeld's folksiness—"goodness gracious" is a favorite phrase—at first added to his appeal. But eventually he began to sound erratic. In the middle of 2005, he unilaterally renamed the "war on terrorism" the "global struggle against violent extremists." Then he decreed that the Iraqi insurgents could not be called "insurgents" but rather "enemies of the legitimate Iraqi government."

By early 2006, even a large number of Republicans were urging President Bush to fire Rumsfeld. Briefly, he tried to calm himself, posing as a sort of Zen Rummy. At a press conference, a reporter asked about demands from retired generals that he resign. "I kind of would prefer to let a little time walk over it," he said. Asked about dissatisfaction in the military, he answered mildly that "there are always differences of opinion." Another questioner asked whether Rumsfeld regarded himself as autocratic. "You know me," was all he would say.

But Zen Rummy was of no use. As the midterm election approached, the *Army Times* ran an editorial concluding: "Donald Rumsfeld must go." Just six days before the election, Bush said Rumsfeld was doing a "fantastic" job and would stay at the Pentagon until the end of Bush's presidency. A day after the election, Bush admitted he was fibbing: By the time he gave those assurances, he had already selected Rumsfeld's replacement. In a White House ceremony showing him the door, Rumsfeld again paraphrased Churchill: "I have benefited greatly from criticism, and at no time have I suffered a lack thereof."

AMAZON WARRIORS

Potomac Land, though backward in many ways, is unusual in that some of its most feared warriors are women. This is in contrast to the Jivaro, for example, who allow women no role in their headhunting activities because they believe that women do not have souls. In this regard, Potomac Man is not unlike the Scythians of antiquity, who occupied land from eastern Europe to the Near East. The remains of Scythian women from the fourth and fifth centuries B.C. have been found with swords and bows. It is possible these women were the inspiration for the Amazons, the female warriors of Greek mythology, who were said to have cut off their right breasts to allow them to use bow and arrow more effectively.

Though Potomac Men are more likely to be warriors, Potomac Women can be just as fierce. The bloodthirstiest of all is Ann Coulter. A product of the Republican staff of the Senate Judiciary Committee, she is now a full-time, multimedia provocateur. She refers to women widowed by the September 11 attacks as "harpies" and "the witches of East Brunswick," observing, "I've never seen people enjoying their husbands' deaths so much." Of the liberal Supreme Court justice John Paul Stevens, she proposed: "We need somebody to put rat poison in Justice Stevens's crème brûlée."

Earlier, she said the question about President Bill Clinton was "whether to impeach or assassinate." Of the American who joined the Taliban, she argued, "We need to execute people like John Walker in order to physically intimidate liberals, by making them realize that they can be killed, too." No fan of the press, she condemns "that old Arab" Helen Thomas, and said of the Oklahoma City bombing, "My only regret with Timothy McVeigh is he did not go to the New York Times Building." Writing for the *National Review,* she said of radical Muslim nations: "We should invade their countries, kill their leaders, and convert them to Christianity." Liberals, she articulated, "are either traitors or idiots," and the United States should deport "all aliens from Arabic countries." In *USA Today,* she described "the corn-fed, no makeup, natural fiber, no-bra needing, sandal-wearing, hirsute, some-what fragrant hippie chick pie wagons they call 'women' at the Democratic National Convention."

A versatile warrior, Coulter defends as willingly as she offends. In June 2004, she pronounced: "The Americanization of Iraq proceeds at an astonishing pace, the Iraqis are taking to freedom like fish to wa-ter, and the possibilities for this nation are endless." But her finest mo-ment probably was the Conservative Political Action Conference in Washington in 2007, when she said, to applause, "I was going to have a few comments on the other Democratic presidential candidate, John Edwards, but it turns out that you have to go into rehab if you use the word faggot."

Elected Potomac Women are more tactful, but only marginally so. Jean Schmidt, an Ohio Republican, made herself known in Potomac Land only ten weeks after arriving in 2005 by going to the House floor to attack John Murtha, a decorated Marine combat veteran who, as a Democratic member of Congress, had proposed pulling out of Iraq. She said she got a call from a Marine colonel, who "asked me to send Congressman Murtha a message: that cowards cut and run, Marines never do."

There were instant boos on the floor, followed by days of denunci-ation. Even the Marine in question denied telling Schmidt any such thing. Schmidt sent a note of apology to Murtha, who campaigned for Schmidt's opponent in 2006. In an overwhelmingly Republican dis-trict, she barely survived Election Day. But nobody could be surprised back in her Ohio district, where she already was nicknamed "Mean Jean" and known for the unpredictability of her utterances. Appearing at an antiabortion rally on the national mall, she announced with con-fidence that the rainy weather "is God's way of cleansing the evil in the world."

The Democratic tribe has some Amazon warriors, too. Among the best is Barbara Boxer, known for her use of weaponry—in this case, props and theatrics—delivered from a portable platform known as the "Boxer Box" so that the barely five-foot-tall Boxer can see over podi-ums. Years ago, she protested Pentagon spending by calling a press conference and wearing a necklace made from an ordinary bracket that cost the Pentagon hundreds of dollars. As a House member during the Clarence Thomas confirmation to the Supreme Court, she led a march of women to the Senate who demanded access to the Democrats' caucus meeting to register their views. Bob Dole, the amiable longtime Republican Senate leader, once called her "the most partisan senator I've ever known."

But that was nothing compared to the Boxer who emerged in 2005, after winning her third term in the Senate. First, she was the only member of the Senate who refused to certify President Bush's re-election, forcing a symbolic but time-consuming debate over the election results. Later, she showed up at a press conference at a gas station one block from her office to bemoan high gas prices—then hopped into a waiting Chrysler LHS, rated at eighteen miles per gallon. Her biggest triumph of the year, though, was in January, when she took a thick stack of posters with her to the confirmation hearing for Condoleezza Rice to be secretary of state. She performed one of the best battle scenes Potomac Land has seen in years.

"You no doubt will be confirmed," Boxer acknowledged to Rice, before blaming her for "the lead role" in the decision to attack Iraq. "And I personally believe—this is my personal view—that your loyalty to the mission you were given, to sell this war, overwhelmed your respect for the truth." She read examples of Rice dishonesty before disclosing: "I don't have any questions on this round."

Rice responded anyway, and the two women engaged in an increasingly tense exchange, leading to Boxer's lecturing: "Well, if you can't admit to this mistake, I hope that you'll—"

"Senator, we can have this discussion in any way that you would like," Rice interrupted. "But I really hope that you will refrain from impugning my integrity. Thank you very much."

"I'm not," Boxer shot back. "I'm just quoting what you said. You contradicted the president and you contradicted yourself."

"I really hope that you will not imply that I take the truth lightly," Rice revised.

"Let me intervene at this point," suggested the mild-mannered chairman, Richard Lugar. He called a recess.

"Perfect," Rice said. The episode led to an immediate send-up on

Saturday Night Live, with the Boxer figure showing Rice a package of bologna. It also earned her the title of "most obnoxious" member of the Senate, awarded by *U.S. News & World Report* for her "take-no-prisoners, snarling speeches."

In January 2007, at a hearing of the Senate Foreign Relations Committee, Boxer again confronted Rice, this time saying she didn't have a personal stake in the Iraq war because she was childless. "You're not going to pay a particular price, as I understand it, with an immediate family," the senator told the witness. Days later, Boxer, on the House floor for the State of the Union address, walked right past Rice without even a pause.

But if Boxer is the most obnoxious, the most successful of all Amazon warriors in Potomac Land is another Californian, Nancy Pelosi. With the Democrats' victory in 2006, she became the first woman to be Speaker of the House. She got there with a superior blend of skill and ferocity. Talking about Social Security in 2005, she told a liberal blog about the Republicans: "You first have to take them down. . . . So we're going after them. We have to destroy their brand."

Lunching with *Time* magazine correspondents one year later, she observed over chicken salad dressed with lemon wedges, "If people are ripping your face off, you have to rip their face off." Other Pelosi-isms spoken at that lunch: "If you take the knife off the table, it's not very frightening anymore." And: "Anybody who's ever dealt with me knows not to mess with me."

Pelosi's warring tendencies occasionally produce a misfire. Just before the election in 2006, she handed the opposition a gift when she said of Osama bin Laden: "To capture him now I don't think makes us any safer." And just a few days after the Democrats won control of the House in 2006, she plunged the party into civil war.

Steny Hoyer, a Maryland Democrat who had been Pelosi's number two in the House for five years, expected to keep that job because of his work getting Democrats elected. But Pelosi, still angry that Hoyer had challenged her for the top job back in 2001, wrote a letter to colleagues endorsing Murtha, the antiwar retired Marine. Instead of savoring their election victory, Democrats spent two weeks in a highly publicized brawl. Pelosi hauled in newly elected Democrats who favored Hoyer, planting an implicit threat that the decision could hurt their committee assignments.

But to no avail: The battle ended in a lopsided defeat for Murtha, and by extension Pelosi, after Murtha branded the Democrats' slate of ethics reforms "total crap." In the first vote of confidence in her leadership, Democratic colleagues voted against their newly chosen Speaker, 149 to 86.

"We've had our disagreements," Pelosi admitted after the vote, urging: "Let the healing begin." Fox News' Major Garrett pointed out that nearly two out of three Democrats voted against her recommendation and asked if she had any regrets. "No," the warrior said. "I'm not a person that has regrets."

And, besides, it was time for Pelosi to turn her attention to another battle: making sure her longtime rival, fellow Californian and Democratic television star Jane Harman, did not get the chairmanship of the Intelligence Committee. Shoving Harman out of the way, Pelosi also had to cut down the next person in line, Alcee Hastings, because of his shady past and his quarrels with party leadership ("Haters," Hastings protested). This purge left Pelosi with no choice but to install Silvestre Reyes, a man so unprepared for the intelligence chairmanship that, in a pop quiz sprung on him by *Congressional Quarterly,* he couldn't identify the terrorist group Hezbollah and mistakenly thought al-Qaeda were Shiite Muslims. "Why do you ask me these questions at five o'clock?" he protested.

REVENGE KILLINGS

Like the Jivaro of the Amazon, much of the aggression among Potomac Man' is driven by revenge for real or perceived slights to person or party. And because political fortunes rise and fall so quickly, there is a built-in electoral cycle that allows Potomac Man to exact his revenge. Couple that with Potomac Man's proven ability to nurse grudges, and almost everybody here is in the process of administering or receiving retribution.

Long ago, during the Ronald Reagan period, a young man named

Jefferson B. Sessions III suffered a grievous injury to his dignity. Nominated to a federal judgeship at the tender age of thirty-nine in 1985, the federal prosecutor from Alabama suffered an almost unknown fate: He was rejected by the Senate Judiciary Committee— one of only two people to experience such a rejection in half a century. Democrats on the committee accused Sessions of racial "insensitivity" because he unsuccessfully prosecuted civil-rights activists for voting fraud. He also admitted that he called the NAACP and the ACLU "un-American," and a former colleague testified that Sessions favored the Ku Klux Klan until learning that its members were "pot smokers."

For a decade, Sessions stewed. Then, his chance came: Howell Heflin, one of the Democrats who voted against him, was retiring. Jeff Sessions won the race to replace Heflin in 1996, then got a seat on the same Judiciary Committee that had rejected him. It was the start of a long campaign to punish Democrats and liberals. Sessions was one of just nine senators to oppose a ban on torture. He raised objections about renewing the Voting Rights Act. In the days after Hurricane Katrina, according to *Time* magazine, Sessions, pushing for repeal of the estate tax, called a former law professor to see if he knew of any business owners who died in the storm so he could use the victims as poster boys in his fight against the tax.

Sessions persuaded his colleagues to support 370 miles of fence along the Mexican border and 500 miles of vehicle barriers. "It's painful to bring people who are unable to speak English or to effectively take advantage of the opportunities our country has," he told his colleagues this week. "They . . . continue to speak their own language, and they don't advance and assimilate." During a Judiciary Committee hearing on immigration in 2006, he noted that "my great-great-great-great-grandfather was an immigrant, I'm proud to say. The last one got here about 1850."

"Did they miss the Civil War, Senator?" asked the chairman, Arlen Specter, a Republican who had also voted against Sessions in 1985.

"Lincoln killed one of them at Antietam," Sessions replied.

The Civil War may have ended seven score years before, but Potomac Man continued to fight it rhetorically. In 1998, Missouri senator John Ashcroft, a Republican presidential candidate, gave an interview to the Confederate publication *Southern Partisan*. "Your magazine," he said, "helps set the record straight. You've got a heritage of doing that, of defending Southern patriots like Lee, Jackson, and Davis." A year later, he proclaimed that in the United States "we have no king but Jesus." He spoke of his defeats as crucifixions and his victories as resurrections, and he had himself anointed with oil each time he took office; when oil wasn't available before his Senate swearing in, he substituted Crisco.

Ashcroft's flaming rhetoric didn't get him much traction in the 2000 presidential race—he pulled out in January 1999—but it did manage to cement his reputation as a far-right politician, which complicated his reelection in the Senate from middle-of-the-road Missouri. In November 2000, he suffered the acute indignity of losing his Senate seat to a Democrat who had died three weeks earlier in a plane crash; the dead man's wife was appointed to fill the vacancy.

It was a humiliating downfall, but Ashcroft quickly got his revenge. Bush appointed him attorney general, and Ashcroft quickly installed Jesus as king of the Justice Department. He started regular prayer meetings in his office. He had drapes installed in the Great Hall of Justice to cover up the statue *Spirit of Justice* because one of her breasts was exposed. The drapes cost taxpayers $8,000. Ashcroft aides claimed the move was to make the room more useful as a television backdrop, but the room was almost never used for such an occasion and Justice Department e-mails surfaced with references to "hiding the statues." The statue had been in place for nearly seventy years and, soon after Aschroft stepped down in 2005, the drapes were removed and the bare breast of Justice again exposed.

Ashcroft got his revenge in more consequential ways, too. Not sixty days after the September 11 attacks, he went to the Senate and announced that critics of Bush eavesdropping policies such as the Patriot Act were aiding and abetting the enemy. "To those who scare peace-loving people with phantoms of lost liberty, my message is this: Your tactics only aid terrorists, for they erode our national unity and diminish our resolve. They give ammunition to America's enemies, and pause to America's friends."

Another time, Ashcroft proclaimed the FBI had "disrupted an unfolding terrorist plot to attack the United States by exploding a radioactive dirty bomb." Other officials quickly made it clear he dramatically overstated the threat. He boasted that "the objective of securing the safety of Americans from crime and terror has been achieved"—a month before the Health and Human Services Secretary marveled that "it is so easy" to attack the nation's food supply.

It was a tumultuous four years, and when Ashcroft stepped down, a colleague spoke at his farewell party about all the cases Ashcroft provoked: *Ashcroft v. Free Speech Coalition, Eldred v. Ashcroft, Ashcroft v. ACLU, Ashcroft v. ACLU* (another one), *Georgia v. Ashcroft, Leocal v. Ashcroft, Ashcroft v. Raich, Ashcroft v. Oregon.* And others. When Ashcroft announced his retirement, David Letterman surmised, "Apparently he wants to spend more time spying on his family."

Ashcroft, in retirement, set up a lobbying operation to cash in on his notoriety. But people paid him less attention once they stopped fearing him. In April 2006, the *Washington Post*'s Al Kamen learned, Washington State University managed to sell only 100 of 1,100 advance tickets to an Ashcroft speech on national security and civil liberties. The College Republicans leader concluded in a local newspaper that Ashcroft was "not an exciting character for a lot of people."

CEREMONIAL BATTLE

In Papua New Guinea, the highlanders have for thousands of years practiced a vengeance system known as payback. It began when warriors raided clans in neighboring valleys to steal food, setting off a chain of increasingly bloody revenge raids. In recent decades, some highlanders have sought to take a step away from violence (and toward tourist dollars) by curtailing the actual battles in favor of battle reenactment ceremonies. They use the same spears, wear the same feathers, and cry the same war cries, but they don't actually kill each other. The problem is the relations between clans remain highly volatile, and a ceremonial battle reenactment can very quickly become the real thing.

This phenomenon occurs periodically in Potomac Land as well. On any given day, Potomac Men level charges against each other as part of the daily give-and-take of politics, not bothering to respond to the other side's predictable jabs. These are the ceremonial battles. But occasionally, one side will launch a genuine raid on an opponent's character. If the aggrieved party does not respond with immediate payback, his reputation can be seriously damaged.

This was the lesson John Kerry, the Democratic presidential nominee, learned on August 5, 2004, when an obscure group called the Swift Boat Veterans for Truth launched TV ads saying Kerry, a Vietnam veteran, lied about his war record to win a Purple Heart and a Bronze Star. Kerry, who favored manicures and haircuts by Cristophe, ordered kir at bars, played classical guitar, and wore Turnbull & Asser shirts, operated under the Marquis of Queensberry rules of politics. Kerry, running against a man who skipped the Vietnam war by serving halfheartedly in the national guard, figured the accusations were too preposterous to merit a response. Big mistake. He waited two weeks to answer the charges, and the delay may have cost him the presidency.

"When you're under attack, the best thing to do is turn your boat into the attack," Kerry finally said. "I still carry the shrapnel in my leg from a wound in Vietnam." To Bush, he challenged: "If he wants to have a debate about our service in Vietnam, here is my answer: Bring it on." But it was too late. Polling showed Kerry's support plunge among veterans as he lost the advantage in the race he had after the Democrats' convention. He never recovered.

Kerry, defeated in the presidential race but planning another try, vowed that he would never again be caught in ceremonial battle mode when his opponents were going for the kill. This caused him to make an equally grievous calculation—in the other direction. At an event in California just before the 2006 midterms, Kerry told a little joke. "You know, education, if you make the most of it, you study hard, you do your homework, and you make an effort to be smart, you can do well," he said. "If you don't, you get stuck in Iraq." Kerry later said he meant to make fun of Bush. But it sounded as if he were calling the troops stupid.

Bush responded with predictable, if feigned, outrage. "The members of the United States military are plenty smart and they are plenty brave and the senator from Massachusetts owes them an apology," he cried. The outrage was an obvious attempt to draw Kerry into a fight to change the subject for the election, in which Kerry wasn't even on the ballot. And Kerry fell for it.

"It disgusts me that a bunch of these Republican hacks who've never worn the uniform of our country are willing to lie about those who did," he said in a long, furious, and televised statement in which he declared, "I apologize to no one."

Democrats, hopeful to turn the discussion back to Bush's problems in Iraq, begged Kerry to shut his mouth. Even the radio host Don Imus pleaded. "Stop talking," he told Kerry. "Go home, get on the bike, go windsurfing, anything. Stop it. You're going to ruin this." Demanded Imus: "Why not apologize for the misunderstanding?"

"Well, I did," the belligerent Kerry said. "I said it was a botched joke. Of course, I'm sorry about a botched joke. You think I love botched jokes?"

"Why not, along with apologizing for the botched joke, at least apologize for the perception and the misunderstanding of your remarks, and then move on?" the sympathetic host pressed. "And, please, I'm just begging you."

Finally, bludgeoned for his overreaction, Kerry put down his weapon. "I personally apologize to any service member, family member, or American who was offended," he said in a statement. Relieved Democrats went on to victory in the election. But Kerry's 2008 presidential hopes were, well, "botched" by what the *New York Daily News* called the "Kerry Kalamity." A Gallup poll asking for responses to another Kerry presidential run found that the top answer was "already lost/had his chance," followed, in order, by "don't like him," "dishonest," "wishy-washy," "poor choice," "needs to think before speaking," "weak," and "traitor." In Papua New Guinea, they refer to such people as dead. In early 2007, Kerry finally accepted his fate and went to the Senate floor to announce he wouldn't run in 2008.

THE ROLE OF THE GADFLY

In a land of warriors, it requires a particular brand of antagonism to stand out. There are but a few who manage to do this, to be so inflammatory that even partisan allies are frequently embarrassed. Such gadflies, of course, have had a place of importance in civilization since ancient Greece, when Socrates, pleading his case in Plato's *Apology*, compared himself to the biting insect: "I am that gadfly which God has given the State and all day long and in all places am always fastening upon you, arousing and persuading and reproaching you." Potomac Man, because of his enjoyment of ideological and partisan combat, finds the gadfly useful.

Because of their extraordinary zealotry, the largest number of these gadflies in Potomac Land are by necessity unelected. The Reverend Patrick Mahoney, for example, who calls himself the director of the Christian Defense Coalition, is the most prolific performer of political street theater in Potomac Land. When John Roberts and Samuel Alito had their Supreme Court confirmation hearings, Mahoney and friends snuck into the hearing rooms in advance and consecrated the furniture with holy oil. Then there's conservative activist Eugene Delgaudio, who performed a "man-donkey mock wedding ceremony" at a Democratic convention and who marked the anniversary of Chappaquiddick by hosting a march of people in bathing suits on Capitol Hill calling themselves the "Ted Kennedy swim team."

But some of these master warriors succeed in getting elected to Congress from highly ideological districts. One such fighter is Henry Waxman, who stands all of five foot five but has been called "Scariest guy in town" by *Time*, the "Democrats' Eliot Ness" by the *Nation*, and "tougher than a boiled owl" by former senator Alan Simpson, a Wyoming Republican. Representing the liberal stronghold of West Los Angeles, he has the safest of perches from which to attack

Republicans on everything from arsenic levels in water to scandals at Enron and Halliburton. Lacking subpoena power in the minority for years, he and his staff managed to produce some two thousand "reports" documenting official (Republican) wrongdoing. Days rarely go by in which Waxman is not firing off an accusatory and unreciprocated letter to the president, the vice president, or lesser victims.

Three days after Democrats won control of the House in 2006, Waxman rushed to the Los Angeles Chamber of Commerce to speak of his new dilemma as chairman of the Government Reform Committee: so much to investigate, so little time. "I'm going to have an interesting time because the Government Reform Committee has jurisdiction over everything," he worried aloud. "The most difficult thing will be to pick and choose." So busy is he with his probes that he only visits California once a month or so.

Occasionally, a gadfly will bite his way to the upper chamber, persuading an entire state that he is stable enough to represent a broad population. In recent years, one of the most successful gadflies has been Russ Feingold, a Democratic senator from Wisconsin. Even a quick look at Feingold indicates he is quite different from his peers. Attending a hearing of the Senate Foreign Relations Committee, he could be seen furiously scratching out items on a twenty-four-point list, which he had scribbled on wrinkled yellow legal paper in black, red, and blue ink. The list, which the senator later tore, folded, and discarded, was entirely illegible even on close inspection.

Feingold relishes a fight wherever he can find one. When the Senate Judiciary Committee took up a constitutional amendment effectively banning gay marriage, Feingold staged a heated walkout from the committee room even though the symbolic measure had no chance of passage in the Senate.

Feingold turned his ire on the chairman, Arlen Specter, even though he, like Feingold, opposed the amendment. "This is a terrible thing, to use the Constitution of the United States to discriminate against some of our citizens," Feingold declared, then left the room.

"I don't need to be lectured by you—you are no more a protector of the Constitution than I," Specter called after him. "If you want to leave, good riddance!"

"I've enjoyed your lecture, too, Mr. Chairman," Feingold retorted. "See ya."

That blowup followed by weeks Feingold's most famous moment of agitation. Without even consulting with his colleagues, he introduced legislation calling for the censure of the president of the United States. Democrats, hoping for 2006 election gains, were horrified that Feingold had allowed Republicans to change the subject from Iraq. Filing in for their weekly caucus lunch in the Capitol, Democrats were stunned into silence.

"I haven't read it," demurred Barack Obama.

"I just don't have enough information," protested Ben Nelson.

"I really can't right now," John Kerry said as he hurried past a knot of reporters—an excuse that fell apart when Kerry was forced into an awkward wait as Capitol Police stopped an aide at the magnetometer.

Hillary Clinton rushed into lunch, shaking her head and waving her hand over her shoulder. When a food cart blocked her entrance to the meeting room, she tried to hide from reporters behind the four-foot-eleven Barbara Mikulski.

"Ask her after lunch," offered her spokesman. But Clinton, with most of her colleagues, fled the lunch out a back door as if escaping a fire.

Republicans were grateful for the gift. The office of Senator John Cornyn (Tex.) put a new "daily feature" on its Web site monitoring the censure resolution: "Democrat co-sponsors of Feingold Resolution: 0."

As Socrates learned, things don't always end well for the gadfly. Fortunately for Feingold, the Senate restaurant didn't serve hemlock, but things ended badly just the same. After a desultory hearing on his censure resolution, the lonely Feingold quietly dropped the effort.

Eight

TABOO

Every civilization has its taboos. And while some—say, incest, can-
nibalism, or dietary prohibitions—are nearly universal, others are
quite unusual. The chief of the Masai tribe of Kenya, for example, believed he would lose his magical powers if he ate anything other than
milk, honey, and roasted goat liver. As the anthropologist Sir James
George Frazer observed, certain Masai were not permitted to pluck
whiskers from their beards because this would have deprived them of
their rainmaking abilities. When the chief of the Namosi in Fiji got a
haircut, he was required to eat a man to remove any evil that may have
come with the trim. Likewise, the Nubas of eastern Africa believed
that anybody who entered the priest's house would die, unless the vis-
itor bared his left shoulder and got the priest to lay his hand on it.

Homo politicus, like many other peoples, adheres to a long and
complex list of taboos involving his clothing, hairstyle, speech, sexual
activities, and even domestic employment. But what sets Potomac
Man apart is the frequency with which he defiles himself by breaking
Potomac Land's taboos. Outsiders visiting Potomac Land are often
surprised by Potomac Man's tendency toward destructive behavior.
Why, they wonder, would a person who had attained a high office risk

his entire reputation by engaging in sex with an intern or a page? Why would a lawmaker sell out his constituents merely to gain a few thousand dollars in campaign contributions? Why would a man with good presidential prospects dissolve his career with a series of racial and religious insults?

The answer is to be found, again, in Potomac Man's unusual view of himself. He is so convinced of his own exceptionalism that he believes himself invincible, invulnerable to accusations of vice, and incapable of failure. This tendency is reinforced by Potomac Man's reliance on paid staffers, whose job it is to affirm to the boss constantly that his actions are the correct ones. The result is a remarkable detachment—some here call it compartmentalization—between the standards Potomac Man expects of those he leads and the standards he sets for himself. He is therefore prone to commit acts with ignorance that other cultures would immediately qualify as self-mutilation.

Anthropologists have observed that many cultures experience a gap between ideal behavior, perceived behavior, and actual behavior. Nowhere, however, is the gap more yawning than in Potomac Land, where virtually every Potomac Man's perceived behavior is identical to his notion of ideal behavior—even if his actual behavior rarely aligns with the Potomac ideal.

The result of this tendency is that Potomac Man often violates taboos without giving them the slightest thought. This danger is enhanced by the fact that the definition of taboo in Potomac Land is constantly expanding. Potomac Man frequently adopts new taboos—say, the failure to pay a domestic worker's Social Security taxes—and punishes offenders retroactively. While Potomac Man is quite flexible in his acceptance of deviations from social norms, there is no such flexibility when a taboo is violated. Then it is highly unusual for the offender to recover his place in Potomac Land.

THE NANNY TABOO

It is the ability to learn from mistakes that has set apart humans from the animal kingdom. Here again, however, Potomac Man demonstrates his exceptionalism. Even when he sees others fall because of a mistake, he willfully and insistently takes the same erring path, assuming against all evidence that the outcome in his case will be different.

A fine illustration of this is what Potomac Man calls the Nanny problem. In 1993, Zoe Baird, President Bill Clinton's nominee to be attorney general, withdrew after word got out that she had employed an illegal immigrant couple in her home and didn't pay their Social Security taxes. The lesson was compounded—or should have been—when the next candidate, Kimba Wood, also withdrew because she had employed an illegal immigrant as a babysitter.

After Baird and Wood, it was widely believed that Potomac Men adjusted, ridding themselves of illegal nannies and paying taxes on their legal nannies. But in 2001 the incoming Bush administration nominated Linda Chavez to be labor secretary—only to discover that she, too, had sheltered an illegal immigrant. Chavez rationalized her case by saying she was merely housing the woman, who cared for her children and cleaned the house, as an act of charity. Nobody accepted that excuse, and Chavez withdrew.

That brings us to the strange case of Bernie Kerik, chosen in 2004 to be Bush's secretary of homeland security. Kerik had been the police chief in New York during the terrorist attacks of 2001, and he became a favorite of the administration. He quit the force and quickly earned $6.2 million as a consultant to a stun gun maker that got lucrative contracts from Bush's department of homeland security. After the Iraq invasion, Bush gave Kerik the job of training Iraq's police. Kerik largely failed in that endeavor but returned from Iraq in time to appear at events in support of Bush's reelection in 2004.

Kerik came highly recommended by former New York mayor Rudy Giuliani, who earned the title "America's Mayor" during the 2001 terrorist attacks and was preparing to convert that popularity into a run for the Republican presidential nomination. Kerik, Bush said, is "one of the most accomplished and effective leaders of law enforcement in America." But that view changed over the next few days.

White House lawyers who interviewed Kerik for the job had

warned him that he would humiliate himself if it turned out that he had hired illegal help or otherwise broken the law. Kerik insisted there were no skeletons in his closet, and he noted no such problems on his screening forms.

But reporters quickly discovered some: he had filed for bankruptcy in 1997; a New Jersey judge had issued a warrant for Kerik's arrest in 1998 over unpaid condominium fees; a flap with the Saudi government had gotten him kicked out of that country; and he was "deeply entangled" with a New Jersey construction company tied to the Gambino crime family. Kerik, it turned out, also accepted $165,000 in free apartment renovations from a contractor and a $28,000 loan from a real estate developer. The *New York Daily News* found out that others paid for his 1998 wedding reception and bought him Tiffany jewelry and Bellini baby furniture.

Worse, the *Daily News* discovered a "secret love nest" Kerik maintained for simultaneous "passionate liaisons" with publisher Judith Regan and prison guard Jeannette Pinero—conducted while Kerik was married to a hygienist he had met at his dentist's office.

These things, however, did not bring Kerik down. What forced him to withdraw his nomination was his discovery that, much to his shock and dismay, he had employed an illegal Mexican nanny. Kerik had somehow "uncovered information that now leads me to question the immigration status of a person who had been in my employ as a housekeeper and nanny. It had also been brought to my attention that for a period of time during such employment, required tax payments and related filings had not been made."

This breaking of the nanny taboo, his lawyer said, was "the sole reason" for Kerik's quick departure from Potomac Land. Never mind that bit about the mob, the love nest, and the arrest warrant; federal prosecutors told Kerik they expected to charge him with several felonies, the *Washington Post* reported. In New York, Kerik's name was removed from a Manhattan jail named in his honor, and, the *New York Daily News* reported, his NYPD windbreaker was pulled off eBay after attracting no bidders. But farther south, Kerik's fall had only cemented his image as a true Potomac Man.

THE HAIRDO TABOO

Potomac Man, it is often said, is extremely proud. He will defend himself against perceived slights even at great cost to himself. Though he deals daily with issues of great consequence that affect millions of people, his most pressing concern is his own status and dignity. What he does not realize is that this hypersensitivity to his own dignity frequently subjects him to ridicule, thereby undermining the very dignity he guards.

Among the proudest members of Potomac culture in recent years is Cynthia McKinney, a Democratic congresswoman from Georgia. The first black woman elected to Congress from her state, she was also the first to wear gold tennis shoes on the House floor. She established as her trademark look a hairdo of thick milkmaid braids. The hairdo, alas, would bring about her downfall.

In the spring of 2006, McKinney walked into the Longworth House Office Building one Wednesday morning. As a member of Congress, she was entitled to the perk of walking around the metal detectors that others must clear before entering the building. Lawmakers get lapel pins that remind Capitol Police of their status. But on this day McKinney chose not to wear hers; she expected to be recognized simply because she was a member of Congress.

That's when the hairdo came in. McKinney had given up the braids and was wearing her hair in a pile of loose twists. The Capitol Police officer at the building entrance did not recognize her with the new look. When McKinney sidestepped the metal detector, an officer directed her to stop and, when that failed, reached out to restrain her. She struck him in the chest with her cell phone.

Capitol Police asked prosecutors to charge her for assaulting their cop; a grand jury was assembled. "Even the high and haughty have to show some ID," the police chief said. By way of reply, McKinney held a press conference at Howard University, a traditionally African American school in Washington, and with Harry Belafonte and Danny Glover joining her, said she was a victim of racial profiling and inappropriate touching.

This was a mistake. Gleeful Republicans seized on her dustup to change the subject from a string of bad news for the party. They began wearing "I Love Capitol Police" buttons and delivered speeches on the House floor in praise of the officers. Democrats shunned their wayward colleague and many of them signed on to a Republican resolution supporting the police. McKinney tried to defend herself on television, compounding the problem.

"What happened?" asked CNN's Soledad O'Brien.

"Let me first say that this has become much ado about a hairdo," McKinney replied. "The real issue—"

"I'm going to stop you there," O'Brien said.

"You can't stop me, Soledad," the congresswoman said.

McKinney refused to describe the incident, and the two battled back and forth, with frequent interventions from McKinney's lawyer.

"We can't have this," O'Brien maintained.

"You can't interrupt me, Soledad."

"Until you answer my question, I'm not sure we can move on."

The televised dispute continued, lawyers and all, until O'Brien reminded McKinney, "This is my program."

After a come-to-Jesus meeting with her Democratic colleagues, McKinney proffered an apology. "There should not have been any physical contact," she said. "I am sorry that this misunderstanding happened at all, and I regret its escalation, and I apologize."

Apology not accepted, the voters replied. That summer, they voted her out of office in a Democratic primary. As she was arriving to give her concession speech, McKinney enjoyed a last hurrah. One of her bodyguards, a karate expert who acted in martial arts films, got in a fistfight with a television cameraman, the last of several scuffles he had with journalists covering the McKinney campaign.

Of course, disgrace needn't be permanent in Potomac Land. McKinney lost a primary once before, in 2002, after a series of bizarre events. She had commented dismissively on Al Gore's "Negro tolerance." Before that, her father memorably described her Republican opponent as a "racist Jew." She wrote a letter to a Saudi prince asking him to send money to aid America's poor and suggesting the United States should rethink its Middle East policy.

Then, in 2002, she said the government should be investigated for conspiring in the World Trade Center attacks. "We know there were numerous warnings of the events to come on September 11," she told a Berkeley radio station. "What did this administration know and when did it know it, about the events of September 11? Who else knew, and why did they not warn the innocent people of New York who were needlessly murdered? . . . What do they have to hide?"

When that outburst resulted in her defeat in the 2002 Democratic primary, her husband offered to spell out the reason for her loss: "J-E-W-S." Two years later, McKinney was elected to Congress again.

THE HYPOCRISY TABOO

Because he mentally separates his own actions from the behavior he expects of others, Potomac Man is frequently accused of hypocrisy. The charge baffles many Potomac Men, who after some time in the capital, assume the world will hold them to the same lenient standards they have adopted for themselves.

This was the assumption that drove Deal Hudson, who as adviser to President Bush and the White House on Catholic affairs, was one of the most powerful actors in Potomac Land. He published *Crisis,* a conservative Catholic magazine. He got money from conservative philanthropists and arranged cruises with the most prominent Christian conservatives in the country.

He earned fame as a moral scold during the Monica Lewinsky scandal. "After we have stripped away all idealism from offices that bind our culture together—president, father, husband—what will be left for us to aspire to?" he demanded. "Who will want to sacrifice personal desires for public responsibilities?" Further, he decried the "lie that a person's private conduct makes no difference to the execution of their public responsibilities. It's this lie, alive in our culture of death, that has shaped the character of Bill Clinton and encouraged the moral softness in all of us."

He had particular venom for Catholics with moderate views, saying they are "duped by the rhetorical evasions, the liberal masquerade, of postmodern dissidents." He bemoaned the "general moral decay . . . in society." He recommended that Catholic clergy should denounce presidential nominee John Kerry, a Catholic, because of his support of abortion rights. He championed "the traditional notion of marriage." He announced that another Democratic candidate, Wesley Clark, "doesn't seem to have any" religious convictions.

Bush adviser Karl Rove came to admire Hudson and signed him up to do the Republican Party's Catholic outreach in the 2000 campaign—which became particularly necessary because of Bush's appearance at the anti-Catholic Bob Jones University.

Hudson became Bush's envoy to Catholic bishops, and he became the leader of the White House's Catholic call to religious leaders every Tuesday morning. He was put on a delegation to the Vatican and had the clout to get people jobs in the administration. When he complained about the Democratic political activities of a staffer at the U.S. Conference of Catholic Bishops, the man was fired. He got regular invitations to the White House—sometimes to the Oval Office—and was publicly praised and embraced by Bush and his aides.

"I continue to lead an informal Catholic advisory group to the White House, as well as communicate with various White House personnel almost every day regarding appointment, policy, and events," he boasted in a letter to *Crisis Magazine* supporters in November 2003. "These efforts have helped to place faithful, informed Catholics in positions of influence."

Hudson was, in fact, at the zenith of his influence in Potomac Land when, in the summer of 2004, the *National Catholic Reporter* discovered that there was more to the man than moralizing.

A few people already knew that Hudson was a thrice-married former Baptist minister who had converted to Catholicism in 1982. But almost nobody knew that he had lost his job as a professor at Fordham for, at the age of forty-four, sexually harassing an eighteen-year-old college student.

The girl, the Catholic newspaper reported, was Cara Poppas, who had been in and out of foster homes since age seven and was a ward of the court. At Fordham she had signed up for Hudson's philosophy class, and when she approached the professor with a question after class one day, he invited her to his office, twice. She confessed that she was depressed and suicidal. He invited her out for margaritas at Tortilla Flats in Greenwich Village.

For hours, they drank rounds of tequila shots. Hudson put his arm around two women from New York University and "was heavily French-kissing both girls," Poppas later recounted. He licked salt from one woman's neck and ate a lime held between her breasts. After midnight, Hudson and Poppas took a train back to the Bronx, and the professor "began to feel my breasts," the student recounted.

He then offered her a ride to school. "Dr. Hudson told me to lay my head on his lap, suggesting fellatio when he unzipped his zipper. I did both," the student reported. He then took her to his office "and laid me down on top of [his desk]. He began touching me, unzipping my jeans, and pulling up my shirt. I was just glad to be laying down, I could barely feel my body." After exchanging "sexual acts," Hudson took Poppas to her dorm, then went home to his wife.

Romantic that he was, Hudson took Poppas to lunch the next day at a McDonald's and directed her not to tell anybody about the previous night. The professor kept sending her notes, and the student, her academic life collapsing, eventually told school authorities about Hudson. The professor, forced to surrender his tenure, eventually paid $30,000 to settle a lawsuit Poppas brought against him.

In other cultures, a man like Hudson might have reacted with shame. But he had been in Potomac Land long enough to shed that shame and to consider himself wronged by the revelation. He quit his position advising the GOP and put the blame not on his own activities but on those of the newspaper.

He said that "a liberal Catholic publication" had engaged in "personal attacks" to retaliate for his support for Bush. "Like many people, I have done things in my life that I regret," he allowed, but "I will not allow lowbrow tactics to distract from the critically important issues in this election."

A month later, with *Crisis* in crisis, he quit that, too. "As you can imagine, the past month has been very difficult for both me and my family," he said. In other cultures, the victim would be young Poppas. In Potomac Land, it was Hudson.

The Methamphetamine Taboo

One man who surely watched the fall of Hudson closely was the Reverend Ted Haggard, a Colorado Springs preacher who in 2003 became president of the thirty-million-member National Association of Evangelicals. Like Hudson, Haggard had the White House's ear; like Hudson, he also had a secret. And, like Hudson, he had the Potomac Man's assumption that he was exempt from the charges of hypocrisy that bring down ordinary people.

Haggard was routinely listed among the most powerful evangelical Christians in America. He liked to boast that he could call the White House with a question and within a day get Bush's response. He participated in weekly conference calls with the White House. He spoke personally with the president on matters ranging from the Supreme Court to steel tariffs. His clout led world leaders to seek his advice.

Addressing the evangelicals' association in 2004, President Bush praised the preacher: "Ted, I think I need to invite you to Crawford so you can drive my pickup truck." Haggard and the others applauded Bush's vow to "defend the sanctity of marriage against activist courts and local officials who want to redefine marriage." Haggard became involved in efforts in Colorado and beyond to ban gay marriage.

The preacher boasted of his power in an interview with Tom Brokaw. "I don't call presidents," Haggard said. "I don't harangue the White House."

"You don't have to call him—he calls you," said Brokaw.

"I'll be talking to the White House in another three and a half hours," Haggard allowed.

But during the period Haggard was on conference calls with the White House, he was also placing calls to Mike Jones, a male prostitute in Denver. Days before the 2006 election, Jones, armed with voice-mail recordings from Haggard, went to the media to claim that Haggard paid him for sex for three years.

In Denver TV and radio interviews, Jones said a man named "Art" paid him $200 for their monthly sex, which the preacher arranged by pay phones and commuted to by motorcycle. Haggard, Jones said, snorted methamphetamine—"he loved it before sex"—and once asked the prostitute to invite some college-age boys to their meetings. "Various acts were done," said the ever-discreet prostitute.

Haggard went through Potomac Man's usual cycle of weakening denials. "I never had a gay relationship with anybody," he said at first.

The next day, Haggard employed some of Potomac Man's hoariest excuses. Of the meth, he said, "I bought it for myself but never used it"—much like Bill Clinton's claim that he "didn't inhale" the marijuana he smoked. Of the sex, he said, it was only a back rub—echoing former senator Chuck Robb's characterization of his nude encounter with a former Miss America.

Inevitably Haggard stepped down from his roles in the church and in the evangelicals' group. The pastor who took his place, Ross Parsley, sent an e-mail to church members. "It is important for you to know that he confessed to the overseers that some of the accusations against him are true," Parsley wrote.

Finally Haggard fessed up to "sexual immorality." Writing to his congregants, he admitted to "repulsive and dark" parts of his life and said he was "a deceiver and a liar"—even as he denied homosexuality. He began a multiyear rehabilitation plan including prayer, confession, and possibly the laying on of hands—presumably not by Jones.

After just three weeks of rehabilitation, one of the ministers overseeing Haggard pronounced him "completely heterosexual." But there would be no rehabilitation in Potomac Land. The White House cut Haggard loose. A spokesman, Tony Fratto, said it's "not true" that Haggard was close to the White House. "He had been on a couple of calls," Fratto said. "I believe he's been to the White House one or two times."

THE OUT-OF-TOUCH TABOO

It has become axiomatic in Potomac Land that the more secure a Potomac Man's position, the zanier the risk he is willing to take. The Kennedy family is particularly noteworthy in this regard, but there is a long list of the powerful humbled by what outsiders would regard as utter foolishness. Perhaps it is the craving for more excitement in an otherwise humdrum life; there are, after all, few adrenaline rushes as potent as a near-death experience on a political campaign.

It was just this sort of thrill that motivated Senator Conrad Burns, a Montana Republican, when he bragged to a picnic crowd in the summer of 2006: "I can self-destruct in one sentence. Sometimes in one word." What's more, Burns was determined to prove it, with a series of statements that risked the most damaging label that can be applied to Potomac Man: that he is "out of touch."

He had always been a bit loose with his tongue. He once said it was a "hell of a challenge" to live in Washington with so many black people. Then, giving a speech to a group of equipment dealers, he referred to Mideast oil producers as "ragheads." But in white, Republican Montana, which President Bush won by more than 20 percentage points in both 2000 and 2004, it would take more than that to put the thrill-seeking Burns into a tight Senate race. So he tried harder.

In June 2006, while Burns was working to crack down on illegal immigration, he decided to make a joke about the "nice little Guatemalan man" who did work on his house. Burns told a crowd he asked the man: "Could I see your green card? And Hugo says, 'No.' I said, 'Oh, gosh.' " This struck the senator as so funny that he repeated a version of it again a week later. Noting that illegal workers were moving east, Burns said, "I told my roofer, 'You better go out and get your help or you won't get my house roofed.' " This was hilarious, Burns decided. So at another event, he pretended to take a cell phone call from "Hugo."

The polls were tightening. Burns's adrenaline was pumping. He was ready to try something even riskier: He would take on one of the most celebrated segments of American life since the September 11 attacks, the firefighters.

In July, Burns was waiting for a flight at the Billings, Montana, airport, when he spied a few firefighters known as the Hotshots who had come out from Virginia to help Montana fight a 143-square-mile wildfire. Burns inquired if the men were firefighters, and when they confirmed that they were, the senator told them "what a piss-poor job" they had done.

"Have a nice day," replied one of the men, Gabe Templeton, according to the Missoula, Montana, newspaper.

Burns further informed them that they were "wasting a lot of money." He said the firefighters weren't doing "a damn thing" and just "sit around" on the job. These firefighters rarely make more than $12 an hour for their dangerous work. Templeton informed him that "we are pretty low on the totem pole."

Even Agriculture Secretary Mike Johanns, a fellow Republican, thought that went a bit far. "To be quite candid, I think it's very unfair to the firefighters," Johanns said, pointing out that three firefighters were killed a few weeks after Burns's outburst. The Montana firemen's association said Burns had "fallen out of touch" with his constituents. Out of touch!

The daredevil Burns was proving his theory correct. He was now down in the polls—a near impossibility for an incumbent Republican senator in his state. The Butte *Montana Standard* mused, "Burns's worst enemy may turn out to be Burns."

Even before Burns started opening his mouth, he had been in some trouble because of his association with Jack Abramoff, the disgraced lobbyist. Burns was the top recipient in Congress of Abramoff funds—$150,000 worth. In exchange, Burns pressured the Interior Department to grant $3 million to one of Abramoff's tribal clients. Abramoff boasted that Burns gave him "every appropriation we wanted." The Justice Department made Burns part of its Abramoff probe. "I wish he'd never been born, to be right honest with you," a regretful Burns said of his old friend.

Republicans, trying to save Burns from himself, flew out from Potomac Land to help his campaign. But he continued to inflict verbal wounds on himself. With First Lady Laura Bush at his side, Burns told a fund-raising crowd there is a "faceless enemy" of terrorists who "drive taxicabs in the daytime and kill at night." The Senate Agriculture Committee held a field hearing in Montana—an easy boost for Burns—but he nodded off during the proceedings. A video appeared on YouTube showing the senator's eyelids drooping and finally closing, to the tune of "Happy Trails." As he departed one press conference, he proclaimed, "I'm ready to go get knee-walking drunk!"

And that wasn't all. At another hearing in Washington, he made a crack about the large number of Italian Americans representing the Federal Aviation Administration. And when he learned that a witness named Andersson used the Swedish spelling, Burns replied, "Oh, ja." He was even caught advising a Northwest Airlines flight attendant to stay at home and be a mother, then on another flight taking a seat in first class while his wife sat in coach.

This was getting out of hand. At a debate at a high school in Hamilton, Montana, Burns was heckled and called a psycho by the crowd. For the rest of the campaign, Burns cleaned up his language, and the polls started improving—but it was too late. On Election Day, Burns achieved what was nearly impossible in Montana. He lost to a Democrat, by three thousand votes. For days, the voluble Burns was uncharacteristically silent, refusing to concede defeat. Then it was time to get knee-walking drunk.

The Macaca Taboo

Potomac Man commonly exhibits a moth-to-a-flame relationship with danger. It is not that he is exceptionally brave; relatively few members of the tribe have fought in the military or otherwise displayed heroism. Rather, he has a powerful tendency to draw attention to his most glaring flaws.

This is in part driven by the town criers, who assign what is called a designated flaw to each public official. Bill Clinton's assigned flaw was sex addiction. John Kerry's was indecision. George Bush's is incuriosity. In each case, the media reinforce this flaw by pointing out every fresh example of it. The political figure invariably shows himself powerless to escape the flaw.

The designated flaw of Senator George Allen, a Virginia Republican, is racism. As with all designated flaws, this is only partially justified. Much of it comes from Allen's efforts to portray himself as a Southern redneck. The California-born son of a professional football coach, he adapted to Virginia by wearing cowboy boots, chewing tobacco, and collecting plastic cups and sample shampoo bottles from budget hotels. While none of this is necessarily racist, Allen did provide some genuine material to support the designated flaw. In his Charlottesville law office, he once displayed a hangman's noose. In his cabin, he hung a Confederate flag. He also had the flag emblem on a lapel pin. He irked Virginia's black leaders by opposing a mention of slavery in Confederate History Month.

The designated flaw did not stop Allen from becoming the popular governor of Virginia, and then a senator from the state. After a few years in the Senate, Allen was being mentioned as a likely presidential contender for the 2008 race, blending George Bush's good-ol'-boy charm with Ronald Reagan's political leanings. To inoculate himself against his designated flaw, he took three "pilgrimages" to civil rights battlegrounds, became a champion of black colleges, and signed on to a resolution apologizing for lynchings. The new and improved George Allen was cruising to reelection in 2006—a springboard to his presidential run.

Then, at midday on August 14, an item appeared on an obscure Virginia political blog called Not Larry Sabato, dedicated to mocking a local pundit of that name. It said Allen, at a campaign rally, had publicly berated a fellow who was videotaping the event for Allen's opponent, Democrat Jim Webb. The young cameraman, an Indian American named S. R. Sidarth, just happened to be the only person at the event who wasn't white. The Designated Flaw! And it was on videotape.

"This fellow here, over here with the yellow shirt, macaca, or whatever his name is, he's with my opponent," Allen is seen saying. "He's following us around everywhere, and it's just great." While his supporters laughed, Allen mocked his opponent's ties to Hollywood and added: "Let's give a welcome to macaca, here. Welcome to America and the real world of Virginia."

Those sixteen words ended Allen's presidential aspirations and his career in the Senate. The *Washington Post,* running the flap on page one, pointed out that "macaca" means "monkey" and is considered a racial slur in some cultures.

The excuses, and the apologies, began immediately. Allen said he confused "macaca" with the word "mohawk" because of Sidarth's haircut, which was actually a mullet. Then it was claimed that he just made up the word. Hours after Allen's campaign manager said the senator has "nothing to apologize for," Allen apologized anyway.

His standing collapsed almost overnight. Over ten days of nonstop macaca, Allen's apologies became ever more profuse and abject. He apologized on Sean Hannity's radio show, in at least seven media interviews, in several statements from his campaign, and eventually in a phone call to the young man himself.

Visiting Harrisonburg, Virginia, he became a one-man apology machine. When Allen arrived to take a factory tour, the local NBC affiliate demanded another apology for the macaca moment. "I made a mistake," Allen obliged. "It was a mistake, and I'm sorry for it, very sorry for it, and I'm going to try to do better."

The words were barely out of his mouth when a reporter from the ABC affiliate requested another pound of flesh. "Oh, goodness," the senator said with a groan. "I regret it; it was a mistake; I'm solely responsible for it; and I'm very, very sorry. . . . It was a mistake; I was wrong; it's my fault; and I'm very, very sorry to hurt anyone."

This was not enough for the reporters, one of whom pressed him on his phone call with Sidarth. "I apologized to all Virginians, I apologized," Allen said. "I finally got ahold of Sidarth, Mr. Sidarth, yesterday, found his cell phone, I talked to him personally."

After another macaca question, and another macaca apology, a reporter from the local newspaper called out, "Can we get a question on the issue of the day?" He could not.

The press pack, having caught Allen exhibiting his designated flaw, was not about to let up. It didn't even help when it was reported that Allen's opponent Webb had once said that the U.S. Naval Academy was a great place for a "horny woman." Allen tried, clumsily, to set things right. He staged what his campaign called an "ethnic rally" so that he could have his photograph taken with nonwhites. Then he announced that he had introduced legislation in Congress to help black farmers—though it was done so late in the session it had no chance of being taken up.

Still, macaca stalked him. At a Tysons Corner debate between Allen and Webb, local TV anchor Peggy Fox asked Allen if he had learned the term "macaca" from his mother, who grew up in Tunisia, where the term is a racial epithet. Allen repeated his apology and said his mother had nothing to do with it. "It has been reported," Fox continued, that "your grandfather Felix, whom you were given your middle name for, was Jewish. Could you please tell us whether your forebears include Jews and, if so, at which point Jewish identity might have ended?"

Allen recoiled as if he had been struck. His supporters in the audience booed and hissed. "To be getting into what religion my mother is, I don't think is relevant," Allen said furiously. He directed Fox to "ask questions about issues that really matter to people here in Virginia" and refrain from "making aspersions."

Uh-oh. Suggesting somebody has Jewish blood is "making aspersions"? Now the town criers could add "anti-Semite" to Allen's designated flaws. Jewish leaders protested. The next day, Allen issued a statement saying he checked into the matter and—what do you know?—his mother's family was Jewish. "Some may find it odd that I have not probed deeply into the details of my family history, but it's a fact," he said, trying to borrow the "incurious" flaw from Bush.

No matter. Allen was by now in a dead heat with Webb, and the town criers were back to the racism flaw. They had found old friends and teammates of Allen who alleged that he used the N word and once put the severed head of a deer in a black family's mailbox.

In the inevitable concession speech that followed his defeat a month later, Allen had the good sense not to blame anti-Semitism for his loss.

A SITUATIONAL CODE OF ETHICS

One of the enduring paradoxes of life in Potomac Land is the universally held view that morality is absolute. Conservatives, reluctantly joined by liberals, have long decried the creep of moral relativism in America. But when it comes to his own life, Potomac Man, regardless of his ideology, is an avowed relativist.

Sometimes this is revealed in ways more amusing than consequential. Conservative radio host Rush Limbaugh (a thorough Potomac Man though he lives in Florida) spent much of the 1990s condemning Bill Clinton for proclaiming that he smoked marijuana but "didn't inhale." Said Limbaugh, "The president's history of drug use is questionable."

More broadly, he said, "There's nothing good about drug use. We know it. It destroys individuals. It destroys families. Drug use destroys societies. Drug use, some might say, is destroying this country. And we have laws against selling drugs, pushing drugs, using drugs, importing drugs . . . and so if people are violating the law by doing drugs, they ought to be accused and they ought to be convicted and they ought to be sent up."

The authorities took Limbaugh's advice. They found nineteen prescriptions for painkillers written for him between April and August 2003 by doctors in New York, Florida, and California. The world found out about it when his maid told the *National Enquirer,* and Limbaugh checked himself in for drug treatment. The radio host eventually surrendered to authorities on a charge of fraud.

But instead of congratulating authorities for doing what he advised them to do, Limbaugh blamed his political opponents. "The Democrats in this country still cannot defeat me in the arena of political ideas, and so now they're trying to do so in the court of public opinion and the legal system," he said. "I guess it's payback time." Actually, payback came in the summer of 2006, when customs agents detained Limbaugh for three hours at Palm Beach airport—because he had a Viagra prescription in somebody else's name.

At other times, the public discovery of a Potomac Man's moral relativism comes as a shock to those, usually outside Potomac Land, who had taken his moral pronouncements at face value. This was the case for Potomac Land's town crier of virtues, who has shown himself to be a man of great moral flexibility.

Bill Bennett, the former cabinet official, has made millions of dollars from books with titles such as *The Book of Virtues, Moral Compass*, and *The Death of Outrage.* He condemned "unrestricted personal liberty" and decried how wealth made it "harder to deny the quest for instant gratification."

"There is much unhappiness and personal distress in the world because of failures to control tempers, appetites, passions, and impulses," he tut-tutted in the *Book of Virtues*. He later condemned Bill Clinton for "raising the threshold of moral outrage." Among many other vices he deplored was gambling. In fact, a group Bennett founded, Empower America, opposed legalized gambling and put out an Index of Leading Cultural Indicators listing "problem gambling" as a negative indicator.

But in 2003, *Washington Monthly* and *Newsweek* reported that Bennett had lost some $8 million over a decade in casinos in Las Vegas and Atlantic City. Given the high-roller treatment at several casinos, he wired more than $1.4 million in one two-month period to cover gambling losses. Word leaked out in part because casino owners were angry that Empower America was trying to block their expansion.

Bennett sensed his obsessive gambling could be a PR problem. His customer profile at one casino warned: NO CONTACT AT RES OR BIZ!!! But when confronted, he said he saw no problem with his gambling. "I've gambled all my life, and it's never been a moral issue with me," he said. "I liked church bingo when I was growing up. I've been a poker player."

The gambler's Potomac friends rallied to his defense. "It's his own money and his own business," said one. "A rather minor and pardonable vice," said another. But those outside Potomac Land found it less pardonable, and far more hypocritical of the newly dubbed "Bookmaker of Virtues."

"He said today, gambling is a personal matter, and he's not doing anything illegal, and it's nobody's business—or as he calls that in his book the Clinton Defense," mused Jay Leno. The late-night comic also noted: "I guess they call him our moral policeman, he's the author of *The Book of Virtues*, admits now he's lost $8 million gambling in casinos. In fact, his newest book—Joe, do you have that here? This just came today. It's *Bill Bennett's Las Vegas on 50 Grand a Day*."

Bennett decided to find refuge in a new virtue: contrition.

"A number of stories in the media have reported that I have engaged in high-stakes gambling over the past decade," Bennett said in a written statement. "It is true that I have gambled large sums of money. I have also complied with all laws on reporting wins and losses." It continued: "Nevertheless, I have done too much gambling, and this is not an example I wish to set. Therefore, my gambling days are over."

The virtues paragon prayed for mercy at the altar of Tim Russert. "My—my—you know, my gambling days are over," Bennett told the *Meet the Press* host. "Those—those kind of—those kind of numbers, that kind of playing, that just can't happen."

Except, of course, that they did. But no matter: Bennett survived the scandal and even continued to violate other taboos. On his radio show in 2005, he made the hypothetical observation that "you could abort every black baby in this country and your crime rate would go down." Bennett went on to land a contract as a commentator for CNN.

THE MOUNT DOOM TABOO

Potomac Man is buffeted constantly by two conflicting winds. First, he must strive, day in and day out, to portray his opponents in the worst possible terms. Second, he must avoid offending the larger public with words that seem extreme or dangerous. Understandably, the two pressures are in constant conflict, and his pursuit of the former frequently causes Potomac Man to run afoul of the latter, thereby undermining his own standing rather than his opponent's. This is why he so often injures himself in an attempt to wound the opponent—or, as many here describe their opponents, "the enemy."

One common misfire in Potomac Land is the comparison of even the most benign developments to those of Adolf Hitler's Germany. In 2002, Senator Phil Gramm, a Texas Republican, said a Democratic tax proposal sounded as if it were "right out of Nazi Germany." Senator Robert Byrd, a West Virginia Democrat, compared Republican efforts to end filibusters to the Enabling Law giving Hitler dictatorial powers. "Witness how men with motives and a majority can manipulate law to cruel and unjust ends," he said. Senator Jeff Sessions, an Alabama Republican, likened embryonic stem cell research to Nazi medical experiments.

Senator Dick Durbin of Illinois, the number two Democrat in the Senate, topped them all when he spoke about U.S. treatment of military prisoners. "You would most certainly believe this must have been done by Nazis, Soviets in their gulags, or some mad regime—Pol Pot or others—that had no concern for human beings," Durbin said.

Republican senators, veterans groups, and the White House pounced, calling this "reprehensible." The man from Illinois knew this wasn't playing well in Peoria, so he issued a statement of "regret." That proved insufficient to quell the furor, so Durbin went to the Senate floor—and wept. "I extend my heartfelt apologies," he said through his tears.

Among those who succeeded in forcing the Durbin tears was Rick Santorum, a brash Republican senator from Pennsylvania who himself had played the Nazi card. He compared Democrats' position on judicial nominees to "Adolf Hitler in 1942 saying, 'I'm in Paris. How dare you invade me. How dare you bomb my city? It's mine.' "

Santorum issued no statement of regret or apology for this—nor, indeed, for the many other strange and angry things he said over a period of years. This was a mistake. For, in refusing to suffer the indignity of apologizing, Santorum put himself in the position of having to defend various remarks that were, at least to people outside Potomac Land, indefensible. Santorum's no-apology problem—brought about by Potomac Man's overinflated sense of pride—became a huge liability as he tried to persuade the people of Pennsylvania in 2006 to return him for a third term in the Senate.

The troubles began in 2003, when Lara Jakes Jordan, a reporter with the Associated Press, interviewed the senator about a Texas law banning sodomy. Santorum argued that if sodomy were legal, "then you have the right to bigamy, you have the right to polygamy, you have the right to incest, you have the right to adultery. You have the right to anything."

Jordan had asked Santorum if he would argue that gay people should not have sex. "In every society, the definition of marriage has not ever to my knowledge included homosexuality," he said. "That's not to pick on homosexuality. It's not, you know, man on child, man on dog, or whatever the case may be."

"I'm sorry, I didn't think I was going to talk about 'man on dog' with a United States senator," Jordan said. "It's sort of freaking me out."

In the furor that followed, Santorum refused to apologize for putting homosexuality on the slippery slope to pedophilia and bestiality. "To suggest that my comments . . . are somehow intolerant, I would just argue that it is not," the proud man said. This caused people to dig up the 2002 article Santorum wrote for the Web site Catholic Online blaming Boston's liberalism for the Catholic Church's pedophilia scandal. "It is no surprise that Boston, a seat of academic, political, and cultural liberalism in America, lies at the center of the storm," he had written.

Would he apologize for that? Not a chance. He repeated his view that "sexual license" and "sexual freedom" nurtured an environment where sexual abuse would occur.

Far from apologizing, Santorum decided to make a habit of such outrages. He wrote a book parodying Hillary Clinton titled *It Takes a Family* by arguing that more mothers should stay home with their children. Then he led the congressional effort to keep Terri Schiavo alive and became the first lawmaker to visit the woman, who lay in a vegetative state in a hospice.

"I strongly believe that rights are being violated here," he told Fox News. "To not let the family give her ice chips . . . not let her get a drink of water—"

This went too far even for conservative host Sean Hannity. "She can't swallow," he pointed out.

"—to me is dangerous," Santorum continued.

"You just heard a doctor say that would be very dangerous for her to do that," Hannity pressed.

Santorum ignored him. "—to me, is an absolute scar on America."

Then Santorum added a pinch of hypocrisy to the mix. A champion of lower taxes, he came under investigation by Pennsylvania authorities for taking taxpayer funds to enroll his children in a Pennsylvania charter school—even though he and his family lived in

Virginia. His local school district in Pennsylvania had to pay $38,000 per year so the Santorum kids could attend an online cyberschool. After news of the arrangement broke, he pulled his children out of the school but declined to reimburse the $100,000 Pennsylvania taxpayers had to provide. No apology was forthcoming.

To nobody's surprise but Santorum's, this put his 2006 reelection in substantial doubt. When the polls turned steeply against him in Pennsylvania, he retreated to *Lord of the Rings* fantasy. Explaining the war in Iraq in October, he posited: "As the hobbits are going up Mount Doom, the Eye of Mordor is being drawn somewhere else." A spokesman explained that he had read *The Hobbit* to his six children; on Election Day, voters decided he should have more time for such activities.

Santorum's demise was a cautionary lesson for Potomac Men of all stripes. Senator Hillary Clinton, a New York Democrat running for president in 2008, had a reputation, much like Santorum's, for polarizing the electorate into fervent supporters or passionate foes. To soften her image, she tamed her language on the campaign trail to a long string of the type of clichés generally found in greeting cards:

"Being there for you means standing side by side with you."

Voting rights: "The gift that keeps on giving."

"I'm in it to win."

"Take our country back and put it on the right track."

"I'm not running for president to put Band-Aids on our problems."

"Standing on the sidelines is no way to stand up for the troops."

This went on until, at a speech to the firefighters union in March 2007, Clinton became entrapped in a wreck of colliding clichés: "I am thrilled and honored to stand with you, and together we will make it clear that those of us who believe that courage and anger about what is leads to hope means that we will change America for the better."

Nine

FESTIVALS AND
SOCIAL RITUALS

For centuries, a people known as the Ik prospered in the mountains of northeastern Uganda, hunting and gathering in the forest. Their land was abundant in wildlife, and the animals killed on a hunt were shared evenly by everybody in the band. The Ik might have remained a happy and prosperous tribe had their more advanced neighbors not tried to "help" them modernize. In the middle of the twentieth century, Ugandan authorities declared the Ik's land a national park and banned hunting. Instead, the Ik were given land to farm; and their new agricultural economy—they grew maize, pumpkins, beans, and more—was, in theory at least, a great advancement over hunting and gathering. But it did not work out that way. The Ik were hunters, and they had difficulty adjusting to farming, while their neighbors kept them from the best land. Today, the Ik are starving and declining in numbers. They steal cattle, force children from the home at the age of three or four, and leave the weak and elderly to die. They have lost most of their rituals and any notion of cooperation.

A tragedy similar to the Ik's has been visited on Homo politicus in recent years; and while it has not harmed the Potomac economy, it threatens to vanquish Potomac Man's unique culture. With the growth of government in Potomac Land, foreign cultures, particularly those of New York and California, sent more and more representatives to the capital to make sure that they were getting (at least) their share of government money. As foreign law and lobbying companies moved to town, and retiring legislators joined the firms rather than return to their own communities, the interlopers brought new and enticing practices to Potomac Land, particularly in the area of socialization. They have introduced to Potomac Man unfamiliar notions such as fashion, fine cuisine, and nightlife. In years past, Potomac Land's social rituals consisted almost entirely of dinner parties at one of several Georgetown salons; now, it seeks to rival the red-carpet glamour of Hollywood and New York. Instead of candlelit salons, Potomac Men frequent restaurants such as Citronelle and CityZen so often that they have forgotten how to use their granite and stainless steel kitchens. But these efforts invariably fall short and make Potomac Man feel inferior to the New York and Los Angeles cultures that occupy his town. Without true stars and celebrities in Potomac Land, Potomac Man must content himself with reading *People* magazine and bragging about spotting James Carville at the Palm.

The most obvious manifestation of the loss of indigenous culture in Potomac Land is the rise of an institution known as the Bloomberg party, which has become the most important annual festival. It began in the early 1990s as the *Vanity Fair* party, then in 2000 was taken over by another New York media company, Bloomberg. Technically, the event is merely an appendage (the after-party) following the annual White House Correspondents' Dinner. In times past, the correspondents' dinner—a torpid black-tie affair where the president speaks and journalism awards are administered inaudibly—was itself the main event. But now the truly important people of Potomac Land leave that dinner (or skip it entirely) and attend the Bloomberg party at a nearby mansion. The Bloomberg guest list of some 750 people is the single most important gauge of stature in all Potomac Land.

The bearer of this Potomac equivalent of Willy Wonka's golden ticket (the Bloomberg invitation was printed on thick Lucite one year and a coaster the next) encounters a land utterly foreign to the common Potomac Man: cucumber-lime drinks; pomegranate martinis;

portable toilets decorated like a rain forest; velvet ropes; a waterfall; a bathtub full of champagne; goodie bags containing Bloomberg slippers; and, of course, a Bloomberg stock ticker. Inside, Potomac Land's equivalent of celebrities—Michael Chertoff! Maureen Dowd! Scooter Libby!—can be found fawning over genuine celebrities—Ben Affleck! Morgan Fairchild! Ludacris!—with a devastating result. Here, Potomac Man discovers that, even if he is important in Potomac Land, he is a nobody compared to the celebrities of New York and Hollywood. Worse, Potomac Man must grovel even to get on the list to be in the presence of greatness. At first, party crashers went early and claimed to be cabinet officers or committee chairmen; now a photo ID is required. Hundreds get turned away at the rope line; thousands more send unanswered e-mails or place unreturned phone calls pleading for a spot "on the list."

The Bloomberg party has brought home the truth of a lament often heard in Potomac Land: Politics is show business for ugly people.

THE FUND-RAISING FESTIVAL

Not long ago, Potomac Man engaged in the most elaborate dinner rituals. Sally Quinn, the society writer and Washington hostess, described the routine, five-course dinner parties that characterized Potomac Land through the 1970s: "There would be martinis and Dubonnet at cocktail time. Dinner would begin with terrapin soup and sherry, then move on to the turbot and a sincere Sancerre. Next would come the beef Wellington, accompanied by a decent Mouton Rothschild. We would stay with the red wine through the salad and cheese course, and naturally crêpes suzette would require Dom Pérignon. After dinner, when the gentlemen retired to the library and the ladies upstairs with the hostess, the postprandial liqueurs would be served."

The hostesses—with names such as Polly Fritchey, Susan Mary Alsop, and Katharine Graham—assembled prominent figures from both political parties at their salons. Joe Alsop's "Sunday night suppers" lured presidents and future presidents to the columnist's home

in Georgetown. Affairs of state were handled over candlelight and genial conversation.

But in the last two decades, Potomac Man's social rituals have
turned more primitive. As party affiliation became the defining feature
of Potomac life, Potomac Man ceased virtually all forms of socializing
with members of the other tribe. After Republicans came to power in
Congress in the 1990s, conservative leaders gathered at Grover
Norquist's Capitol Hill town house for beer and contributed $5 apiece
for the Chinese food. Others met with conservative editor Bill Kristol
for pizza.

Members of Congress rearranged work schedules so that lawmakers need only be in town from Tuesday through Thursday, so that
when Potomac Man held his parties, only a few lawmakers from
nearby districts were likely to be in attendance. President Bush,
meanwhile, held only four state dinners in his first four years in the
White House; his father held as many in six months. The early-to-bed
president and his top aides rarely attended parties outside the White
House or visited restaurants unless for fund-raising purposes. White
House Christmas parties have been abbreviated so the president can
make his 9:30 P.M. bedtime, a deadline he even upheld the night his
inaugural balls were held. "I'm really not a part of the Washington society," Bush told a sympathetic journalist Fred Barnes. "I've got a lot
to do. We're at war, and I've got a lot of reading to do in the evening."

Now social rituals in Potomac Land serve primarily as another
means for partisan advantage—principally, fund-raising. Some fund-
raisers accommodate thousands at a convention center or sports
arena. Others are in private homes. Virtually all are strictly segregated
by party.

The doyenne of this new, balkanized social scene in Potomac Land
is Hillary Clinton, former first lady, now senator and presidential aspirant. Leaving the White House in 2001, she and her husband bought
a home at 3067 Whitehaven Street, Northwest, for about $3 million,
then put the place through a big renovation. The 5,500-square-foot
home, near the vice president's residence and the British ambassador's
home (the first lady and the ambassador used the same interior deco-

rator), was nearly perfect for entertaining. But not perfect enough: Four years after moving in, Clinton announced a $900,000 expansion.

Clinton's pace of entertaining was impressive: more than fifty fund-raisers in her first two years in the residence. Sometimes she held more than one event on the same night. Those willing to cough up $25,000 got to sit down with the senator for group dinners. Those whose contributions were in the four figures were ushered into a tent outside; wandering the house was not permitted, even for a U.S. senator. Dianne Feinstein of California, leaving a fund-raiser at the Clinton home in 2001, told a *New York Daily News* reporter outside: "There was someone standing at the living room door, which said to me, 'Do not enter.'"

The only way a Republican could get into Clinton's parties was by giving a lot of money to a Democratic candidate. Republicans, for their part, partied at the home of a Clinton neighbor, Republican lobbyist Wayne Berman and White House social secretary Lea Berman. The *Washington Post*, which dubbed Clinton's home "Maison Blanc Cheque," reported that when Republican lawmakers and donors attending a 2001 fund-raiser at Berman's house wandered over to have a look at the Clinton house, they found that Secret Service agents in front of the house prevented them from approaching.

On one night when the Clintons and Bermans held dueling parties, then Health and Human Services secretary Tommy Thompson managed to get into the Clinton party, a fund-raiser for Senator Maria Cantwell. According to the newspaper *Roll Call*, Terry McAuliffe, then the Democratic chairman, approached Thompson and asked, "Do you have a check for Maria?" Another night, the quiet neighborhood was clogged with black sedans and Secret Service vans, as Clinton hosted Democratic donors and the Bermans hosted Bush, Karl Rove, and big Republican donors.

For her first few years in the Senate, Clinton invited Democratic donors from around the country to have dinner with her at Whitehaven in exchange for checks for her political pursuits. Her events, generally limited to two hours, could bring in as much as $2.5 million. As the 2008 elections grew closer, she invited Democratic activists from Iowa and New Hampshire, the first states to vote in the primary season, to dine at Whitehaven as part of what her staff described as "intimate" evenings, thirty people at a time.

In 2007, with a Clinton presidential campaign official, the price of admission to Whitehaven grew higher. In February, she hosted a gathering for seventy "bundlers"—those who bundle together others' smaller contributions—who agreed to raise $250,000 apiece, including $50,000 by the end of March. The choicest seats at the dinner belonged to those who agreed to raise $1 million. Those who couldn't keep up with these lawyers, venture capitalists, and Hollywood investors—the poor relatives who pledged to raise only $25,000—had to settle for a briefing by the senator at the middlebrow Hyatt Regency. She called the junior varsity donors Hill-raisers.

Clinton's advisers, celebrating her fund-raising prowess, described her as the "new Pamela Harriman," the great Georgetown hostess who died in 1997. But that comparison required a bit of selective history. Harriman was, indeed, a leading Democratic fund-raiser during the 1980s. But for years before, Harriman's role was that of Georgetown hostess, admitting to her home on a typical evening more Republicans than cross the threshold of the Clinton home in a year.

Unfortunately for Clinton, fund-raising friends prove uncomfortably fickle. During the Clinton presidency, Hollywood magnate David Geffen was a major donor who, in exchange for his largesse, got to sleep in the Lincoln Bedroom at the White House. But in February 2007, Geffen turned on his old friends, telling *New York Times* columnist Maureen Dowd that he disapproved of the "Clinton royal family." Geffen suggested that Bill Clinton's sexual indiscretions continued— "I don't think anybody believes that in the last six years, all of a sudden Bill Clinton has become a different person"—and ridiculed Hillary's position on the Iraq war: "It's not a very big thing to say, 'I made a mistake' on the war, and typical of Hillary Clinton that she can't."

It was no way to treat the hostess.

COMING OF AGE

On the night of June 26, 2002, the president's twin daughters, Jenna and Barbara Bush, went into Stetson's, a grungy bar on U Street in Washington. They chain-smoked cigarettes and drank Budweiser beer into the wee hours. When word of the outing appeared in the *Washington Post*, it created a scandal—not because the underage girls were again drinking alcohol (this had been going on for years and more than once earned the intervention of Texas authorities) but because they were doing it in a *Democratic* bar.

In Potomac Land, where most everything is segregated by party allegiance, Potomac Man's choice of nightlife is just another way to demonstrate partisan leaning. Democrats party with Democrats, Republicans party with Republicans, and each tries to use the other tribe's social rituals against him. Democratic congressman Harold Ford, Jr., a young bachelor who attended a Super Bowl party in 2005 sponsored by Playboy, found that this indiscretion cost him a Senate seat a year later; the Republican National Committee ran an ad showing a blonde in a slinky dress saying she met Ford at a Playboy party and cooing, "Harold, call me." Even social rituals far from Potomac Land can become political. Republican congressman Denny Rehberg of Montana fell off a horse while under the influence of alcohol during an official visit to Kazakhstan; the Democratic Party filed a Freedom of Information Act request demanding documents related to the trip.

To minimize such embarrassing incidents, Democrats and Republicans frequent separate watering holes, where the risk of bad publicity is minimized by the absence of members of opposing tribes. For young Democrats, the iconic bar is Stetson's Famous Bar and Grill, a cowboy-themed bar at Sixteenth and U Streets, a mixed neighborhood. As with other Democratic bars, it evokes a common man's way of life that Potomac Man finds alluring, if unfamiliar. Buffalo wings can be had for $6.75, chili fries for $4.50, and rail drinks for $2.50 during happy hour. Stetson's offers billiards, darts, pinball, and a jukebox—activities young Democrats believe, from watching movies, are associated with "real Americans"—those who do not live in commuting distance of Potomac Land.

Stetson's has filled this role for Democrats for more than twenty years, but young Republicans had no equivalent. Finally, in 2000, a young man named Bo Blair satisfied this need. He opened Smith Point on Georgetown's main strip, Wisconsin Avenue. It rejected everything about Stetson's, offering a first course of barbecue-lacquered quail with quinoa, dried cherries, toasted pine nut stuffing, and marjoram quail jus for $9. Instead of burgers, it had pan roasted jumbo sea scallops with celery root puree, lobster mushroom flan, and tarragon for $26. More important, it had Jenna and Barbara Bush.

Except for their one brief fling at Stetson's, the twins were faithful to Smith Point, and their presence made the bar the center of Republican nightlife. Though their reputation outside Potomac Land was not the best (Jenna was photographed sticking out her tongue while riding in her dad's presidential motorcade), among Potomac Men the twins were the embodiment of culture. After a few sightings of one or both of the twins at the bar, word spread among White House aides, young staffers on Capitol Hill, and Republicans throughout Potomac Land's legal-industrial complex. Ropes and bouncers were erected on the sidewalk outside. To weed out Democrats and other undesirable elements, Blair gave the bouncers—themselves Republican staffers—a list of 1,500 people approved for admission after 11 P.M. Once inside, the Republicans, most in their twenties, could relive the music of their toddlerhood (the 1980s) until 3 A.M.

Smith Point, with its Nantucket-themed interior, helps Republicans keep their lineage pure. Blair once boasted to a Cox News reporter that he knew at least twenty-two married couples who had met in his bar. Smith Point also teaches young Republicans to act like older Republicans: they must raise money for the party. On the night before Bush's second inauguration, a group of young Republicans who had each raised $50,000 for the reelection campaign partied at Smith Point. The Bush campaign referred to these khaki-clad young Republicans as the Mavericks.

Blair's bar suffered when the Bush twins left town, Barbara for New York and Jenna for Central America. And on the night of the

2006 elections, a Smith Point party became funereal. For brief moments, the grief could be forgotten, as when, in January 2007, Barbara returned for just one night to party at her old haunt. But for the most part, the combined loss of the twins and the 2006 elections sent the action back to Stetson's.

Foraging and Sustenance

For Michael Steele, it was a rookie mistake. Steele, the lieutenant governor of Maryland and a Republican candidate for the Senate, wanted to meet some Washington reporters, so he agreed to a lunch at the Charlie Palmer steakhouse near the Capitol. Steele, thinking his anonymity was protected because the reporters had agreed not to identify him by name, soon discovered that nothing at Charlie Palmer is anonymous. Halfway through the lunch, Bill Frist, then the Senate Republican leader, walked into the room to greet Steele. So when Steele was quoted—anonymously—in the next day's *Washington Post* disparaging the president and the Republican Party while lunching at a Capitol Hill steakhouse, Frist and his allies in the White House and the Congress knew the culprit immediately. Steele confessed to his disloyalty before nightfall.

As every Potomac Man knows, lunching at an expensive Potomac Land restaurant is about as discreet as granting an interview to CNN. These restaurants serve as the primary conduits through which lawmakers' affections and votes are purchased by lobbyists and interest groups. With names such as Charlie Palmer Steak, Bistro Bis, Oceanaire, the Caucus Room, and Capital Grille, these restaurants allow well-financed interests to entertain lawmakers and their staffs and, crucially, to raise money for the lawmakers' reelections.

Charlie Palmer's steakhouse alone was the host of more than 335 campaign-related events before the 2006 election, according to the PoliticalMoneyLine Web site—and this doesn't even include senators' events. A Republican group called Texans for Henry Bonilla dropped $3,800 there for an event in July 2005. The American Psychiatric Association's political arm gave about $4,500 worth of martinis and

New York strips in March 2005. The Committee for the Preservation of Capitalism invested $1,800 for a dinner. The Democratic National Committee ponied up $145,000 for fund-raisers at the restaurant.

The steakhouse is the rare Potomac Land institution that opens its doors to both tribes. Though events and even tables are segregated by party, restaurants are happy to serve any who will pay $38 for a Kansas City rib eye. The fund-raising arm of Nancy Pelosi, who would become House Speaker, spent more than $10,000 at Charlie Palmer, narrowly eclipsing the amount spent by fund-raisers for Tom Reynolds, the man who led House Republicans' election efforts. The one notable exception to this is the Republican Party's Capitol Hill Club, adjacent to GOP headquarters. It hosted 2,720 events before the 2006 election, all for Republican causes.

Potomac Man can be fickle in his dining tastes. Jack Abramoff's restaurant, Signatures, had 105 events before the 2004 election, but, as the Republican lobbyist's legal troubles grew, that shrank to 27 in 2005, before the restaurant closed. Lawmakers apparently favor restaurants nearest to their place of work: Charlie Palmer and Bistro Bis, both on Capitol Hill, are the most popular, followed by the Capital Grille at Sixth and Pennsylvania. Even a few blocks can be crucial, because Potomac Man does not like to work hard for his lunch. At Ninth Street is the Caucus Room, a steakhouse opened by lobbyists Haley Barbour and Tommy Boggs with help from Potomac Land fixtures Terry McAuliffe and Boyden Gray; but PoliticalMoneyLine listed only twenty-six political events before the 2006 election.

In the popular imagination, the quintessential power scene in Potomac Land is the Palm, a clubby steakhouse in DuPont Circle. On its walls are the caricatures of its clients: powerful Potomac Men from times past, such as Bob Strauss, Vernon Jordan, James Carville. But the venerable Palm and others of its ilk no longer impress modern Potomac Man. Only twelve political events at the Palm were listed before the 2006 election. Another ancient steakhouse, K Street's Prime Rib, had eight. This says much about the evolving appetites of Potomac Man. No longer does he desire his likeness on the wall and a friendly maître d'; now he prefers money in his campaign account in exchange for helpful legislation.

The Innate Need to Be Seen

Very little about Potomac Man's social life would be considered social in other cultures. Conversations are brief and superficial, generally conducted with each party looking over his interlocutor's shoulder in search of a more glamorous partner. Intimate gatherings are eschewed in favor of drop bys, in which participants arrive, quickly circulate through a crowded room, and then depart. The central feature at many a Potomac gathering is a receiving line in which the participants wait to have their photograph taken with the famous host, often without even a perfunctory conversation; the president conducts some twenty such parties during the Christmas season, shaking perhaps ten thousand hands, pausing not for eggnog but for Purell hand sanitizer.

The reason for this strange behavior is relatively simple: The purpose of these interactions is not human contact but visibility. In Potomac Land, an individual's social worth has little to do with his charm and personality and everything to do with his perceived importance. If he is seen by sufficient eyeballs at a top A-list party, his stature is enhanced, as is his host's. If he arrives late and can mention an important meeting that just ended, or is still wearing the studio makeup from a television appearance, so much the better. In fact, many a Potomac Man's social life is conducted entirely on television, using his appearances on cable and network television to achieve the visibility he would otherwise acquire by attending social events.

Arguably the most competent practitioner in this field is Joe Wilson, who in the space of a year managed to turn himself from an unknown to a fixture of the Potomac social scene. In the summer of 2003, Joseph C. Wilson IV was a retired diplomat known primarily for the bit role he played in Baghdad in the days before the first Persian Gulf War. But then, in an op-ed in the *New York Times* and an article in the *Washington Post*, Wilson went public with a secret trip he took for the CIA that had debunked one of the White House's main justifications for war in Iraq. Administration officials then exposed his wife, Valerie Plame, as a CIA operative. And Wilson went on an unrivaled media tour of righteous indignation.

In August 2003, he said at a forum that he would like to see Karl Rove "frog-marched out of the White House in handcuffs." He became a regular on the network and cable news circuit, appearing on everything from *Meet the Press* to *Imus in the Morning* to *The Daily Show.* His cause quickly mushroomed, from defender of his wife to booster of John Kerry's presidential campaign to all-purpose antiwar critic. He held press conferences with regularity at the National Press Club and on Capitol Hill.

Gradually Wilson grew less concerned about the injuries done to his wife by the disclosure of her identity. On one *Meet the Press* appearance, he announced that Plame "would rather chop off her right arm than say anything to the press and she will not allow herself to be photographed." A few months later, Wilson and Plame appeared in a photo spread in *Vanity Fair*. In one, the two sat in his Jaguar, the spy only partially disguised by a scarf and sunglasses. In another, the couple sat on the terrace of their home in the Palisades section of Washington, Plame hiding behind a newspaper.

What little cover Plame had was quickly dissipating, but Wilson's presence on the Potomac scene was exploding. He was summoned west to have lunch with Norman Lear and Warren Beatty. He published a ghostwritten book titled *The Politics of Truth*. He appeared with his wife at the Press Club, weeping as he told Plame, "If I could give you back your anonymity." He started calling her "Jane Bond." They consented to more photos, in *Time* magazine.

The invitations poured in. Wilson and Plame appeared at a Georgetown party hosted by Ben Bradlee and Sally Quinn. He mixed with Bruce Springsteen and musicians from the band R.E.M. at a party at Zaytinya restaurant downtown. They met P. Diddy at the *Vanity Fair* Tribeca Film Festival party in New York. The pair went to the White House Correspondents' Dinner as a guest of ABC News. They smiled for the cameras—no more camouflage for her—on the red carpet, and attended a party hosted by the glossy magazine *Capitol File* at the upscale Cafe Milano. He went to a party at the Spy Museum to hobnob with Hillary Clinton and veterans of the Clinton White House. The two went to a party at NBC correspondent Campbell Brown's home in Washington's Adams-Morgan neighborhood, bravely mixing with media figures and even a few White House officials; this time, no frog march was proposed.

The New Republic found Wilson so ubiquitous that it offered tourists to Washington a warning along with a photo of Wilson: "Be on the lookout for this man," it cautioned. "If you encounter him, at all costs, do not let yourself get between him and a camera, a lectern, or a buffet, or you will likely be trampled."

THE ROLE OF GATEKEEPERS

Potomac Man's social universe is surprisingly small. There are more than seven million people living in the Baltimore-Washington metropolitan area, but there are perhaps five hundred people in Potomac Land whose opinions matter to Potomac Man. These are the lawmakers, strategists, journalists, and officials who, collectively, define the social order of Potomac Land: who's up, who's down, and who's rising or falling.

Mark Halperin, who stepped down as ABC News political director in 2007, even gave the band a name, the Gang of 500. He described them as "the group of columnists, consultants, reporters, and staff hands who know one another and lunch together and serve as a sort of Federal Reserve Bank of conventional wisdom." Conveniently, Halperin placed himself as the leader of this exclusive gathering; in his daily tip sheet called the Note, he even had this fanciful group meeting for brunch each weekend at Lauriol Plaza, a Tex-Mex spot in Adams-Morgan. He believed there are many more people who aspire to be in his club. The "political class" he wrote, consists of "the Gang of 500, plus the 33,000 people who aspire to be gang members."

In late 2006, Halperin took the extraordinary step of writing about his own book party in the Note, where he boasted about the "bold-faced names" in attendance:

> *Tim Griffin, Grover Norquist, and* Time's *Mike Allen kicked off the party. Senator John McCain lent his sanguine, merry presence, and was quickly enveloped by the crowd. Unflappable Congressman Rahm Emanuel accepted the good vibes of*

*Democrats who greeted him as a potential savior. Governor Mitt
Romney arrived, with venerable party animal Ron Kaufman in
tow, direct from a fund-raiser with President Bush for three
gubernatorial candidates (including Iowa's Jim Nussle). Senator
Hillary Clinton exclaimed to boyish trio Jonathan Prince, Jake
Siewert, and Mike Feldman that they looked all "grown up."
Charles Gibson chatted with Karl Rove. The homophonous duo
of Terri McCullough and Terry McAuliffe hung out with
Senator John Sununu.*

Judging from the guest list of this party, there are relatively few
elected officials in Halperin's conception of the Gang of 500. There
were but a dozen senators on the list, including party mavericks such
as John McCain, Chuck Hagel, and Lindsey Graham, and a handful
of House members, particularly press-friendly leaders such as Rahm
Emanuel, Roy Blunt, and Tom Davis. There are only a trio of White
House aides—Josh Bolten, Dan Bartlett, Karl Rove—and but a score
of congressional staffers. Foreign diplomats—once a mainstay of
Potomac Land's elite—were absent.

The largest category on the list are the journalists, who are about
a quarter of the total and range from hotshots such as Rick Berke of
the *New York Times* and Ron Brownstein of the *Los Angeles Times* to
lesser known but influential producers for MSNBC's *Hardball* and the
National Journal's Hotline, an online compendium of political news.
By far, the most prominent group in the Gang of 500—50 percent of
the total—are the strategists and lobbyists. They have names such as
John Weaver, Mark Penn, Charlie Black, Harold Ickes, Mark McKinnon,
and Anita Dunn. They come from firms such as Glover Park Group,
Public Strategies, National Media, Quinn Gillespie, Patton Boggs.
They are largely unknown outside Potomac Land but are the people
who tell the nation's ostensible leaders how to think, talk, and vote.

Though he fancied himself the arbiter of elite thinking in Potomac
Land, Halperin, who lived in New York, in fact had relatively little say
in determining social stature here. That task has fallen to Juleanna
Glover Weiss, a thirtysomething Republican lobbyist. Weiss has
worked for various types of powerful figures: Vice President Cheney,

Rudy Giuliani, John Ashcroft, Steve Forbes. But her fame comes from her role as a giver of large parties at her neo-Georgian home among the embassies of Washington's Kalorama neighborhood. Weiss and her husband, fellow Republican operative Jeffrey, bought a run-down group home and refurbished it into a grand space for entertaining. Once a month or so, she sends invitations, by e-mail or the old-fashioned way, then hires valet parkers and a bartender and fills the place with finger food and specialty martinis for nearly three hundred of her closest friends.

Others perform similar roles as party host, such as Republican lobbyist Ed Rogers in McLean, Virginia; Democratic fund-raiser Nancy Jacobson in Georgetown; and Republican ad man Jim Courtovich in Kalorama. But Weiss attracts the most frequent and consistent gatherings of Potomac Land's powerful: Democrat, Republican, and media. Occasionally this means a high-ranking official such as Cheney; generally it means an assembly of the aides and strategists who tell the titular leaders what to do.

How Weiss adds and subtracts names from her list is something of a mystery. After receiving a promotion to an important job, the rising Potomac Man frequently will receive a congratulatory e-mail from Weiss, possibly followed by an invitation to the next event. Conversely, it's not uncommon for somebody who has disappointed Weiss to be dropped for a couple of months. Banishment, however, is rare, and requires a serious offense, such as that done by Weiss party regular Mark Foley of congressional page scandal fame.

For each event, Weiss scrolls through her e-mail address book and selects names from a pool of 1,700 people. Only four or five people on the list are actual lawmakers; they are, after all, rarely in town on a Saturday night. Instead, there are a few hundred staffers from Capitol Hill, one hundred or so from the White House, and another few hundred lobbyists. The rest are journalists who are certain to talk (and possibly write) about the party, thereby adding to the mystique.

The disproportionate number of journalists on the list might explain why a procession of writers, from *Vogue, Elle,* the *New York Times,* the *Washington Post,* and *Washingtonian* magazine, have written flatteringly about Weiss. In *Washingtonian,* Ed Henry wrote:

Flashbulbs have been popping all night as [NBC News'] Norah O'Donnell greets well-wishers ranging from Fed chair Alan Greenspan and NBC's Andrea Mitchell to White House political director Ken Mehlman. Newsweek's Michael Isikoff is dishing out rapid-fire anecdotes in one corner while top Republican lawyer Ben Ginsberg shares war stories in another. An aide to Senator Hillary Clinton, Philippe Reines, is chatting up Vice President Dick Cheney's spokeswoman, Jennifer Millerwise, near the front door.

Henry later scored a party in his honor when he moved to CNN.

That must have inspired Jennifer 8. Lee, herself an aspiring party giver, to write a similar ode in the *Times*: "With ivory skin and reddish-blond hair, the willowy Mrs. Weiss resembles the women from Vermeer's paintings—if Vermeer's ladies had dressed with the flair of a 21st-century professional woman."

The stories invariably identify Weiss as the "Washington hostess" or the keeper of a "salon." But she resists both labels, and in fact neither archetype fits. Her gatherings have little resemblance to the intimate Georgetown dinner parties of earlier days in Potomac Land thrown by women with names such as Graham and Harriman. These are standing-room-only affairs, where conversations are brief and eyes are wandering toward the next cluster of people as each participant plots a route across the room. These parties are largely about networking for Potomac Man; they allow introductions to be made and business cards traded with the hint of future deals, scoops, and jobs.

The events have not hurt the business interests of the Weisses either, of course. Sometimes the parties are thrown in honor of lobbying colleagues or prominent journalists. Sometimes they are for good causes: aid for tsunami victims, educational groups, and an Iraq charity. And sometimes they are for lobbying clients. But this bit of awkwardness is willingly overlooked by the Potomac elite for the rare chance to see Democrats and Republicans together when they are not fighting. Indeed, if the bar is not too crowded, it is a chance for that rarest of things in Potomac Man's social life: the unguarded moment. It was at the Weiss home, after all, that a leading adviser to Bush on the Iraq war could be found not long after the toppling of Saddam Hussein singing the theme song from the film *Team America: World Police.*

"America F@#k Yeah.
Comin' again to save the m@#!$@#!$@#!g day, yeah."

PURIFICATION FESTIVALS

As part of the twelve-day New Year festival in ancient Babylon, the king had to undergo a purification ritual on the fifth day. Inside the Esagila temple, the king laid down his scepter, his ring, his crown, and his weapons. The king then sat on a chair before a statue of the god Marduk, and the high priest struck the king forcefully on the cheek, then brought the king to his knees. The king delivered a confessional prayer, after which the priest struck him again, hard enough to draw tears. After this, the king was handed back his royal equipment and given absolution to reign for another year.

Potomac Man practices a ritual strikingly similar to that of the Babylonian festival of antiquity. He calls it the silly season. In the late winter and early spring, the president is expected to attend four formal dinners: those of the Alfalfa Club, the Gridiron Club, the Radio and Television Correspondents' Association, and the White House Correspondents' Association. At each of these, the president is expected to sit through a program in which he is ridiculed and roasted; typically he will answer this with a speech poking fun at himself. He is then applauded, and the business of the republic returns to normal the next morning, with the president again in charge.

For years, the Gridiron Club's annual white-tie dinner was the main event; the capital's gray-haired journalists performed a musical revue lampooning political figures. At the end of the night, the president gently made fun of himself. Nursing a low approval rating at one such dinner, Bush told the crowd: "By the way, when Dick [Cheney] first heard my approval rating was thirty-eight percent, he said, 'What's your secret?'" Bush also played with the notion that Cheney runs the government. "The truth is that I do run the country," he said. "But Dick runs me and Lynne runs Dick. So actually Lynne runs the country. And, Lynne, I think you're doin' a heckuva job."

But the dinner, untelevised and nominally off the record, has become hopelessly quaint in modern Potomac Land. The Gridiron's motto—"Singe but never burn"—has been ruled anachronistic in a town that now prefers to go for the burn. The dinner has been upstaged by the larger, televised dinners hosted by the White House and radio and television correspondents.

The modern era of the dinner roast began in 1996, when radio host Don Imus, invited to speak to the Radio and Television Correspondents' Dinner, spoke, with Bill Clinton sitting on stage, about the Clintons' marital infidelities and legal troubles. "We all know you're a pot-smoking weasel, that you once ate an apple fritter the size of a baby's head, and that you actually run a twelve-minute mile," Imus said of the guest of honor.

The worst part for the president is that while the audience in the hall knows he is lampooning himself, those watching the broadcast from outside Potomac Land have a dangerous tendency to take his statements at face value. At the 2004 Radio and Television Correspondents' Dinner, Bush went through a slide show in which he searched the White House for Iraq's missing weapons of mass destruction. "Those weapons of mass destruction got to be here somewhere," Bush narrated. Then, "Nope, no weapons over there. Maybe over there?" This led to endless grief from Democrats, liberal commentators, and earnest people everywhere. "BUSH SHOULD KNOW BETTER," ruled the august *Akron Beacon Journal*.

Bush finally got the self-deprecating requirement just right at the 2006 White House Correspondents' Dinner, when he stood on the stage with an impersonator who spoke Bush's inner thoughts. "I get to pretend I like being here," the Bush id complained. "How come I can't have dinner with the thirty-six percent of the people who like me?"

On Cheney's shooting of a hunting partner, the impersonator voiced: "Where is the great white hunter? He shot the only trial lawyer in the country who supports me. . . . He was drunk as a skunk! On one beer! Light beer! Oh, people were duckin' and divin' for cover. I wish I'd been there. I saw him coming down the hall the other day. I looked at him and said, 'Don't shoot!' "

The president had confessed his sins, and it was now time for Marduk to pardon the king of Babylon. But in Potomac Land, absolution never comes. Instead, Bush had to listen to comedian Stephen Colbert deliver a twenty-minute evisceration of the president and his character. Bush, Colbert said, "believes Wednesday what he believed Monday, despite what happened Tuesday." With Bush on the stage, Colbert announced: "I stand by this man because he stands for things. Not only for things, he stands on things. Things like aircraft carriers and rubble and recently flooded city squares. And that sends a strong message, that no matter what happens to America, she will always rebound—with the most powerfully staged photo ops in the world."

Quarreling with the notion that the Bush administration was "rearranging the deck chairs on the *Titanic*," Colbert roared: "This administration is not sinking. This administration is soaring. If anything, they are rearranging the deck chairs on the *Hindenburg*."

The president grimaced his way through the speech and went home angry. White House reporters mused about whether Colbert had been too harsh—which generated furious defenses of Colbert, and denunciations of the White House press corps, from foes of the president who had watched the event on C-SPAN.

The Correspondents' Association needed a way out. For its next dinner, it hired Rich Little, a little-known comedian who hasn't made fun of a president since Ronald Reagan. He performed on television and in Las Vegas—in the 1960s and 1970s. His performance—mostly impersonations of dead people—was such a bomb that President Bush was asked by a reporter the following Monday whether he would consider a pardon for Little. For Bush, the silly season flagellation was nearing an end and absolution was finally at hand.

Ten

HUMAN SACRIFICE

In the late fifteenth century, Aztecs in the capital of Tenochtitlan, now buried beneath Mexico City, built enormous temples in the form of pyramids. By the thousands, prisoners covered in blue chalk were forced to walk up the steps of the pyramid and, reaching the summit, were thrown onto their backs and held down by five men. As trumpeters played, a priest dug a hole in the prisoner's abdomen with a flint knife, then pulled out the victim's still-beating heart, which the priest held up as an offering to the sun god. The priest then put the heart in a bowl and the victim was tossed down the steps of the pyramid, where the corpse was cut into pieces to be given as gifts and possibly eaten by the Aztecs. In a busy year, tens of thousands of people were sacrificed.

Some believe the practice was a religious ritual gone awry. Others believe it was an economic necessity for the Aztecs, who did not have a sufficient number of large animals to fill their dietary need for protein. Still others say that it was the Aztecs' way of preventing civil unrest: The visibility of the sacrifices made the government appear invincible and discouraged citizens from making themselves noticed. Whatever the motive, the sacrifices were the most elaborate the world had ever seen—at least until Potomac Land got into the business of human sacrifice.

When it comes to matters of crime and punishment, Homo politicus fancies himself to have a highly advanced civilization. This is in large part because such a high percentage of Potomac Men are trained in the law; it is common at Washington gatherings to hear jokes about somebody being the only nonlawyer in the room. Whatever their numbers, there can be no doubt that Washington has more lawyers per capita than any other location.

But this reverence for law is misleading. On deeper investigation, Potomac Man's view of justice is crude, and he demonstrates a preference for harsh punishments associated with the most barbaric of cultures. Long after other civilizations abandoned the practice, Potomac Man continues to subject offenders to human sacrifice.

When photos surfaced of U.S. troops abusing prisoners at the Abu Ghraib prison in Iraq, Defense Secretary Donald Rumsfeld said he took "full responsibility"—then demonstrated that by sending low-level soldiers for court-martial and demoting a single general to colonel. When wounded soldiers were found to be living in deplorable conditions at Walter Reed Army Medical Center, the Army's top medical officer, Lt. Gen. Kevin Kiley, pronounced, "I'm accountable" but clung to his job while subordinates were fired or reassigned; Kiley, too, was eventually sacrificed. When the Justice Department was caught firing U.S. attorneys for political reasons and then telling Congress otherwise, Attorney General Alberto Gonzales proclaimed, "I am responsible"—then fired his chief of staff.

Whenever a scandal occurs among Potomac Men, there is a ritual demand for human sacrifice—even if the individual sacrificed is not the perpetrator of the offense. As soon as a misdeed comes to light there are immediate calls for "heads to roll" and demands for a series of resignations—a ritual as public as painting the victim blue and removing his heart for the sun god. The motives for such ritual slayings—appeasing the gods of public opinion or discouraging other would-be dissidents and whistle-blowers—are strikingly similar to those of the Aztecs.

THE SACRIFICIAL LAMB

Potomac Man lives by the maxim "It's not the crime, it's the cover-up." The phrase is heard in Washington almost as frequently as "It's not the heat, it's the humidity." In both cases, Potomac Man will invariably nod. For, in Washington, the misdeed itself is rarely punished; it's the effort to conceal the original misdeed that can cause an individual to be sacrificed. President Nixon was forced to resign not because of a burglary but because of his cover-up. President Clinton was impeached not because of his affair with an intern but because he lied about it.

For Potomac Man, it's not what you do but how you spin it.

This brings us to I. Lewis "Scooter" Libby—a man of great mystery in the capital. Even his first name is a matter of intrigue. Libby does not tell even friends what the initial stands for. Public records indicate it's "Irve," though others go with "Irv" or "Irving." Then there's the question of "Scooter." Libby has, at various times, said he acquired the nickname because of the way he crawled as a child and because of New York Yankees shortstop Phil Rizzuto.

The mystery "I" only added to Scooter's aura. In the last months of the Clinton administration, he helped fugitive financier Marc Rich win a pardon—causing no end of ridicule for Clinton and getting Libby hauled before a congressional committee.

In the Bush administration, Libby, as the powerful chief of staff to a very powerful vice president, was among the most important of all Potomac Men. Or he was, at least, until it was determined that the White House needed to make a human sacrifice to purge the crime of unmasking a CIA operative. Thus did Scooter Libby get indicted by a grand jury looking into a crime that Libby did not commit.

The matter began on Bastille Day 2003, when conservative columnist Bob Novak reported that "two senior administration officials" told him that Bush critic Joe Wilson's wife, Valerie Plame, was a CIA "operative." Wilson had embarrassed the administration by writing an op-ed article in the *New York Times* saying that a central claim the president made—that Iraq had tried to buy yellow cake uranium in

Niger for nuclear weapons—was false. Wilson, a former ambassador, had been sent previously by the CIA to look into the allegation and found it bogus.

The matter quickly became a scandal. First, there was the phony "sixteen words" from Bush's State of the Union address: "The British government has learned that Saddam Hussein recently sought significant quantities of uranium from Africa." Then two administration officials had outed a CIA agent—a possible crime that could compromise the lives and careers of Plame and hundreds of her contacts. Worse, it appeared that they outed the agent to punish her husband for exposing that the administration had, as Wilson put it, "twisted" intelligence "to exaggerate the Iraqi threat."

Wilson immediately accused Karl Rove of the crime and famously demanded a frog march. After howls from liberal publications and some Democrats, the Justice Department, at the request of the CIA, began an investigation in September 2003.

Three years later, it turned out Wilson wasn't far from the mark. Rove was indeed identified as the second source who confirmed Plame's identity to Novak. And eventually, Richard Armitage, the number two person at the State Department, confessed to being Novak's primary source.

Never mind that Armitage was a critic of the war who obviously wasn't identifying Plame to punish Wilson. And never mind that Libby wasn't one of Novak's sources. At the end, Libby was the one who got indicted; Rove and Armitage weren't charged, much less frog-marched.

How's that? Remember: For Potomac Man, it's not the crime, it's the cover-up.

The prosecutor, a no-nonsense kid from Brooklyn named Patrick Fitzgerald, discovered that Libby, though not Novak's source, had given the information about Plame to other reporters. More to the point, he tried to conceal his role when investigators asked him about it. Libby told prosecutors that he learned about Plame's role at the CIA from, of all people, NBC News Washington bureau chief Tim Russert. In fact, Russert did not ask Libby about Plame, and Libby at the time was well aware that she worked for the CIA. He had heard it from Vice President Cheney himself, from two CIA officials, and a State Department official.

Libby knew he was doing something naughty. He asked *New York Times* reporter Judith Miller to identify him not as a "senior administration official" or even the more vague "Republican source" but as a "former Hill staffer"—which, while technically true, applied to perhaps 50 percent of all Potomac Men and was about as useful as describing President Bush as a former fraternity member.

At first, Scooter's colleagues in the White House dutifully cooperated in his cover-up. Scott McClellan, who succeeded Ari Fleischer as press secretary, stated without qualification that neither Rove nor Libby was involved in outing Plame. "If anyone in this administration was involved in it, they would no longer be in this administration," he said.

Finally, Bush aides decided Fitzgerald was not falling for their bluff. It was time for a human sacrifice—and Libby was the likeliest candidate. In October 2005, Rove, in danger of being indicted, told the grand jury that, after thinking the matter over some more, it just may have been Libby who had first told him about Plame's identity. Libby, who learned of Rove's perfidy the same day his mother died, was indicted within days. A few months later, Rove was cleared. Libby, who had broken his foot, was seen on television hobbling out of the White House on crutches.

In court in early 2007, Libby's lawyers demonstrated convincingly that Libby was a scapegoat for more powerful figures. They demonstrated that both Rove and Fleischer (dubbed "Slick Willie" by the jury) leaked the same information about Plame and then told the grand jury otherwise—yet were not prosecuted. They demonstrated that Cheney himself had scribbled in the margins of Wilson's column: "Did his wife send him on a junket?"

Libby's lawyer, Ted Wells, told jurors about Libby's plea to his boss, Cheney: "They're trying to set me up. They want me to be the sacrificial lamb. I will not be sacrificed so Karl Rove can be protected." Cheney took notes during his meeting with Libby: "Not going to protect one staffer and sacrifice the guy that was asked to stick his neck in the meat grinder because of the incompetence of others."

But Libby was sacrificed—because, Wells argued, Bush needed Rove more than Libby. "Libby was an important staffer," he argued, "but Karl Rove was the lifeblood of the Republican party."

Maybe so, but that was of little importance to Fitzgerald, who stuck his flint knife into Libby's rib cage and removed his heart.

When the jury found Libby guilty on four of five counts in March 2007, the new felon's wife, Harriet Grant, went over to her husband with a furious, teeth-baring look and said, "We're gonna fuck 'em." Who the 'em was wasn't entirely clear, but her anger was understandable. Even the spokesman for the jury, Denis Collins, said as he left the courthouse: "It was said a number of times, 'What are we doing with this guy here? Where's Rove, where's—you know, where are these other guys?' We're not saying that we didn't think Mr. Libby was guilty of the things we found him guilty of, but that it seemed like he was . . . the fall guy."

The fall guy was sentenced to thirty months in prison. The sacrifice complete, Bush quickly commuted Libby's sentence.

USE OF SCAPEGOATS

By tradition, Aztec prisoners were expected to go to their deaths willingly; if they proved resistant, there were drugs to make them more compliant. Even among those not condemned to be sacrificed, the notion of self-sacrifice was common in cultures similar to the Aztecs'. Rulers offered blood drawn from their tongue, ears, or genitals; it was a way of communicating with the gods.

While Potomac Man is expected to embrace sacrifice with a similar attitude of acceptance, the sacrifice victim commonly does not play along with this conceit. This is most likely to occur when the sacrificial offering is new to Washington culture. In this instance, the victim fights his fate and refuses to be disemboweled—at least without bringing several others into the grave with him.

One such man is Michael Brown, Bush's choice to lead the Federal Emergency Management Agency. Brown was a former municipal official who ran for Congress in 1988 and got 27 percent of the vote. He was at the end of a tumultuous nine-year reign over the International Arabian Horse Association when his longtime friend from Oklahoma, Joe Allbaugh, invited him to come work at FEMA. It wasn't immediately apparent how his history with horses prepared Brown to run the government's disaster operations, but Brown worked his way to the top job after Allbaugh left to make money in Iraq.

Most of the world didn't know about Brown until the government's disastrous response to Hurricane Katrina and President Bush's visit to Alabama where he said eight words that turned Brown into a national joke: "Brownie, you're doing a heck of a job."

New Orleans was flooded with sewage and toxic chemicals. Corpses littered the streets. Looters took control of the town. Desperate citizens were begging to be rescued from the Superdome and the convention center. Enter Brownie, who told CNN that FEMA didn't even know people had been suffering for days in the convention center.

"Sir," replied CNN anchor Paula Zahn, "you're not telling me you just learned that the folks at the convention center didn't have food and water until today, are you? You had no idea they were completely cut off?"

Said Brown: "Paula, the federal government did not even know about the convention center people until today."

Within days, Brownie was forced to resign, becoming the administration's official scapegoat for the problems in New Orleans. A few weeks later came the human sacrifice, at the altar of the House Select Bipartisan Committee on Hurricane Katrina.

Members of Congress danced around the pyre.

Christopher Shays, a Connecticut Republican, called Brown's account of events "feeble," "clueless," "shocking," and "beyond belief." Said Shays, "I'm happy you left, because that kind of . . . look in the lights like a deer tells me that you weren't capable to do the job."

Kay Granger, a Texas Republican, told Brown: "I don't know how you can sleep at night. You lost the battle."

Gene Taylor, Mississippi Democrat, said Brown was in way over his head. "You folks fell on your face. You get an F minus in my book," he attested. The Mississippian added, "Maybe the president made a very good move when he asked you to leave your job."

Chairman Thomas M. Davis III, a Virginia Republican, gave members unlimited time to abuse the witness and added his own barbs.

When a lawmaker complained about the lack of ice in New Orleans, Brown replied, "I think it's wrong for the federal government to be in the ice business, providing ice so I can keep my beer and Diet Coke cool."

Taylor, incredulous, asked, "How about the need to keep bodies from rotting in the sun?"

Brown, losing control, demanded four times that Taylor not "lecture" him.

"I have come to the conclusion that this administration values loyalty more than anything else," Shays said, "more than competence or, frankly, more than the truth."

Shays was correct, to a point. Brown got his job because of a friend's loyalty rather than his own skills. But when the administration offered him as a sacrifice, Brown was expected to accept his fate and go quietly. He did not.

In an interview with *Playboy,* he called Congressman Taylor "that little twerp," adding, "He can just bite me, for all I care." He said Senator Norm Coleman, a Minnesota Republican, was "chickenshit." Bush is "a cheerleader," Brown said, and he "doesn't have an incredible command of the English language." Brown also issued a belated "screw you" to Homeland Security secretary Michael Chertoff and said of his equine experience: "Dealing with horses' asses taught me how to deal with the federal government."

Brownie got a break when the White House accidentally released the video and transcripts of pre-Katrina meetings. In them, Brown sounds alarms about the disaster, but Bush and Chertoff appeared passive; the president asked no questions, then declared, "We are fully prepared."

Before the storm hit, Brown said he was concerned that there weren't enough crews to evacuate and treat victims at the Superdome, what he presciently called "a catastrophe within a catastrophe."

"We're going to need everything that we can possibly muster, not only in this state and in the region, but the nation, to respond to this event," Brown told Bush on the tape. He called the storm "a bad one, a big one" and said disaster workers should bend the rules if necessary to help people.

"Go ahead and do it," Brown said. "I'll figure out some way to justify it. . . . Just let them yell at me."

Brownie was right about the yelling part, but his bosses weren't prepared for his defense. "You were the scapegoat there for a while," the comedian Stephen Colbert told Brown. "But it's no good if the goat wanders back into town and starts pointing fingers at people."

BURIAL ALIVE

Among the more peculiar aspects of Aztec sacrifice was the annual festival in honor of the god Tezcatlipoca, which required the sacrifice of the most handsome young man in the area. The victim spent a year receiving the best of treatment, including the services of four beautiful maidens; priests escorted him and people bowed to him. But all this was a prelude to the ultimate and inevitable removal of his beating heart atop a pyramid.

Likewise, even the most revered public servant in Potomac Land must have a reasonable expectation that he will be sacrificed. Further, he must embrace his own demise cheerfully when his time comes. Because of the Potomac tradition that the victim must go willingly to the sacrifice, it is almost unheard of for a Potomac Man to be fired or even asked to resign; rather, he is given a hint that he might, of his own volition, consider drafting a resignation letter.

This is what happened to Colin Powell eight days after the 2004 election. Powell, more popular than his boss, President Bush, got a call from Bush's chief of staff, Andy Card. "The president would like to make a change," Card said, even supplying the date Powell should use on his resignation letter. Powell hand delivered the letter but, the *Washington Post*'s Karen DeYoung found out, White House aides found a typo and sent it back for Powell to redo. "I believe that now that the election is over the time has come for me to step down," Powell wrote.

But what happens if somebody is not steeped in the ways of Potomac Man? There is a danger that he will misinterpret the hint that he should resign and ignore it. This results in an awkward period in which colleagues of the person chosen for sacrifice make increasingly public statements speculating about the official's imminent departure.

This was the sad case of John Snow. As the head of rail giant CSX, he was a titan in the private sector. As secretary of the treasury from 2003 to 2006, he was an emasculated and uninspiring mouthpiece voicing official administration pronouncements. And of the several million people living in the Washington area, Snow was the last to know he was being fired.

Unlike Powell, Snow didn't get the hints that were dropped by the White House—so his colleagues had to get increasingly murderous in their anonymous quotes. After the 2004 election, a senior administration official told the *Post* that Snow could "stay as long as he wants—providing it's not very long."

More than a year later, Snow was still on the job, saved only by the White House's inability to find a suitable replacement. The hints were getting less and less subtle. "They're waiting for Snow to do the right thing," a source "in close contact with the West Wing staff" told the *New York Times*. "They thought he would have gotten the message by now and submitted his resignation."

In public, Bush offered the most tepid of support when, at a meeting with Snow, he was asked about the secretary's future. "Secretary Snow is here at the table," Bush said, pointing out the obvious. "He's been a part of this discussion. I'm glad you brought him up. He has been a valuable member of my administration, and I trust his judgment and appreciate his service."

The *Post*'s political gossip, Al Kamen, recommended that if "Snow doesn't know he's outta there, he might want to study President Bush's response to a reporter's question yesterday at a health-care meeting about whether Snow is 'expected to stay on.'"

Kamen provided a simultaneous translation of Bush's statement:

"Secretary Snow is here at the table," Bush said. "He's been a part of this discussion." [Note past tense.] "I'm glad you brought him up." [No doubt.] "He has been a valuable member of my administration [Past tense again.], and I trust his judgment and appreciate his service. [It's been great.]"

Incredibly, Snow still didn't get the hint, even as his eventual successor, Hank Paulson of Goldman Sachs, was floated for the job. The *Financial Times* reported that he was "tolerated more than respected." A Hearst Newspapers columnist asserted that his "presence has barely registered."

Appearing on the Hill for a hearing in April 2006, Snow was the victim of one dis after another. The hearing was about a 2007 Treasury Department budget he wouldn't be around to spend, and only three of the nineteen senators on the panel showed up. Even packing the underattended hearing with about twenty Treasury aides didn't help Snow avoid a dressing-down.

The committee chairman, Christopher Bond, a Republican from Missouri, complained that various Treasury projects "experienced significant problems" and demanded: "I expect answers, Mr. Secretary, not excuses." Snow took a big gulp of water.

Finally, Snow was prepared to be sacrificed. "As you know, I have been anxious for some time to return to private life," he wrote to Bush. "Now with the economy so clearly on a good path, it is time for me to step down."

He didn't take the hint a moment too soon. His resignation letter was dated May 30, the same day of the Rose Garden ceremony announcing Paulson as his replacement.

PREVALENCE OF SELF-IMMOLATION

After capturing the Tlaxcallan leader, Tlahuicole, the Aztecs gave him a military command, according to legend. But Tlahuicole, after serving in that position for a time, eventually insisted on being sacrificed. This view, that self-sacrifice is a preferable to serving dishonorably, can be found in Potomac Land, too. It helps to explain the unusual case of John DiIulio, a University of Pennsylvania academic who took a job as director of the White House's Office of Faith-Based and Community Initiatives.

DiIulio, who possessed an outsider's naïveté that Potomac Men found charming, quit his job after just seven months when he concluded that the White House was using the faith office not to enact legislation but to cater to right-wing supporters. "The need to frame a proposal broad enough to capture people of goodwill on the left and right seemed a really obvious way to proceed," the perplexed DiIulio said when he left.

The professor was wise enough to keep private his most candid assessments—and for this, his White House colleagues were grateful. "John DiIulio has done a wonderful job," the White House press secretary, Ari Fleischer, said when DiIulio quit; he called him "a sage and a saint."

Then, DiIulio lapsed. Back in Philadelphia, he forgot what he learned among Potomac Men about the need to be stingy with the truth. He dashed off an e-mail to the journalist Ron Suskind, who was writing an article for *Esquire,* then granted an interview.

"There is no precedent in any modern White House for what is going on in this one: a complete lack of a policy apparatus," DiIulio said. "What you've got is everything—and I mean everything—being run by the political arm. It's the reign of the Mayberry Machiavellis."

DiIulio blamed chief Mayberry Machiavelli, Karl Rove, and said what House domestic policy adviser Margaret LaMontagne "knows about domestic policy could fit in a thimble." DiIulio found "a virtual absence as yet of any policy accomplishments that might, to a fair-minded nonpartisan, count as the flesh on the bones of so-called compassionate conservatism . . . the administration has not done much, either in absolute terms or in comparison to previous administrations at this stage, on domestic policy."

Fleischer turned on the sage and sainted DiIulio with ferocity. "Any suggestion that the White House makes decisions that are not based on sound policy reasons is baseless and groundless," he said.

DiIulio, though just a passerby among Potomac Men, was savvy enough to know that he was about to become a human sacrifice.

Shrewdly, he decided to do the deed himself before he could be savaged any further.

At first, he issued a statement saying the article was "unjustly hard on Mr. Rove and over-the-top complimentary to me, thereby creating a too-pat contrast that is, I feel, most unfair to Mr. Rove. . . . I regret any and all misimpressions." But he quickly concluded that this apology was not abject enough; within hours, he issued one of the most memorable apologies Potomac Man has ever seen.

"My criticisms were groundless and baseless due to poorly chosen words and examples," DiIulio wrote, using almost the exact formulation Fleischer did. "I sincerely apologize and I am deeply remorseful."

It had the sound of a forced recantation, as when John Cleese, being dangled from a window by Kevin Kline in the 1988 film *A Fish Called Wanda,* vowed: "I offer a complete and utter retraction. The imputation was totally without basis in fact, was in no way fair comment, and was motivated purely by malice, and I deeply regret any distress that my remarks may have caused you, or your family, and I hereby undertake not to repeat such a slander at any time in the future."

More ominously, it echoed the confession of Soviet official Gregory Zinoviev before his 1936 execution: "I am fully and utterly guilty. I am guilty of having been the organizer, second only to Trotsky, of that bloc whose chosen task was the killing of Stalin. I was the principal organizer of Kirov's assassination. The party saw where we were going, and warned us; Stalin warned us scores of times; but we did not heed these warnings. We entered into an alliance with Trotsky."

Of course, everybody in Potomac Land knew DiIulio's confession was phony and his original charges were true. Four years later, DiIulio's former deputy in the White House faith-based office provided a posthumous defense of DiIulio's honor. The deputy, David Kuo, wrote a book substantiating his old boss's claims—and then some.

Kuo said White House officials, though ostensibly courting the religious right, privately described its leaders as "ridiculous," "out of control," and "goofy." Pat Robertson? "Insane." Jerry Falwell? "Ridiculous." James Dobson? "Had to be controlled."

He described how the leaders were easily won over with cuff links, pens, and stationery bearing the White House logo. Meanwhile, Bush declined to deliver the billions of dollars in grants he had promised to religious charities. "Making politically active Christians personally happy meant having to worry far less about the Christian political agenda," Kuo wrote in the book *Tempting Faith*.

Kuo described how, under the direction of White House political advisers, the faith-based office held taxpayer-funded events in twenty states and districts the Republicans were targeting in the 2002 election; Republicans won nineteen of the twenty. Kuo concluded that the White House was "mocking the millions of faithful Christians who had put their trust and hope in the president."

The White House immediately prepared a pit in which to bury Kuo alive. In front of the cameras, White House press secretary Tony Snow read Kuo's letter of resignation, which contained the usual praise for the president that is standard in all such letters. "I'm proud of all the initiative has accomplished," Snow read. "It's your staff's keen awareness of your unwavering support for this initiative that's made the difference."

Dobson, the Christian organizer and radio commentator, proclaimed the book a "mix of sour grapes and political timing." Tony Perkins of the influential Family Research Council, added: "I feel sorry for him, because once you do something like this, you get your fifteen minutes in the spotlight, but then after that nobody will touch you."

The attacks were worse in the blogosphere. Michael Medved said Kuo's book "isn't even subtle in its attempt to . . . hand victory to the Democrats." A former colleague of Kuo in the administration likened him to Judas, saying he wanted to "line his pockets with thirty pieces of silver." A Christian publisher called Kuo "an addition to the axis of evil." Kuo discovered that the White House intervened with Fox News to have segments about Kuo's book killed.

"The hardest thing to come of this has been the White House lies and the absolute willingness of conservative Christian activists to lap it up," Kuo wrote in his blog.

It was a true live burial for a Potomac Man. But Kuo was an unusual case, immune to the character assassination. He wrote the book after having a seizure in 2003 and surgery on a malignant brain tumor. That gives Kuo the courage of a man who needn't fear for his political future.

"I keep wondering why it is that the White House keeps putting up people to respond to me who are not from the White House," he wrote. "Then the realization hits me—there is no one left at the White House who could. Compassionate conservatism is so dead that there is now no one at the White House who can talk about it."

KILLING THE MESSENGER

The prevalence of human sacrifice in Potomac Land has what the natives call a "chilling effect" on dissent. Just as the constant spectacle of blood and organs pouring from the temple had a deterrent effect on those who would consider questioning Montezuma or another Aztec leader, so does the ritual sacrifice of whistle-blowers and other truth tellers in Potomac Land discourage others who would do the same.

After the invasion of Iraq, for example, the Bush administration and Congress established an inspector general to monitor and audit the billions of dollars being spent to rebuild the country. But then an unexpected thing happened: Stuart Bowen, the inspector general, began to uncover vast wrongdoing by U.S. officials and government contractors, causing major embarrassment. Congress, working with the White House, sought to remedy the situation. Rather than fix the problem in Iraq, which would be too costly, they moved to abolish the Office of the Special Inspector General for Iraq Reconstruction. Bowen would have to be sacrificed for telling the truth.

In earlier times, the journalist Michael Kinsley observed that a gaffe is when a politician tells the truth. While this has long been true—candor is invariably at odds with reelection—Potomac Man has taken this view to extremes in recent years. Now a high officeholder who lapses into the truth can expect capital punishment.

In February 2003, on the eve of the war in Iraq, General Eric Shinseki, the army chief of staff, was being questioned by Democratic senator Carl Levin of Michigan before the Senate Armed Services Committee.

"General Shinseki," the senator asked, "could you give us some idea as to the magnitude of the Army's force requirement for an occupation of Iraq following a successful completion of the war?"

"In specific numbers, I would have to rely on combatant commanders' exact requirements," Shinseki answered carefully.

"How about a range?" Levin proposed.

The general took the bait. "I would say that what's been mobilized to this point—something on the order of several hundred thousand soldiers are probably, you know, a figure that would be required."

This was, indeed, a true reflection of military planners' private estimates. But in public, Defense Secretary Donald Rumsfeld was spreading the word that a much smaller force would be needed. Shinseki's truth telling was a serious gaffe.

"Way off the mark," countered Paul Wolfowitz, Rumsfeld's deputy.

"Far off the mark," Rumsfeld agreed, joining the public rebuke of the general.

Wolfowitz complained about Shinseki's truth telling to Thomas White, the secretary of the army. White refused to reprimand his general. A little more than a month later, White himself was fired.

History, of course, proved that Shinseki was right about the need for vastly more troops in Iraq. But Shinseki, a decorated Vietnam veteran, lost his job for that kind of truth telling. A year earlier, he disagreed publicly with Rumsfeld's plan to kill the army's new howitzer, the Crusader; in response, Rumsfeld let it be known in April 2002 that he would replace Shinseki when his term expired, essentially turning the chief of staff into a fifteen-month lame duck.

After marginalizing Shinseki, Rumsfeld ignored the warnings he and the other military leaders told their civilian bosses. And the secretary ignored the general's warnings that the Army was not big enough to handle the demands of Iraq. In his retirement address in 2003, he cautioned: "Beware the twelve-division strategy for a ten-division army."

Shinseki got his revenge, of sorts. At his fortieth reunion at West Point in 2005—after it became universally acknowledged that

Rumsfeld's occupation force in Iraq was far too small—Shinseki's classmates wore caps with his nickname declaring RIC WAS RIGHT. And half a dozen retired generals, freed from the chain of command, called for Rumsfeld's resignation for ignoring their warnings about the difficulties in Iraq.

But Rumsfeld kept his job, tens if not hundreds of thousands died in Iraq, and Shinseki was pushed into retirement. For Potomac Man, telling the truth is a perilous activity.

This is true regardless of rank or role. Indeed, Potomac Men with less visibility than Shinseki put themselves in much greater danger by telling the truth—particularly if that story contradicts the officially authorized version of events.

Halliburton Corporation, the company Vice President Cheney once led, received billions of dollars in government contracts related to the Iraq war, without suffering the indignity of going through a competitive bidding process. The Army Corps of Engineers granted Halliburton an "emergency" contract that lasted five years—overruling the agency's chief procurement officer, Bunny Greenhouse, who pointed out that a true "emergency" contract should not last more than a year.

Greenhouse's objections leaked to the media, and she granted interviews. The FBI opened a probe into price gouging, overbilling, and the awarding of no-bid contracts to politically connected companies. When Democratic senators inquired, Greenhouse ignored her bosses' warnings and declared: "I can unequivocally state that the abuse related to contracts awarded to KBR [a Halliburton subsidiary] represents the most blatant and improper contract abuse I have witnessed during the course of my professional career." Indeed, Halliburton couldn't justify $1.4 billion in charges to the taxpayers.

In other civilizations, Greenhouse would get a commendation for her action. In Potomac Land, Greenhouse lost her job. A few weeks after her public statement, she was removed from the contracting position, banished from the civil service's senior executive ranks, and given a pay cut. The corps said her demotion was "not in retaliation for any disclosures of alleged improprieties."

USE OF SUMMARY EXECUTIONS

Just as the Aztecs used human sacrifice to deter social unrest, what makes Potomac Man's penalty system so frightening is the possibility that virtually any individual can be sacrificed without warning and with no justification. This is possible because of Potomac Man's extensive criminal code, packed with long-forgotten statutes that were written to deal with long-expired emergencies.

The Espionage Act of a 1917 was a nasty little piece of legislation, signed into law by Woodrow Wilson just after the United States declared war on the Kaiser's Germany. It is full of quaint notions from another time: references to coaling stations, telegraphs, code books, signal stations, blueprints, and photographic negatives. It was even dubious at the time, used to imprison conscientious objectors to World War I and to lock up the Socialist leader Eugene Debs. It was forgotten about soon after the war and almost never enforced for ninety years.

But in recent years, lawyers working for President Bush revived the dusty statute as a way to deter people who leak information to the media, and to punish media outlets for publishing the leaked information. They determined that the law makes it possible to prosecute people who even *possess* classified information—even if they are private citizens. This was a brilliant discovery: Suddenly, thousands of journalists and lobbyists in Washington could be prosecuted for doing business the way they have routinely done it for decades. Any one of them could be sacrificed.

The unlucky victims turned out to be two officials from the pro-Israel lobby, the American Israel Public Affairs Committee (AIPAC). The FBI arranged a sting operation to catch the lobbyists doing what they did quite openly: collecting information about American foreign policy and talking about it with anybody who would listen. They were "caught" having lunch with a mid-level Pentagon analyst, Larry Franklin, in 2003, above the Rosslyn Metro station at an Italian restaurant called Tivoli.

After the FBI confronted Franklin, they demanded he help them net Steve Rosen, who had built AIPAC into a powerful lobbying out-fit, and AIPAC official Keith Weissman. Franklin had little choice but to agree, donning a wire and passing information to Weissman outside Nordstrom at the Pentagon City mall in Virginia. The two lobbyists understandably saw no reason to keep their information secret; the law, as everybody understood it, punished leakers, not leakees. The spoke about it with journalists, friends at the White House, and the Israeli embassy.

But under the newly revived Espionage Act, the two men were in-dicted, along with Franklin. Weissman and Rosen earned the distinc-tion of being the first nongovernment officials to be prosecuted for merely possessing classified information. The prosecutors said this would teach people that they "must resist the temptation to acquire" classified information.

The two lobbyists sought to toss out the charges, pointing out, ac-curately, that what they did "is what members of the media, members of the Washington policy community, lobbyists, and members of con-gressional staffs do perhaps hundreds of times every day." The judge pointed out that it's "irrelevant" whether the law makes sense or not, because it's still on the books.

Though it owed its very existence to Rosen, AIPAC quickly joined in the sacrifice, firing him and Weissman for behavior "beneath the standards AIPAC sets for its employees." This was clearly false—Rosen and Weissman were doing exactly what they were paid to do—but AIPAC was eager to keep itself from being added to the sacrifice. It eventually stopped paying legal bills for the two.

At AIPAC's 2006 convention, some delegates were asked about the treatment of Rosen.

"I'm not the person to ask about that," said Nathan Diament, a Washington representative for Orthodox Jews.

"Who?" responded Neil Cooper, a delegate from the Philadelphia area.

"Rosen? Which one is he?" answered a charity executive, with a smile.

"I need to read more about it," demurred Etan Cohen, a college student.

Only secretly would they admit the obvious. "I don't like the way AIPAC handled it, hanging them out to dry," said one West Coast delegate, after delivering an on-the-record no comment. "They didn't do anything different from what everybody else does in this town every day."

SIN EATERS, FLACK CATCHERS

The notion of a scapegoat is, of course, a biblical one. As part of the Hebrews' atonement, the sins of the tribe were transferred to a goat, which was driven into the wilderness. The Aztecs had a similar device: the goddess Tlazolteotl ate the sins of those who confessed to her.

One fascinating aspect of Potomac culture is that some members of the community exist almost entirely to be abused for sins committed by others. One of the most common work roles among Potomac Men is the flack, a person who serves as a spokesman for another person or agency. The flack's job is to prevent the public from knowing what the person or agency he represents is actually doing. This can be accomplished either by creating false accounts or by refusing to answer questions at all, a process known as stonewalling.

Predictably, this role sets the flack up for a great deal of hostility from people in the news media who are trying to obtain a correct version of events. The journalists, unable to get the information they seek, resort to heckling the flack in televised briefings.

The most memorable of these spear catchers in recent years has been Scott McClellan, a White House press secretary who had the bad luck to be speaking for the president during the Valerie Plame scandal. McClellan, wittingly or unwittingly, conveyed to the press the utter falsehood that neither Scooter Libby nor Karl Rove had leaked the identity of the CIA operative.

When McClellan was later proven to be either a dupe or a liar, he was exposed to televised taunts in the White House briefing room.

"This is ridiculous!"

"You're in a bad spot here, Scott."

"Have you consulted a personal attorney?"

"You're not saying anything."

"There's been a wound to your credibility here."

"Your credibility . . . may very well be on trial with the American public. Don't you agree?"

The spokesman absorbed the blows so that his superiors didn't have to. His responses were suitably meek. "I'm very confident in the relationship that we have in this room and the trust that has been established between us," the spokesman said.

"We can't vouch for you," one of his interrogators shot back. "That's not our job."

"Have you considered resigning?"

McClellan did not consider resigning. Right up until March 2006, he told colleagues he planned to stay on the job. But Bush had other ideas, and the loyal McClellan was told he had to go. Having exhausted all his credibility in defending the White House's falsehoods, he was no longer of use—other than as a sacrifice. "I have given it my all, sir," he said to Bush, choking up on the South Lawn. The two then boarded Marine One for a symbolic farewell—but the helicopter wouldn't fly and they had to depart by car.

McClellan had the bad luck of following an earlier flack, Ari Fleischer, who had the advantage of freeing himself from the normal bounds of logic that constrain human conversation. When troops failed to find the weapons the White House insisted Iraq had, for example, Fleischer reasoned: "I think the burden is on those people who think he didn't have weapons of mass destruction to tell the world where they are."

After McClellan's sacrifice, President Bush quickly found a new flack, conservative commentator Tony Snow from Fox News, who armed himself with a new defense: ignorance.

"You're asking me a state-of-mind question that predates me," Snow said at his first briefing. "I'm not even going to try to fake it."

"I will apologize, as the new kid on the block. For today, I'm not going to handle international issues or currency issues. I do not wish to set off global tempests because I frankly just don't know enough on those."

"You'll forgive me, but I'll do the talking points on this because, again, as the new kid on the block, I'm not fully briefed into everything."

"You're getting me ahead of my brief. I don't know any more than I told you."

"I won't get ahead of my brief on this."

"You'll have to ask General Hayden. . . . You'll have to ask the folks on Capitol Hill. . . . You will have to ask the Senate committee."

"Can't confirm or deny."

"I can't comment."

Such answers would buy Snow time until the inevitable point when, his credibility also in tatters, he, too, would be sacrificed.

While reporters content themselves with the humiliation of flacks, those Potomac Men in elected office demand the ritual sacrifice of higher level officials. Lawmakers prefer to confront their victim in a committee hearing room—not a briefing room—staring down from the dais at their victim in the witness stand.

Sometimes, Potomac Man demonstrates his power over other cultures by forcing people from outside Potomac Land to appear before their committees: baseball players who used steroids, oil company executives reaping windfall profits, or corporate wrongdoers from companies such as Hewlett-Packard. Far more often, the elected officials demand that a representative of the administration be offered as a sacrifice.

A classic of this form was the ritual sacrifice demanded on Capitol Hill after the Department of Homeland Security cut counterterrorism funding for New York City and the Washington area by 40 percent, even though the two had suffered 100 percent of al-Qaeda's terrorist attacks on American soil. DHS concluded that the nation's capital is a "low-risk" city for terrorism and that the Statue of Liberty, Brooklyn Bridge, and Empire State Building are not worthy of "national icon" status. Instead, terrorism magnets such as Kansas City and St. Louis got increases, as well as the horses of Louisville, the cattle of Omaha, the bison of Montana, and five cities in Florida, where the president's brother was the governor.

The White House had no intention of changing its mind. It

wouldn't even release the data it used to make its decisions. But it was willing to make one concession: It would offer George Foresman, the DHS official in charge of disaster preparedness. Foresman was hauled to two committees so that everybody could toss their spears at him.

First came the House Government Reform Committee.

"One of the greatest displays of incompetence," judged Congresswoman Carolyn Maloney of New York.

"It does boggle the mind," agreed Jim Moran of Virginia.

Florida's John Mica added, "I've never seen a goofier list of priorities."

"You really think," Chairman Tom Davis demanded, that "Montana is at a higher risk than D.C.?"

Foresman, his hands trembling slightly, replied weakly, "Congressman, there are all kinds of intricacies."

Next came the House Homeland Security Committee.

"It was indefensible; it was disgraceful; and to me it raises very, very real questions about the competency of this department in determining how it's going to protect America," said the chairman, Peter King of New York. "This was a stab in the back to the city of New York."

Several others piled on with similar epithets. Foresman, seated in the first row, fidgeted, scratched his brow, and pinched his nose.

As befits a sacrifice victim, he had no real defense, just some technical talk about "empirically driven, analytically based ability to allocate dollars."

Sheila Jackson Lee of Texas proposed Foresman stop the "nightmares of philosophical gobbledygook."

"I don't like the situation we all find ourselves in," Foresman admitted at one point.

"I'm sure it wasn't a pleasant experience," King sympathized.

But Foresman knew his role was to accept sacrifice willingly. "It was actually a phenomenally positive experience," he said gamely.

Eleven

FERTILITY RITES AND MATING BEHAVIORS

In his study of the Nuer, a tribe of herdsmen in the Nile basin, the anthropologist E. E. Evans-Pritchard detailed the elaborate bride-price that must be paid by a groom to the family of his bride. The father of the bride gets eight head of cattle: three cows, three calves, and two oxen. A brother of the same mother gets seven head: two oxen, four cows, and one calf. The mother of the bride gets a cow, a calf, and a heifer; while the bride's brother from another mother gets two cows. Another twenty head are divided among siblings of the bride's father and mother.

The tendency to view courtship as an extension of commerce is, of course, as ancient as the Roman abductions of the Sabine women. In modern times, the custom has faded except among certain primitive tribes such as the Yanomami of the Amazon. When running low on women, bands of Yanomami men arrange raids on neighbors to kidnap their women and make the captives their wives.

Among advanced civilizations, sexual relations are considered to be a pleasurable activity, and love is widely viewed to be a human need—a worthwhile end in itself. But Homo politicus regards love and mating as he does all aspects of life: an opportunity to demonstrate—or enhance—power. Here, men and women at the low end of the power structure treat sex and love as means of obtaining power; those at the upper end use these relationships to display to the larger community the status they have already attained. It is generally not as formal as the Nuer bride payments or as violent as the Yanomami abductions, but Potomac mating is every bit as commercial.

What Potomac Man considers to be a love relationship would, in other civilizations, be called a strategic alliance. Because of the transactional nature of Washington love, relationships here tend to end badly—not necessarily with broken hearts but often with broken contracts. Sometimes the less powerful partner in the relationship concludes that the partnership is not providing the increased status sought. Other times, the more powerful partner, having exhibited power by winning the lover, loses interest in the transaction. In either case, it is common for Washington lovers to resolve disputes with the assistance of lawyers and public relations consultants; these are the people who must negotiate and arrange any refund of the bride-price.

The transactional nature of love and sex in Washington today owes much to former president Bill Clinton, who, by receiving oral sex in the West Wing on Easter Sunday, redefined for Potomac Man the boundaries of acceptable romantic activity. Clinton—affectionately described as a "pussyman" by his friend and confidant Vernon Jordan—survived the resulting impeachment by the House of Representatives, leading many other Washingtonians, in the years since then, to follow the trail he blazed.

In a sense, Clinton was merely continuing a long-standing Washington practice. Senator Chuck Robb, a Virginia Democrat, was bedeviled by the nude back rub he received from a former beauty queen; Clinton adviser Dick Morris was banished because of an episode of toe sucking at the Jefferson Hotel; Bob Livingston declined to be Speaker of the House because *Hustler* magazine was on the trail of his infidelities.

But the knowledge that a married president of the United States could have an affair with an intern but not lose his job emboldened Potomac Man to see just how much he could get away with.

Can a married congressman settle a lawsuit claiming he spent years beating and abusing a woman half his age—and still cruise to re-election? Of course he can.

Can a leader of the House of Representatives win a promotion after divorcing his wife and marrying a lobbyist while doing legislative favors for the lobbyist's company? Absolutely.

Can a senator win reelection after the discovery that one of his staff members was using Senate computers to write a sex diary and run a prostitution business while at work? Why not?

Can a legislator keep his job even after the skeletal remains of his mistress were found in Rock Creek Park? Well, even modern Washington has its limits.

POWER AS APHRODISIAC

Potomac Man is frequently surprised to find that his power does not necessarily serve as an attractant to potential mates who are not part of the political sphere. It can be a devastating discovery for a powerful Potomac Man to learn that his appeal is limited only to fellow Potomac Men. This was the painful experience of Mike Ferguson, a Republican congressman from New Jersey, when he visited the Rhino Bar and Pumphouse in Georgetown one spring night in 2003.

Ferguson had developed Potomac Man's trademark sense of entitlement at a tender age. For his thirtieth birthday in 2000, Ferguson's wealthy parents bought their son a seat in Congress. The Federal Election Commission later assessed him a $210,000 penalty for taking more than half a million dollars in "excessive contributions" from his parents, but Ferguson got to keep his congressional seat.

And so Ferguson found himself at the Rhino Bar at 1 A.M. on a weeknight and decided to help himself to one Michelle Mezoe, a Georgetown undergraduate. Ferguson grabbed her by the arm and, introducing himself as a member of Congress, pulled out his congressional ID card. Next, she recounted to the *Washington Post,* Ferguson offered her his congressional pin—which allows members to avoid metal detectors in the Capitol—if she would "come back and have a drink" with him. The young lady declined to leave with Ferguson, but affixed the pin to her shirt and refused to give it back unless he apologized.

The congressman, through his aides, disputed Mezoe's account, though he had no good explanation for how his pin wound up on her shirt. Undisputed: that Mezoe was offered a $50 gift certificate to return the pin, and that she relinquished it only after police arrived.

Power may be the "ultimate aphrodisiac," as Henry Kissinger put it. This is the mantra of Potomac Man. But it doesn't necessarily apply at the Rhino Bar.

Still, with hard work, and proper incentives, Washington love sometimes blossoms into storybook endings. Consider the tale of Roy Blunt and Abigail Perlman—a love story as heartwarming as that of John and Abigail Adams in revolutionary days.

By other cultures' aesthetic standards, Blunt would not have been considered a desirable mate when he caught Perlman's eye: He was in his fifties, had been married to the same woman for thirty-five years, and had had a kidney removed and surgery for colon cancer. But Perlman was no ordinary woman. She was the top lobbyist for Altria, Philip Morris's parent company—and Roy Blunt had the power to help the tobacco company.

Perlman struck up what the *Washington Post* discreetly described as a "personal relationship" with Blunt, who, in late 2002, became the third-ranking leader in the House of Representatives. Within hours of that promotion, Blunt gave Perlman the Washington equivalent of a diamond engagement ring: He secretly inserted, into a bill creating the Department of Homeland Security, two provisions that would help Philip Morris sell more cigarettes.

Blunt, naturally, said this had nothing to do with Perlman—nor the fact that his son was also a lobbyist for the company. Neither was it related to the more than $150,000 Philip Morris had given to Blunt-affiliated political committees in the previous two years.

"It's good policy," came Blunt's inevitable if implausible explanation.

The Philip Morris provision never made it into law. But "good policy" makes for good bedfellows. Five months later, Blunt got a divorce from his wife, and six months after that, Blunt and Perlman, twelve years her lover's junior, were wed at the Four Seasons in Georgetown. In celebration of the nuptials, the House Ethics Committee granted Blunt's request for a waiver exempting him from rules that would have forced him to disclose the biggest wedding gifts the happy couple received, even those from lobbyists. The *St. Louis Post-Dispatch* reported that their bridal registries at Neiman Marcus and Williams-Sonoma alone showed gifts exceeding $12,000.

It was, by Washington standards, a happy ending for all concerned, with the possible exception of the first Mrs. Blunt. Blunt has since been elevated to House majority leader, which means it can now be said, without a hint of disrespect, that the House's second-ranking lawmaker is in bed with a lobbyist.

There was a time when a sex scandal meant instant disgrace. When House Ways and Means chairman Wilbur Mills was pulled over by police at the Tidal Basin, he was found to be with a stripper known as Fanne Foxe, better known as the "Argentine Firecracker." Mills was gone two years later.

In 1976, similarly, House Administration chairman Wayne Hays resigned after it was reported that he had put on his staff, for amorous purposes, twenty-seven-year-old Elizabeth Ray, who famously boasted: "I can't type, I can't file, I can't even answer the phone."

Gary Hart, an adulterous Democratic senator from Colorado, saw his 1988 presidential campaign collapse after he was photographed with a twenty-nine-year-old model, Donna Rice, on his lap while aboard a boat improbably named *Monkey Business*. And Bob Packwood, an Oregon Republican accused of, among other things, fondling aides and forcing his tongue into their mouths, resigned in 1995 before he could be expelled.

But for Potomac Man today, the sex scandal does not necessarily mean the end of a career. Ask Bill Thomas, the recently retired chairman of the House Ways and Means Committee.

In 2000, the California Republican was second in line to become the powerful committee's chairman. But then his hometown paper, the *Bakersfield Californian*, reported what had been rumored for a year: that the congressman, as one aide put it, was having "an intensely personal" relationship with a health-care lobbyist, Deborah

Steelman. Thomas's wife, meanwhile, had moved back to Bakersfield alone.

By pure coincidence, naturally, Steelman was representing pharmaceutical companies just as Thomas's committee was working on prescription-drug legislation. Thomas denied a potential conflict of interest—but he did not deny an affair with Steelman. In a statement alluding to "personal failures," he argued that he was not swayed by pillow talk. "I have never let anyone substitute their judgment on public policy for mine," he said.

No matter: The congressman, having demonstrated his virility, was given the chairmanship.

Indeed the casual observer of Potomac Man might well conclude that having a lobbyist for a lover is an asset that increases an officeholder's power. Tom Daschle, the South Dakota Democrat who served as Senate majority and minority leader, married a lobbyist after moving to Washington and divorcing his first wife. Dick Durbin, the Illinois Democrat who joined Senate leadership after Daschle's defeat, also has a lobbyist wife. The wives of senators Byron Dorgan and Kent Conrad, both North Dakota Democrats, and Alaska Republican Ted Stevens have also worked as lobbyists. Kit Bond, a Missouri Republican, separated from his wife in 1994 and, as a senator, married a Republican fund-raiser in 2002.

Diane Allbaugh, the wife of Bush's 2000 campaign manager Joe Allbaugh, clearly wasn't very worried about perceptions. She registered as a utilities lobbyist in the Senate in September 2000—four months before her husband moved to Washington to head the Federal Emergency Management Agency. Similarly, Stephanie Herseth, a South Dakota Democrat running for Congress, fell in love with Max Sandlin, the congressman assigned by the Democratic leadership to be her "mentor." Sandlin retired from Congress and joined Greenberg Traurig, Jack Abramoff's former lobbying firm. Mentor and protégée married in March 2007. And lobbyist Doris Matsui took things one step further: After the death of her husband, Robert Matsui, a Democratic congressman, the widow won an election to succeed him.

With so many "intensely personal" relationships proving profitable for lobbyist and lawmaker alike, Potomac Man suffers little public disgrace for such actions. But some, perhaps remembering earlier sex scandals, still regard these relationships with guilt and shame.

This explains why, just before the 2000 election, a *60 Minutes* television crew caught Bud Shuster, a Pennsylvania Republican, hiding in the backseat of a female lobbyist's car as the lobbyist left home—on eleven different mornings.

The woman, Ann Eppard, had been Shuster's chief of staff when he was chairman of the House Transportation Committee. She left Shuster's office—but not Shuster—in 1994 and opened a transportation lobbying firm. The two continued to dine together frequently at the Capital Grille, and Eppard introduced Shuster to several of her new clients. She continued to advise Shuster's congressional staff about who should get a meeting with him, and her clients paid for a Christmas vacation in Puerto Rico for the Shuster family.

The House Ethics Committee called Shuster's behavior "serious official misconduct," and found the "appearance" of a conflict of interest. That appearance got a bit worse when *60 Minutes* caught him in her car. Mike Wallace reported that Eppard would make several turns and then get out of the car and walk home, while Shuster, wearing a baseball cap, then drove Eppard's car to Capitol Hill.

Shuster disputed the "maliciously untrue innuendo" that the two had a love interest, but he did not dispute that he stayed, rent free, in Eppard's home when in Washington.

Eppard died in 2005, at age sixty-two. Shuster, for his part, survived the revelations relatively unscathed. When he stepped down for health reasons in 2001, his son, Bill, had no trouble winning an election to succeed him.

VIEWS ON PROSTITUTION

Potomac Man frowns on prostitution—not because it is seen as immoral, as it is in some cultures, but because the need to pay for sex betrays a lack of power. For example, back in 1993, Ken Calvert, a Republican congressman from California, was caught by police in his car, partially undressed, with a prostitute. He denied the incident for five months before admitting it. More recently, the journalist Jeff Gannon, representing a conservative Web site at White House news briefings, felt it necessary to resign after photos of him offering himself as a prostitute were posted online.

But such stories cannot compete with the brief but glorious career of congressional staffer Jessica Cutler, who, in a period of just thirteen days in 2004, became Washington's most famous sex worker.

From the time she arrived in Washington, there was something, well, screwy about Cutler: she said she was twenty-four but public records showed her to be twenty-six; she claimed an international relations degree from Syracuse University, but the school did not have a record of that. At any rate, Cutler's interests were decidedly more domestic than international. After a brief internship with Senator Joe Lieberman, a Connecticut Democrat who prides himself on the highest moral standards, she landed as a staff assistant in the office of Mike DeWine, then a diminutive Republican senator from Ohio who brought to mind the film *Honey, I Shrunk the Kids*.

That's when the fun began. Cutler began to accept money for her sexual services. And, using her Senate computer, the naughty brunette published an anonymous sex diary called Washingtonienne on the Internet.

"I have a 'glamour job' on the Hill," she began, on May 5. "That is, I could not care less about gov or politics, but working for a senator looks good on my resume. And these marble hallways are such great places for meeting boys and showing off my outfits."

The next day, she celebrated "how hard-up the men are" in Washington. "What is my position?" she asked herself on May 12. "I am a staff assistant, or 'staff ass,' as the men on the Hill like to say. It's the entry-level job in each office."

Complaining about her meager salary of $25,000, she confided: "Most of my living expenses are thankfully subsidized by a few generous older gentlemen. I'm sure I am not the only one who makes money on the side this way: how can anybody live on $25K/year?? If you investigated every Staff Ass on the Hill, I am sure you would find out some freaky shit. No way can anybody live on such a low

salary. I am convinced that the Congressional offices are full of dealers and hos."

The Cutler blog was packed with helpful proverbs ("A man who
tries to fuck you in the ass when you are sober does not love you") and
details of her moonlighting as a prostitute. She spoke of the man who
"peeled off a few hundred from that roll of cash he carries around, and
put the hundreds in my hand as I was getting out of the car. I acted
indignant, like I don't need his help, but I kept it: why punish myself?
I should get something for putting up with his tired old ass." She decided to end it with this man but reconsidered. "What can I say, I like
the money," she explained.

Her last entry, on May 18, mentioned another man. "I just took a
long lunch with F and made a quick $400."

Helpfully, Cutler identified her lovers by their initials, including:
"F = married man who pays me for sex. Chief of staff at one of the gov
agencies, appointed by Bush." "W = a sugar daddy who wants nothing
but anal. Keep trying to end it with him, but the money is too good."
"RS = my new office BF with whom I am embroiled in an office sex
scandal. The current favorite."

At the end of the list, she added: "Shit. I'm fucking six guys.
Ewww."

But it was "RS," the current favorite, who would prove the most
memorable.

We meet RS, once identified as "Rob," on May 6. "A new contender for my fair hand," Cutler announced. "He works in one of the
committee offices. . . . RS had my boss ask me out for him! She actually came in here and said, 'He thinks you're hot.' How junior high! So
all three of us are getting a drink at Union Station after work. Looking
forward to an evening full of awkward moments."

The next morning, Washingtonienne described the night: "RS
looks just like George Clooney when he takes off his glasses. I am serious. Has a great ass. Number of ejaculations: 2. He likes spanking
(both giving and receiving). So I'm seeing ANOTHER person on the
Hill. At least this one is counsel, and not an aide."

The bulletins continued:

"He took me out for drinks, took me back to my place, and we fucked every which way. THEN he tells me that he heard I've been spreading the spanking rumor around the office!"

"He likes talking dirty and stuff, and he told me that he likes submissive women. Good, now I can take it easy in bed. Just lay back and watch him do freaky shit."

"Bad news: the rumor has spread to other offices."

"I'm afraid I really like him. I like this crazy hair-pulling, ass-smacking dude who wants to use handcuffs on me. Shit."

"So it turns out that RS cannot finish with a condom on."

"I also learned that he was a cop, so he has scary police shit like handcuffs in his closet. He implied that we would be using them next time."

"I like him very much and he likes me. But can it go anywhere, i.e., marriage? I don't know. He's Jewish, I'm not. And we have nasty sex like animals, not man and wife. But we work together, so there is an incentive to stay together and avoid an awkward breakup. And after a few months, people around the office will start 'hearing wedding bells.' I really just want to be a Jewish housewife with a big rock on my finger."

Such literary musings came to an abrupt end on May 18, when a blogger with salacious sensibilities and a large following, Ana Marie Cox of Wonkette, posted a link to Washingtonienne. Cutler pulled her site down, but not before she was suspended by DeWine. Three days later, she was fired for "unacceptable use of Senate computers" and use of work time "to post unsuitable and offensive material to an Internet web log." Cutler immediately hit the streets looking for work. When she gave her résumé to one secondhand clothing store, the clerk realized who she was and alerted Washington Post columnist Rich Leiby.

Why, she wondered, were people so interested in her? "I'm a no-body and the people I write about are nobodies," she protested. But she wasn't any longer. She accepted an offer to pose nude for Playboy. She got a contract to write a smutty novel. HBO wants to adapt it for television.

Copycats followed Cutler's example. In 2006, Senator Jeff Sessions directed his scheduler to shut off access to her MySpace.com site, which featured a photograph of her in bare midriff and unbuttoned jeans. "Single, straight, and a Scorpio," wrote the scheduler, Stormie Janzen.

In other cultures, the story would have ended there. Washingtonienne's half-dozen sex partners would have suffered embarrassment as coworkers and Internet sleuths figured out who they were, but their identities would not have become widely known.

Washington, however, is a different place. And Robert Steinbuch, the "RS" in Cutler's blog, is a Potomac Man.

Steinbuch filed a twenty-one-page civil lawsuit in federal court for invasion of privacy. Cutler filed a forty-page response seeking dismissal of the Steinbuch suit. Steinbuch filed a forty-page motion objecting to Cutler's objections. Cutler filed a twenty-one-page motion rebutting his objections to her objections. And so the scandal remained very much alive, tied up in federal court almost two years later.

The Steinbuch lawsuit argued that Cutler described "in graphic detail the intimate amorous and sexual relationship between Cutler and the plaintiff." This, he said, subjected "him to humiliation and anguish beyond that which any reasonable person should be expected to bear in a decent and civilized society."

Steinbuch argued that he was "clearly identifiable to a substantial segment of the community" as Cutler's RS. But the lawsuit had the effect of confirming his dalliance with Cutler, and outing him to a much broader audience. In case anybody missed it the first time around, Steinbuch reprinted eleven pages of the Washingtonienne words that had so humiliated him.

"Cutler caused widespread publication of private intimate facts concerning plaintiff in a manner that would be deemed outrageous and highly offensive to an ordinary reasonable person of average sensibilities," RS protested. "The private facts revealed include such facts as the number of times he ejaculated, his difficulty in maintaining an erection while wearing a particular condom provided by Cutler, spanking and hair pulling during their sexual activity (but conveniently leaving out Cutler's request for both), his intimate personal conversations

with Cutler during sexual activity and during the course of their relationship, physical descriptions of his naked body, the physical details
of the sexual positions assumed by Cutler and plaintiff during sexual
activity, plaintiff's suggestion that he and Cutler be tested for sexually
transmitted diseases so that they would not have to use condoms,
statements made by plaintiff regarding sexual positions."

Steinbuch then reprinted three more pages of Cutler's writings.

Surely, Steinbuch knew he was only drawing more attention to his
nocturnal antics. A Nexis search found no mention of him and Cutler
before his lawsuit—but thirty mentions after he filed. More likely,
Steinbuch's filing had less to do with protecting his privacy than with
making some effort to give his side of the story in public. This need to
have the last word is referred to as spin by Potomac Man, and it is a
powerful instinct.

Washingtonienne's legal response? Caveat emptor. "Steinbuch entered into a sexual relationship with Cutler knowing practically nothing about her character, her attitude toward sexual relations, her
relationship with others, or anything else by which he could assess
whether he could reasonably expect her to keep their sexual relationship private," her lawyers argued.

Steinbuch's case plodded through the court system. In early 2007,
he talked the judge into extending the discovery period so he could
have more time to build his case. In May 2007, Cutler filed for bankruptcy, citing legal bills. But the court of public opinion was less kind:
Steinbuch was done in Potomac Land. He sold his house in Bethesda
("Needs work, but v. cute" was Washingtonienne's description),
moved to Little Rock, and took a job as an assistant law professor at
the University of Arkansas.

Age of Consent

It is a hallmark of Potomac culture that what comes out of a man's
mouth has little if anything to do with how he lives his life. In no area
has this been more apparent than in Potomac Man's view of homosexuality. In his private life, Potomac Man tolerates—and generally ap-

proves of—homosexual relationships. But because officeholders in Potomac Land must answer to constituents who live in less tolerant climes, his public rhetoric indicates nothing about his personal views.

Vice President Dick Cheney, for example, has a lesbian daughter who had a child with her partner. But Cheney declines to push on his boss his own belief that such unions should receive equal treatment. Likewise, Bill Clinton, ostensibly a champion of gay rights, signed legislation giving states the power to reject such unions and developed an avert-your-glance policy named "don't ask, don't tell" governing homosexuality in the military.

Among the most tortured on the topic is Mitt Romney, the former governor of Massachusetts and a Republican presidential candidate. Campaigning unsuccessfully against Ted Kennedy for the Senate in 1994, Romney wrote to a gay Republican group: "I am more convinced than ever before that as we seek to establish full equality for America's gays and lesbian citizens, I will provide more effective leadership than my opponent."

But when that letter resurfaced during Romney's campaign for the Republican presidential nomination, Romney revised his view to speak about "my unwavering advocacy for traditional marriage." With his eye on the nomination, Romney asserted that "I have been rock solid in my support of traditional marriage." As punishment for this shift, Romney, on the presidential campaign trail in 2007, was stalked by a man in a dolphin costume, calling himself Flip Romney, "Just another flip flopper from Massachusetts."

Any chance that Potomac Man's private view of homosexuality would become more public was set back severely by Republican Congressman Mark Foley, whose antics, exposed in 2006, cost him his job and may have cost his party control of Congress.

A former real estate broker and owner of a restaurant called the Lettuce Patch, Foley came to Washington as a Republican member of Congress from Florida after his party's landslide win in 1994. The powerful Foley became even more powerful when he got a seat on the Ways and Means Committee. He eventually joined the party leadership as a deputy whip. Foley used his clout to fight against illegal immigration and to boost the fortunes of his citrus growers back home.

He also had an intense interest in children. He became chairman of the House Caucus on Missing and Exploited Children, and he wrote legislation to toughen penalties for sex offenders. At home, he fought nudists who wanted to run a summer camp for children. "I want to make sure that they're properly regulated, properly secure, and that they're not going to have kids come in contact with undesirables," he declared in 2003.

Foley might have ridden that odd assortment of issues all the way to the U.S. Senate. But then, as he was vying for the Republican nomination, a Florida alternative publication outed him as gay. Foley called a press conference in May 2003 to announce that, well, he had nothing to say about reports that he is gay. "People can draw whatever conclusions they want to," he said.

It was a dangerous challenge for Foley to make, for that very spring, the chairman of the House Caucus on Missing and Exploited Children had been exchanging some most unusual instant messages with teenage boys who had been in the House page program.

One night in April 2003, when the House was voting on an emergency spending bill to fund the war in Iraq, Foley was evidently having Internet sex with one such teenage boy. After an exchange in which both the congressman and the boy describe having orgasms, Foley wrote: "ok. i better go vote. did you know you would have this effect on me."

"can I have a good kiss goodnight?" the congressman requested.

"<kiss>" the teen complied.

After ABC News wrote a report about Foley's electronic communications, more examples flowed in from former pages.

"your not old enough to drink," Foley observed in one exchange.

"shhh . . ." said the teen. "That's not what my ID says."

"ok," said Foley, "we may need to drink at my house so we don't get busted."

Three years later, Foley was very much busted. Resigning in disgrace, he first blamed alcohol, then the Catholic church.

A few years before Foley's demise, Ed Schrock met a similar end. A conservative Republican from Virginia, he abruptly announced his resignation in the middle of the 2004 Republican National

Convention. A Web site devoted to outing hypocritical gay politicians had just targeted Schrock—but this time, there was purported evidence. The site claimed that it had recordings of Schrock using a phone service for gay men seeking assignations, and it posted an audio clip purported to be Schrock's voice.

Schrock, then sixty-three, married, and a retired Navy officer, had favored a ban on gays serving in the military. "You're in the showers with them, you're in the bunk room with them, you're in staterooms with them," Schrock had been quoted in the *Virginian-Pilot* as saying. "It's a discipline thing."

Schrock's former colleagues took pity on him and gave him a staff job on his old committee.

But if a Potomac Man—even a Republican—is discreet, sexual orientation can be overlooked, to a point.

For example, an alternative publication in California has tried to out David Dreier, a Republican who is part of the House GOP leadership. Dreier said his private life is private, and most colleagues respect that position. He remains the top Republican on the House Rules Committee, although unconfirmed rumors about his sexuality dogged his unsuccessful effort to be the acting House majority leader in 2005. Media reports said he didn't get the job because his Republican colleagues found him too "moderate"—to which Barney Frank, the openly gay Democrat from Massachusetts, replied on the Web site Raw Story: "Yes, in the sense that I marched in the moderate pride parade last summer and went to a moderate bar."

Hypocrisy and Forgiveness

Washington celebrates mergers of the mighty: Clinton & Clinton, Cheney & Cheney, Dole & Dole, Matalin & Carville, McConnell & Chao, Mitchell & Greenspan. Mary Bono, who succeeded her rock singer husband, Sonny, in Congress after he was killed in a skiing accident, fell for fellow member of Congress Connie Mack, who divorced his wife in 2006.

But if there is an archetypal love story in Washington today, it is that of Don Sherwood and Cynthia Ore. They are the Antony and Cleopatra of Potomac Land.

Sherwood, the owner of a Pennsylvania car dealership who won election to Congress in 1998, was a righteous and devout man. A conservative Republican, he championed causes such as the "sanctity of marriage," and earned top ratings from religious organizations such as the Family Research Council, the Christian Coalition, and Concerned Women for America. He has been married to the same woman for three decades and is father of three grown daughters. Approaching his sixtieth birthday, he attended a Young Republicans gathering in 1999—and was smitten by a twenty-three-year-old Peruvian immigrant by the name of Cynthia Mirella Ore.

Ore, the daughter of grocery owners, lived in an apartment complex nestled among the strip malls of Rockville, Maryland, a D.C. suburb. In Sherwood, two and a half times her age, the young Peruvian beauty saw an opportunity. "When I first told my girlfriends I was dating a politician, they said, 'Stay away from him,'" Ore later told the *Wilkes-Barre Times-Leader*. "I never saw the negative. Maybe if I got with someone who I thought was a player, I'd be okay."

She was okay, for a while. Her congressman boyfriend, she said, helped her land an internship with another congressman who worked down the hall from him. Sherwood also tried to get her a White House internship, Ore said. The young woman drove a Porsche.

Young Cynthia admired Don's "pink, rosy skin," and "those big glasses" melted her heart. She liked him because, while "guys in D.C. are players" who drive expensive cars, Don drove a truck. "We went to movies, dinners," she told the *Times-Leader*. "He is very charming, very gentleman. The wine and roses—that got me. . . . With Don, it was exclusive. He always said, 'You're my number one.' He got on his knees many times just to kiss my hand. He called me his angel."

Later, when the fairy tale reached its inevitable end, she lamented: "We had such a good chemistry. I miss the touchiness and the passion."

Ah, but the touchiness was just beginning.

Early on the afternoon of September 15, 2004, Cynthia paid a visit to Don at his pad, apartment 215 at 110 D Street Southeast, in a complex called Hill House that provides shelter for many members of Congress when the legislature is in session. Sherwood was angry that she was late, Ore later recounted. He became more angry when she asked to visit his hometown and his house in Pennsylvania, where Mrs. Sherwood happened to be living.

"He pushed my forehead down on the futon and started pounding on me," she reported. "He grabbed my throat. . . . I screamed and wiggled away." She locked herself in the bathroom, turned on the shower to mask the sound, and called 911 on her cell phone.

Police arriving on the scene were perplexed. Ore, the officers wrote in a police report, "did not seem to be of sound mind" and shifted her account. Sherwood explained that he was merely giving Ore a "back rub" when she suddenly "jumped up" and ran to the bathroom. Both Cynthia and Don "left out significant information or are not willing to discuss in detail what actually happened." At any rate, police said they found "no probable cause to make an arrest."

A few weeks later, President Bush was traveling near Sherwood's district in Pennsylvania. The congressman joined Bush on stage and heard him pledge to "always stand firm to protect the sanctity of marriage." The speech included nothing about back rubs.

But while the congressman was busily protecting the sanctity of marriage, the police report leaked to his hometown papers. Sherwood, in response, dismissed Ore as "a casual acquaintance" while, somewhat inconsistently, apologizing "for the pain and embarrassment I have caused my family and my supporters."

The "casual acquaintance" slur only inflamed Ore. On June 15, 2005, she filed a lawsuit in D.C. Superior Court seeking $5.5 million from her legislator lover. In the soap-operatic legal filing, plaintiff Cynthia Mirella Ore said that, after meeting defendant Sherwood in 1999, they soon "formed a close romantic and intimate personal relationship which continued for approximately five years." For much of this time, the complaint charged, "the plaintiff was cohabitating with defendant Sherwood at his place of residence." Here, Ore helpfully provided the congressman's address and apartment number.

"Throughout this long-term relationship," it continued, "defendant Sherwood repeatedly and violently physically assaulted and abused plaintiff. These assaults and abuses included, but were not limited to, defendant Sherwood repeatedly striking plaintiff on her face, neck, chest, and back; violently yanking on plaintiff's hair; and repeatedly choking and attempting to strangle plaintiff by placing his hands around her neck."

Ore now said Sherwood had beaten her repeatedly. "Following each unprovoked and vicious attack, defendant Sherwood reaffirmed his romantic intentions and promised the plaintiff that he would not assault her in the future and pleaded for her to remain in the relationship." So why did the mistress keep coming back? "Plaintiff remained in the intimate relationship with the defendant's repeated promises to marry plaintiff and start a family."

Sherwood was accused of inflicting a grisly list of injuries: "facial lacerations; bruises about the head, neck, and other portions of her body; head injury, injuries to her teeth, mouth, and gums; back and neck strain; injuries to her scalp." Now, she alleged, the man with the pink and rosy skin made her fear for her life.

Cynthia accused Don of two specific assaults: a June 24, 2004, incident in which the honorable gentleman from Pennsylvania punched and tried "violently choking" her while "plaintiff was lying on the defendant's bed, attempting to sleep." She also detailed the September 15 episode, in which the representative of the 10th district allegedly "violently struck the plaintiff on her face, neck, chest, and back with a closed fist [and] repeatedly attempted to choke and/or strangle the plaintiff by grabbing her neck with his hands and squeezing tightly."

Whatever happened on September 15, Sherwood now sounded as if he were ready to choke and/or strangle somebody. "I will defend myself to the fullest extent possible against these malicious and baseless allegations, which in large part have been fully investigated and rejected by law enforcement officials," read his statement.

Sherwood seemed to be referring to the police view that his mistress wasn't "of sound mind." But the *Wilkes-Barre Times Leader,* which pounced on the story from the start while other outlets in the area ignored it, dug in further. They found a D.C. police officer who took photos of Ore's injuries later on September 15 and told the paper

Sherwood should have been arrested. The paper also reported that there were "smudges on a police report that suggest the incident number had been changed" and found that the time on the police report was two hours before the 911 call was logged.

Also, Ore had compiled an extensive collection of her medical and dental records. The files, which she shared with the *Washington Post,* appeared to support her claims of injury.

Sherwood, who had by now hired a lawyer and a media consultant, had the case moved to federal court and tried to get the trial postponed until after Election Day in 2006. Meanwhile, his denials grew less vehement with each version. First, the charge was "absolutely not true" and came from a "casual acquaintance." Next came his move-it-along statement: "I'm truly sorry. Now, I have work to do."

Finally, in a July court filing responding to Ore, Sherwood admitted the relationship. "For about five years, I had an affair I deeply regret. Although it was intermittent and ended last year, nothing I say can diminish the pain and hurt I have caused my wife and family. . . . At the same time, I want to be absolutely clear that I never physically hurt or abused Ms. Ore."

By September, Sherwood was rethinking the part about defending himself to "the fullest extent possible." Seeking a confidentiality order, his lawyer said that because of his "status as a United States congressman, release of his mobile telephone records may raise unique security issues."

In November, Don and Cynthia announced that they'd reached a settlement—part of which called for them to keep mum about the details. The legal dispute thus ended, it was time for the final stage of any Washington love affair: the spin. It was still a year before Sherwood's election—plenty of time for a good politician to recover.

Phyllis Schlafly's Eagle Forum, dedicated to "respect for family integrity" and "public and private virtue," awarded Sherwood a 73 percent rating in 2005, up from 69 percent in 2004. Three weeks before the election, President Bush flew to Sherwood's home district to eat ice cream with Sherwood and tell his supporters at a fund-raiser, "I'm pleased to be here with Don Sherwood. . . . He has got a record of accomplishment." The president, who had earlier proclaimed the week to be "National Character Counts Week," omitted the usual references to family values.

＊The voters were somewhat less forgiving. After Sherwood's Democratic opponent in 2006 ran an ad about the affair and the allegations of violence, Sherwood issued his own ad denying the abuse allegations again and asking forgiveness. "While I'm truly sorry for disappointing you, I never wavered from my commitment to reduce taxes, create jobs, and bring home our fair share," the congressman said. He lost by a wide margin.

Love in the Workplace

Long hours on the job and devotion to work in Potomac Land often mean that love originates in the workplace. This has been true at least since Franklin Roosevelt's time, and generally attracted little attention. When President-elect George H. W. Bush was rumored to be having an affair with an aide in 1989, the *Washington Post* delicately noted that the woman "has served President-elect George Bush in a variety of positions."

But things took a turn during Clarence Thomas's confirmation hearing, when former aide Anita Hill said she had been harassed and threatened by the future Supreme Court justice, who identified his genitalia as Long Dong Silver. Mating relationships between high officials and their staffers suffered another blow when Bill Clinton spied Monica Lewinsky's thong underwear—leading to his impeachment and a year's worth of cigars, Altoids, and blue dresses.

Now, in the Bush era, Potomac Man's relationships with his staffers must be navigated with great care. Senator Tim Hutchinson, for example, lost his reelection in 2002, largely because, three years earlier, he divorced his wife of twenty-eight years and married a younger legislative aide a year later. Hutchinson, an Arkansas Republican who is also a Baptist minister, never regained his "family values" credentials.

Newt Gingrich had a similar situation but handled it quite a bit better. The former House Speaker, a Georgia Republican, had a seven-year affair with a congressional aide, Callista Bisek. But he waited until after he had already left Congress to admit the affair and to file for a divorce from his wife. Bisek became Gingrich's third wife in August 2000.

Done properly, the lawmaker-staff love affair can benefit both parties. Senator Debbie Stabenow, a Michigan Democrat, was long divorced when she started dating, and eventually married, a younger campaign aide. The former aide, Tom Athans, runs a liberal talk-radio outfit called Democracy Radio—so the merger helps Stabenow and her colleagues get the word out while giving Athans a steady supply of talkers.

But political figures must constantly live in fear of the kiss-and-tell staffer who will share details of the affair with the media. In 2001, Diana Davis, a young aide to Republican congressman Mike Rogers of Michigan, provided *Vanity Fair* magazine with photos of her and her girlfriends posing with five Democratic congressmen at a "rowdy" party just two days after the September 11 terrorist attacks. In the accompanying article, she explained why she slept with one staffer: "He was powerful. He knew Tom DeLay."

Even worse than the kiss-and-tell staffer is the kiss-and-disappear staffer. In fact, any Potomac Man pondering romance with a less powerful figure in Potomac Land must pause to consider the cautionary tale of Gary Condit.

In the spring of 2001, Condit, a Democratic congressman from California, was fifty-three years old. He had struck up an affair with Chandra Levy, a twenty-four-year-old intern with the Bureau of Prisons making $27,000 a year. The relationship, already a small problem for the married lawmaker, became a much bigger problem when Levy disappeared. Suddenly Condit was suspected of murder. He denied it—and he was never charged—but the episode ended his career and made him a national disgrace.

Levy was a typical intern, making phone calls and doing research for her agency, wearing her Justice Department credential around her neck. But after she visited the congressman's office in the fall of 2000, the two quickly became entangled. "She liked guys in uniforms," her aunt told the *Post* after she had disappeared. "She liked that power."

As her aunt recounted it, Levy and Condit devised a paging system to arrange meetings in his apartment. There they cooked, ate take-out food and Ben & Jerry's ice cream, and had the body-oil massages that always seem to accompany such affairs. On outings, Condit would disguise himself with a baseball cap. He gave her airline tickets, a bracelet, and on Valentine's Day Godiva chocolates. She had begun to talk about moving in and about starting a family with him.

Then, just as Condit's wife was coming to Washington for a week-long visit, Levy disappeared. A little more than a year later, a man looking for turtles found her skeletal remains in Rock Creek Park. Authorities say Condit isn't a suspect, but that does him little good now. He's banished from the land of Potomac Men—and he's the inspiration for an Off-Broadway show, *Aphrodisiac*.

Twelve

THE CHORUS

The Oxford classicist Oliver Taplin, a specialist in ancient Greek drama, told Britain's *Guardian* newspaper in 2006 that "Greek tragedy is an odd form of drama because the plot keeps getting interrupted by this chorus, who keep insisting on singing and dancing."

Over the millennia, the Greek chorus has evolved into the more sophisticated theater seen in most advanced cultures. But it remains in almost its pure form in Potomac Land, where it is the primary means of communication for large segments of the population. Here, the local chorus members, or choreutai in the Greek, call themselves journalists or reporters. But in fact they are very much like the ancient Greek chorus, constantly interrupting the narrative of Potomac life to draw attention to themselves. Further, each party in Potomac Land has its own chorus, which will sing praises about its partisan protagonists and moan constantly about the failings of the other side.

The Greek chorus itself evolved from fertility and burial rites practiced by primitive cultures in pre-Hellenic times. The choreutai are believed to have been inspired by the cult of Dionysus, the god of wine, which is thought to have come to Greece from North Africa or the Middle East, where similar cults have been found. Cult members tended to be slaves, criminals, and other outsiders. They were known for their trance states; their group dances to drum music; and, of course, their wine consumption, which led to drunken orgies.

For Homo politicus, the choreutai are strikingly similar to their ancient counterparts: in their alcohol consumption, in their unruliness, and in their habit of commenting on Potomac Man's every action and identifying each actor as hero or villain. One group of choreutai, from organizations such as Fox News, the *Washington Times*, the *Weekly Standard*, and the *Wall Street Journal* editorial page, form a chorus that champions Republicans; these choreutai have chorus leaders, choragi in the Greek, such as Roger Ailes, Paul Gigot, and Bill Kristol.

The opposing choreutai—the *New York Times;* CBS News; and the other major newspapers, magazines, and broadcasters—are broadly assumed to be friendly to the Democrats. The Democratic leanings of this latter group of choreutai are not monolithic, however, and entire organizations such as the Media Research Center and Media Matters have been created to identify choreutai as "biased" toward either the Democrats or the Republicans. In fact, the choreutai from what is disparagingly called the mainstream are not reliable partisans and are more interested in drawing attention to themselves and otherwise honoring the cult of Dionysus.

The role of the choreutai is particularly pronounced in Potomac Land because Potomac Man, despite his possession of advanced technology, is strikingly limited in his ability to communicate. Tribal identity has become so powerful that Democrats and Republicans seldom interact with each other. Their communications are almost entirely formal and ritualistic, such as the annual State of the Union festival, when the president speaks to lawmakers from both parties in one room. Otherwise, it is rare to find Democrats and Republicans in the same room. Even on the floor of the House and the Senate, each speaker addresses not his colleagues but a television camera in an empty room.

This lack of interaction between the two tribes has elevated the importance of the choreutai, because almost all intertribal communications between Democrats and Republicans are delivered through the choruses. While unwilling to talk informally, the feuding tribes watch each other's press conferences and speeches on television and read about each other's statements and plans in newspapers, magazines, and Internet publications. Partisans on both sides vie to use the choreutai to spread their own folktales while discrediting the other tribe's mythology.

The Dionysian Orgy

Among the most celebrated of the Potomac choreutai in recent years has been Jeff Gannon, the pen name of one James Dale Guckert. Gannon worked for two Internet sites, Talon News and GOPUSA, owned and funded by a Republican activist and devoted to heralding the wisdom of President Bush. Before the 2004 elections, Gannon began attending televised White House briefings, where he asked questions designed to disparage Democrats and praise the president. The other choreutai disapproved of Gannon but generally tolerated him until it was discovered that he was a gigolo who created a gay escort site on the Internet showing nude photos of himself. Worse, in the eyes of the choreutai, was that Gannon was an avowed partisan. It is part of the cult philosophy that, however partisan a chorus member behaves, he must officially declare himself to be nonpartisan. Gannon was cast out of the cult of Dionysus.

Far more acceptable in the view of Potomac Man is the activity of the *Weekly Standard*, a magazine created by the conservative publisher Rupert Murdoch, who also operates Fox News. The magazine has been cultlike in its support of Bush's actions, but it is officially nonpartisan. Its number two editor, Fred Barnes, wrote a book titled *Rebel-in-Chief: Inside the Bold and Controversial Presidency of George W. Bush*. Among his dispassionate descriptions of Bush, Barnes found the president to be "a visionary" who has "achieved big things." Though Bush had the support of barely more than three in ten Americans, Barnes judged that he delivered "five or six of the most important and eloquent presidential addresses of the last half century," putting him in league with John F. Kennedy and Ronald Reagan.

Among Barnes's other observations: "Bush revealed his proactive tendencies after Hurricane Katrina devastated New Orleans," a period in which even fellow Republicans condemned Bush's inaction. And: "Bush loves to smash conventional wisdom and destroy myths." And: "Bush is a big picture person, eager to concentrate on major issues and delegate smaller ones. That explains why he let Laura design the Oval Office rug." Barnes predicted that "thanks to Bush, a Republican era is now at hand." Not long after this forecast, Republicans lost control of both chambers of Congress, and Bush's support dropped below 30 percent.

Barnes's boss at the *Weekly Standard*, Bill Kristol, was perhaps the most outspoken supporter of the Iraq war in all Potomac Land. While others soured on the war as conditions in Iraq deteriorated, Kristol became only more fervent. In 2007, after four years in Iraq, the *Washington Post*'s Elizabeth Williamson compiled Kristol's greatest hits on the war.

"The war itself will clarify who was right and who was wrong about weapons of mass destruction," he wrote in March 2003, before U.S. weapons inspectors failed to find any of the forbidden weapons. "We would note now that even the threat of war against Saddam seems to be encouraging stirrings toward political reform in Iran and Saudi Arabia," he continued. This did not, in fact, occur.

"I think there's a certain amount of . . . pop sociology in America, you know, somehow the Shia can't get along with the Sunni and the Shia in Iraq just want to establish some kind of Islamic fundamentalist regime," he told National Public Radio in April 2003, before a civil war between Shia and Sunni broke out. That same month, before the insurgency in Iraq threw U.S. forces on the defensive and the Taliban in Afghanistan proved resurgent, Kristol concluded, "The battles of Afghanistan and Iraq have been won decisively and honorably."

In March 2004, before the Iraqi government foundered over ethnic squabbles, Kristol wrote that Iraqis "have in fact demonstrated something remarkable in Iraq: a willingness on the part of the diverse ethnic and religious groups to disagree—peacefully—and then to compromise. This willingness is the product of what appears to be a broad Iraqi consensus favoring the idea of pluralism."

With each false prophecy, Kristol became only more certain of success. Eighteen months later, just before the magnitude of the violence in Iraq began to overwhelm U.S. forces, Kristol predicted that "it is much more likely that the situation in Iraq will stay more or less the same, or improve." Even after the bombing of a holy mosque in Samarra set off what the CIA would come to label a civil war, Kristol wrote in April 2006: "The fact is that we are not facing a civil war in Iraq. . . . Moreover, we can very likely prevent this outcome, and, even better, make real progress toward victory." Writing with a colleague, he continued: "The country's vital institutions seem to have grown strong enough to withstand even the provocation of the bombing of the golden mosque."

As choragus of a pro-Bush chorus, Kristol's intensity was reaching that of a Dionysian orgy. Fortunately, unlike Gannon, he had the good sense to keep his clothes on.

COURTING THE CHORAGUS

Choreutai in Potomac Land have a status order unto themselves, an order confirmed by the seating assigned in the White House briefing room. To many outsiders, the pecking order seems similar to that established in other cultures by high school children. In the rear of the room are the cameramen and sound technicians—the shop class students in high school. Scurrying in the aisles are the still photographers—Potomac Land's equivalent of the art students. In the last few rows are foreign correspondents and representatives of obscure publications; in high school, they would be the average students heading for the local community college. Next come the magazine and national newspaper correspondents—the mathletes and other smart but geeky students. In front of them are the television correspondents (the football team captain, the cheerleader, and the homecoming queen) and the wire correspondents (the class president and head of the student government).

Back in news bureaus distributed throughout Potomac Land are the bureau chiefs and political correspondents whose status is lofty enough that they needn't attend briefings at all. Important people will return their calls and give them private briefings. But above the bureau chiefs—above even the editorial writers, the executive editors, and the publishers—sits one man: Bob Woodward. The man who brought down Richard Nixon is Potomac Land's authoritative choragus. "Bush is a self-confident man," observed conservative writer Andrew Ferguson. "But he's not self-confident enough to say no when Bob Woodward asks if he's got two hours to chat. Cockiness has its limits, even with Bush. This is Woodward's town; the president just lives in it."

Nominally, Woodward remains affiliated with the *Washington Post*, where he worked when he broke the Watergate story. But he is larger than the *Post*. When he released his book *Plan of Attack* in 2004, the Associated Press was the first to report on its contents. When it came time for Mark Felt to identify himself as Watergate's Deep Throat, the honor went not to the *Post* but to *Vanity Fair*. Reporters from the *Post* asked Woodward to reveal the parking garage where he had his clandestine meetings with Felt thirty years earlier, but Woodward instead disclosed the Arlington garage's location to NBC News. His colleagues spent two years probing the CIA leak case before he let them know that he, too, had been told of Valerie Plame's identity; even after confessing, he wouldn't talk to *Post* reporters about it. Finally, when his book *State of Denial* came out in 2006, the *New York Times*, the *New York Daily News*, and CBS News got the story first.

Said Woodward to the *Post*'s media critic, Howie Kurtz: "It's the world we live in." Namely, Woodward's world.

Woodward's singular importance to Potomac Man has allowed him to weather criticism that would have doomed lesser choreutai. After he once obtained a deathbed confession from CIA director William Casey about the Iran-Contra weapons trade, critics argued that Casey's stroke had left him unable to speak and that Casey's hospital room was guarded by CIA security and attended twenty-four hours a day by Casey's family members.

As his stature has grown greater than the Potomac Men he writes about, Potomac Land's most famous choragus has also evolved. When he broke the Watergate story in the 1970s, he was seen as an "adversarial" writer, working without access to the most powerful figures. Over time, however, he became the choragus most often favored by the powerful as an outlet for their own tales. Presidents and others concluded that, if they talked to Woodward, he would be kind to them in his books; ignore him, and history's view of you will be unkind.

President Bush saw both sides of that equation. The White House showed great fondness toward Woodward when he wrote his book *Bush at War* in 2002. After getting unprecedented access to Bush and his top aides, Woodward portrayed Bush as an extraordinary and decisive leader. He defended Bush against accusations that he mishandled his initial response to the September 11 attacks, that Dick Cheney was overly influential in the administration, and that the administration stifled dissent.

The narrative showed a macho president. "Bush had just finished his daily physical fitness routine and was still in his exercise clothes. He was not dripping sweat but had cooled down," Woodward wrote. It showed a forceful president. "Hand-wringing? He hated, absolutely hated, the very idea, especially in tough times." It showed a clear-thinking president. "He wanted action, solutions. Once on a course, he directed his energy at forging on, rarely looking back, scoffing at— even ridiculing—doubts and anything less than 100 percent commitment."

Woodward also described a bold and confident president. "There is an aspect of baseball-coach, even fraternity-brother, urgency in Bush at such moments," he wrote. "He leans his head forward and holds it still, makes eye contact, maintains it, saying, in effect: You're on board, you're with me, right?" After one such performance, one Bush aide "thought the tension suddenly drained from the room. The president was saying he had confidence and they should have confidence."

Woodward described his tour of Bush's ranch and its rock formations. "Bush started tossing rocks at the overhang, and I briefly joined in," the choragus told, then recounted Bush's guidance to him. "You have the story," Bush told him.

At least he had Bush's story of events. The response in Potomac

Land to Woodward's laudatory Bush biography was typified by a *New Republic* spoof of a Woodward conversation with *Post* executive editor Len Downie. " 'I have a senior White House aide who says that Bush was'—he paused to look at his meticulously crafted notes—'brave, decisive, and never-wavering' in the days after September 11. 'The president set the course for the war on terrorism and everyone else fell in behind him.' My source says that Bush's performance was reminiscent of Roosevelt—both of them."

The White House itself was pleased with the result. "The president rightly believed that Woodward, for good and ill, warts and all, would chronicle what happened," Cheney adviser Mary Matalin told the *Washington Post*. "It's in the White House's interest to have a neutral source writing the history of the way Bush makes decisions. That's why the White House gives him access." The Republican National Committee plugged the book. Journalistic critics piled on Woodward, particularly as Bush's foreign policy ran aground in Iraq.

Woodward's second book about Bush, *Plan of Attack,* was more down the middle, and when he started interviews for his third book, *State of Denial,* the White House shut the door. Bush aide Dan Bartlett noticed "a different tone and tenor to this project," according to Kurtz. "Some pretty hard conclusions had already formed in Bob's mind."

Bartlett sensed correctly. Without Bush's cooperation, the third book sharply revised the first, concluding in 560 pages of savage revelation that the Bush administration had bumbled into endless errors and couldn't settle disputes among its warring factions. The chief of staff and the first lady tried to get the defense secretary fired. The defense secretary, Donald Rumsfeld, refused to return calls from the secretary of state. Woodward wrote that Rumsfeld's carelessness made him "speechless." The same people who saw Bush as firm and confident now saw him as anxious, insecure, and dishonest, unwilling to believe how bad things had gotten in Iraq. Revisiting the same heroic early years of the Bush presidency, Woodward now portrayed the president as ignorant and crude.

"I found out new things," the choragus explained.

USE OF MERCENARIES

The cost of communicating in Potomac Land can be daunting. Television advertisements cost tens if not hundreds of thousands of dollars. And it is still true, as A. J. Liebling said long ago, that freedom of the press belongs to the man who owns one. Murdoch knew this when he bought Fox News and started the *Weekly Standard*. In an earlier time, Ted Turner knew this when he started CNN. Even the Reverend Sun Myung Moon surely had Liebling on the brain when he created the *Washington Times*.

But the ever resourceful Potomac Land choreutes, always looking out for the little guy, is finding ways to allow people of lesser means to buy themselves a voice. The Potomac choreutes is fond of saying that he cannot be bought; he does not mind, however, renting out his services on occasion.

Armstrong Williams, a columnist and television commentator, approached Education Secretary Rod Paige in March 2003 with just such a rental plan. He said that he was willing, for a low, low rate, to write columns and make pitches on radio and television for the Bush administration's No Child Left Behind education policy. The Bush officials thought this to be a bargain, and they ultimately agreed to pay Armstrong $186,000 through a contract with the Ketchum PR firm. They had rented a choreutes.

Williams, as good a businessman as he was a commentator, promised specific "deliverables," among them: invitations to administration officials to be on his TV and radio shows; ads featuring Williams, including a "bonus ad" that Williams, a black conservative, would put out during Black History Month. Williams's bills were duly itemized: here was a "two (2) minute commentary devoted to NCLB" on Sinclair Broadcasting, there was a column "devoted to NCLB" that ran in thirty-four newspapers. When word of this arrangement got out, the department's inspector general investigated, but he seemed less interested in whether the Williams rental was proper than whether or not the department got a good deal. The inspector was not pleased that Williams was paid for ads that didn't run.

Congressional investigators with the Government Accountability Office had a less charitable view. They thought that the administration, by paying for the favorable commentary without requiring Williams to disclose his payments, was breaking laws against covert propaganda. The investigators also had problems with $38,000 the Education Department spent on a television "news story" in hopes that television stations would run it without identifying it as a government production.

Unfortunately for Williams, the administration had to cut short his contract before paying all of the $240,000 he had expected to receive. Worse, prosecutors eventually forced him to return $34,000 in overpayments. Williams got to keep the other $152,000 and didn't have to admit wrongdoing.

And why should he have admitted wrongdoing? Paying Potomac Land writers for their services has become a common practice in recent years. One columnist, Maggie Gallagher, wrote favorably about the Bush administration's marriage policies while taking $21,500 as a consultant on the issue. Another columnist, Michael McManus, also got government money for help with the marriage program. The Agriculture Department, getting in on the action, paid a freelance writer $7,500 to write stories touting government conservation programs. Then came word that the Bush administration paid ten journalists, including three from the *Miami Herald*'s Spanish-language publication, hundreds of thousands of dollars to provide anti-Castro commentary on television and radio. Even Castro was aware of the rental scheme, at one point calling one of the journalists a "mercenary."

The pay-for-press program was working so well in Potomac Land that the Bush administration decided to expand it. The Pentagon topped all payouts, spending millions of dollars to plant propaganda in the Iraqi media and to pay off Iraqi journalists. Eventually, individual Potomac Men picked up the approach. Jack Abramoff started paying journalists about $2,000 for each column they wrote supportive of one of Abramoff's clients. Doug Bandow, a columnist with Copley News, lost his column after writing a dozen for Abramoff. But another Abramoff-funded pundit, Peter Ferrara, kept his job at the Institute for Policy Innovation. His boss, Tom Giovanetti, proved most innovative in defense of the ways of Potomac Land. "There have been no clear policies, no rules, no precedents," he wrote in the *National Review.* "Rather, the rules are being asserted now, in hindsight—and the new rules are being reinforced by the hesitancy of organizations to stand up against the accusers." His lament was a Potomac Land inversion of Edmund Burke: All that is necessary for the triumph of good is that evil men do nothing.

THE PATRON-CLIENT RELATIONSHIP

Since ancient times, primitive and advanced cultures alike have relied on some form of the patron-client relationship. The patron, an elite member of the tribe, extends to the client either money or access; the client in turn dedicates himself and his work to the patron. Potomac Man embraces this relationship in many areas; lawmaker-staff, partner-associate, president-intern. But perhaps the most important patron-client relationship in Potomac Land is that between a prominent Potomac Man and his choreutes.

In May 2003, about two months into the Iraq war, the *Washington Post* media critic, Howie Kurtz, got his hands on an e-mail from *New York Times* reporter Judy Miller to the *Times'* bureau chief in Baghdad. Miller was explaining why she wrote a story about Iraqi politician Ahmad Chalabi without alerting her colleagues in Baghdad. "I've been covering Chalabi for about 10 years, and have done most of the stories about him for our paper, including the long takeout we recently did on him," she wrote. "He has provided most of the front page exclusives on WMD to our paper."

That offhand e-mail confirmed what most every Potomac Man already suspected: that Miller had been fed a series of fantastic, and fallacious, stories about Saddam Hussein's weapons programs by Chalabi and other Iraqi expatriates. Without the resulting stories—particularly the (fabricated) claim that Iraq had mobile biological and chemical weapons labs—it is possible the administration wouldn't have gone to war in Iraq. After the U.S. invasion, when there were no illegal weapons found and Chalabi was exposed as a fraud, his offices were raided as part of an FBI probe into whether he passed American secrets to Iran.

Still, the claims, bogus though they were, earned Miller nationwide attention. After the invasion, she "embedded" herself with the Army unit looking for the forbidden weapons, drawing allegations that she was serving as a conduit between the soldiers and Chalabi, passing information from him to them. When the Army proposed withdrawing the unit because there were no weapons to be found, Miller wrote a letter of objection. She cheerfully identified herself to a colleague as "Miss Run Amok."

The patron-client relationship had worked well for Miller—but with Chalabi in disgrace, she needed a new patron. Back in Potomac Land, she found one in Scooter Libby, chief of staff to Vice President Cheney.

A month after her e-mail skirmish, Miller visited Libby in his White House office to talk about the failure to find the promised weapons. Libby told her about Joe Wilson, the former diplomat and Bush critic whose wife worked at the CIA. Two weeks later, Miller met Libby again, for breakfast at the St. Regis Hotel, where Libby expanded on his unmasking of CIA operative Valerie Plame. They spoke about it again by phone. Miller unsuccessfully lobbied her editors to write a story about Wilson and Plame.

A year later, when Libby was being pursued by a prosecutor for his role in the leak, Miller had little reason not to cooperate: the prosecutor already knew what Libby did, and Libby had signed a voluntary waiver releasing Miller from their confidentiality agreement. But Miller had a different idea: She would defend and honor her patron. In doing so, she could also become free-press martyr, ending the ridicule for her false reports about the Iraqi weapons. The *Times* had recently published an editors' note disavowing five stories Miller wrote about the weapons, with headlines such as "Iraqi Defector Tells of Work on at Least 20 Hidden Weapons Sites."

But in her eighty-five days in the jail, the revived Miller received a procession of luminaries: UN ambassador John Bolton, Tom Brokaw, Bob Dole, publisher Mort Zuckerman, book editor Alice Mayhew,

Senators Arlen Specter and Chris Dodd, and even Charles Duelfer, whose survey of Iraq concluded that Iraq had no weapons of mass destruction. The *New York Times* published more than fifteen editorials supporting her.

But the client's celebrated refusal to testify against her patron ended with a whimper. Facing a longer jail stay, Miller was ready to stand down. She spoke with Libby, who said it would be just fine for her to testify. Her publisher and editor took her from the jail to the Ritz-Carlton in Georgetown for a massage and a manicure, but the recriminations began immediately.

The *Times'* top editor, Bill Keller, accused Miller of having an unspecified "entanglement" with Libby and of misleading her colleagues about what she had been told about Valerie Plame. If "I had known the details of Judy's entanglement with Libby," he wrote, "I'd have been more careful in how the paper articulated its defense and perhaps more willing than I had been to support efforts aimed at exploring compromises."

Within months, Miller and the *Times* parted company. "I have become the news," she wrote in a departing letter. For a Potomac Woman, that wasn't the problem. The problem was that in her loyalty to her patrons over her newspaper, she had become *bad* news.

SHADOW PUPPETRY

In Asian cultures, storytellers since ancient times have relied on puppets to tell their tales. Beginning in India, puppetry is believed to have spread to China before becoming a dominant art form in Indonesia sometime after the seventh century. There, shadow puppets, their elaborate images cast onto screens, are understood to have spiritual powers. The storyteller, or dalang, uses the puppet show, wayang kulit, to tell stories of good triumphing over evil.

Potomac Man, too, has a rich tradition of puppetry. In Potomac Land, the choreutai frequently rely on their own form of puppet, known locally as the pundit, or talking head, to act out his tale and to illustrate his points. This need is shared by almost every choragus, whether it's CNN's Wolf Blitzer (who spends so many hours on the air that his Sunday show, *Late Edition*, was dubbed "Long Edition" by his coworkers), MSNBC's Tucker Carlson (who gained celebrity first by wearing a bow tie and then by making an early exit in *Dancing with the Stars*), or Fox News' Brit Hume (who lends conservatives a sympathetic ear, as when Vice President Cheney shot a hunting partner instead of a quail). Blitzer, Carlson, and Hume all need puppets to help make their points—and this need inevitably leads them to the doorstep of Larry Sabato.

Sabato, a political science professor at the University of Virginia, is the most ubiquitous shadow puppet in all Potomac Land. Need a comment on a House race in Washington state? He has it. A thought on presidential candidate Mitt Romney's Mormonism? Sabato's got it. Racial politics in the South? Go to Sabato. How about something obscure, such as the experience of athletes in politics? Sabato can wing it. Some have dubbed him Dr. Dial-A-Quote. Others call him a "quote whore." Virginia political operative Ben Tribbett started a political blog called Not Larry Sabato to break clear of the Sabato monopoly (its homepage has shown a Sabato hairpiece popping off its cartoon head). Some news outlets have tried, unsuccessfully, to ban Sabato quotes from their pages and broadcasts.

The professor takes this ubiquity as a matter of pride, according to his own bio. "According to the *Wall Street Journal*, Dr. Sabato is 'probably the most quoted college professor in the land,' while the *Washington Post* called him 'the Mark McGwire of political analysts,' " it boasts. Indeed, if there were steroids that increased quote output the way it did McGwire's home runs, Sabato would likely take them. The bio further notes that he is "author of over twenty books and countless essays." Further, "Dr. Sabato has served on many national and state commissions," and "is the recipient of more than two-dozen major scholarships, grants and academic awards." It continues: "Lexis/Nexis lists over 400 citations by the media during just the last two years. Every major national newspaper is included, repeatedly. In 2004–2005, Sabato logged nearly 200 television appearances, including multiple appearances."

Sabato has achieved this superpuppet status by being available to any and all media callers on any and all subjects. He's also a great quote. Appearing on Chris Matthews's *Hardball* in 1998, he proclaimed that Bill Clinton "is, after all, a self-certified liar."

"I'm sure he would phrase it differently," Matthews pointed out, "as would a lot of other people."

"Well, I'm not a Clinton flunky," Sabato rejoined.

Eight years later on the same show, Sabato was discussing Senator George Allen's "rural, redneck image," when Matthews asked if Allen had used racially charged language. "He did use the N word, whether he's denying it now or not," said Sabato, who attended college with Allen. Sabato admitted the next day that he'd never personally heard Allen say the naughty word.

Sabato knows his stuff, although his crystal ball has been known to fog over from time to time. In the late summer of 2004, he said that President Bush "really will need a miracle" to defeat John Kerry. More crucial in his role as puppet is his ability to entertain. Hosting a Senate debate in 2000 between Allen and then-Senator Chuck Robb, Sabato hijacked the proceedings by demanding the two agree to ban negative ads. "Why don't you two shake on it?" he asked. "Do it right here." Sabato offered to enforce it; then, when the candidates declined, he told the viewers: "I just want to apologize to my fellow Virginians. I tried."

"Some viewers came away from the hour with a sense that there were three candidates on the stage," was Libby Copeland's review in the *Washington Post*. She got a rival puppet, Virginia Tech's Robert E. Denton, to call Sabato "unprofessional," saying, "This was every bit the Larry Sabato show."

The politicians often don't enjoy the puppet show. Former Virginia governor Gerald Baliles postulated that "the shortest distance between two points is Larry Sabato and a TV camera." And a Robb campaign manager once told the *Richmond Times-Dispatch* that "if it weren't for the media, Larry Sabato would be nothing more than a college professor with an old Volvo and two pairs of Hush Puppies."

Perhaps, but in Potomac Land there is always demand for a good puppet show.

THE CHORAGUS AS HERO

In native cultures across the globe, storytelling plays a crucial role. It is the way history, values, and practical knowledge are passed from generation to generation. The storyteller conveys theories about creation and the natural world and such daily necessities as how to hunt. In Potomac Land, however, the vital tradition of storytelling is severely hobbled by Potomac Man's inherent self-absorption: The Potomac choragus is most interested in stories about himself.

Mark Halperin, until 2007 the ABC News political director, became one of Potomac Land's most influential choragi because his daily memo, the Note, was read by most Potomac Men. In it, the choragus explained the true significance of the previous day's events and forecast the significance of events to come. But it was perplexing to those from other cultures who happened upon the Note, for they were given the impression that the most important person in all Potomac Land was Halperin himself.

In the fall of 2006, Halperin had just written a book with John F. Harris, then political editor of the *Washington Post, The Way to Win*, a self-help guide for political figures and Potomac Land advisers who were seeking to capture the presidency in 2008. Even though the midterm elections were approaching, the Note dedicated itself with firm single-mindedness to the sale of the book. Halperin's method: give a mention in the Note to anybody who had praised his book. The result was a curious echo chamber.

"*USA Today*'s discerning Bob Minzesheimer touts the forthcoming book *The Way to Win*."

"*Publishers Weekly* says about *The Way to Win*: 'Though very topical, the book's comprehensiveness should make it a lasting piece of scholarship.' "

"E. J. Kessler, in a *Forward* profile of Halperin, writes that *The Way to Win* . . . is 'likely to emerge among the top political-journalism titles of the century's first decade.' (We forgive the use of 'likely,' on the assumption that an editor inserted it.)"

"Eric Alterman's review in *The Nation* can't help but say that *The*

Way to Win 'contains a razor-sharp analysis of the upper stratum of American politics available nowhere else.'"

"Here's what Sunday's *Kansas City Star* said about *The Way to Win*: . . . the most fascinating and insightful political book of the year."

This went on daily in the Note for more than a month and included bulletins on the authors' speaking engagements and contests to drum up interest and outright pleas to purchase the book. But the authors' greatest triumph was getting a mention on the Drudge Report, a conservative Web site with millions of viewers. It was easy, actually: Halperin and Harris wrote a flattering passage about Matt Drudge, "leaked" the passage to Drudge himself, and then enjoyed the resulting triumphant Drudge headline:

"ABC NEWS, WASH POST REPORTERS:
'DRUDGE RULES OUR WORLD' "

"The political director of ABC NEWS and the national politics editor of the *Washington Post* make it official in their new insider tome on D.C. politics and how it's played: The four words in every newsroom and campaign headquarters are: Have you seen Drudge?" Drudge wrote. "In an extended fifteen-page homage to the glories of this site, they report: "Matt Drudge is the gatekeeper . . . he is the Walter Cronkite of his era."

In the end, though, it was a humbling tale for Potomac Land choreutai. For all the promotional activity, Potomac Man's circular fascination with the Halperin-Harris book did not spread beyond the borders of Potomac Land. *The Way to Win* didn't sell. Worse, readership of the Note declined, and Halperin eventually stepped down in favor of an editor who turned the focus to Potomac Men other than himself.

REMNANTS OF FEUDAL LAW

One of the many paradoxes about Potomac Man is his view of speech. Ostensibly, free speech is the highest value of the land, ranking at the top of the Bill of Rights. But in Potomac Land proper, communications more closely resemble those under the feudal laws of lèse-majesté. In feudal times, any speech considered insulting to the sovereign or his government was punished severely because it meant a breakdown of the feudal bond. In Potomac Land, similarly, loyalists of the president make efforts to suppress any words that could cause the administration to come under ridicule. The result is something akin to a pagan-state cult, in which words harmful to the president's dignity are scrubbed from the record and replaced with praise for the ruler.

In Potomac Land, the chief author of such praise is Karen Hughes, a longtime adviser to President Bush. She has entered into the national debate a number of trenchant observations about her boss, among them: "The president has a wonderful sense of humor, which is one of the reasons it is so much fun to work for him." And: "I've worked for the president for ten years now, and I've never been in a meeting where he didn't ask tough, probing questions." And: "This president has delivered on his promises, and is doing in office what he said he would do."

Yet Hughes's gift for the banal is not what sets her apart. It is her ability to expunge from public view language that undermines the president. As Bush's top communications strategist, she brought elaborate new powers to the federal government to find and neutralize cases of lèse-majesté. Hughes eventually left the White House and became a private adviser to Bush, but not before she launched a potent—and enduring—effort to protect the president from harmful words.

When Andrew Natsios, administrator of the U.S. Agency for International Development, said on ABC News' *Nightline* that U.S. taxpayers would not have to pay more than $1.7 billion to reconstruct Iraq—an absurd understatement, in retrospect—the administration found an effective away to reduce the embarrassment: It ordered the transcript containing the statement removed from the USAID Web site. Likewise, when the Iraq fighting proved more stubborn than expected, the White House edited the original headline on its Web site of Bush's May 1, 2003, speech, which had said: "President Bush Announces Combat Operations in Iraq Have Ended." The word "Major" was inserted before "Combat."

The language policing spread. The federal Centers for Disease Control and Prevention removed or revised fact sheets on condoms, excising information about their effectiveness in disease prevention. The National Cancer Institute removed information on its Web site saying there was no link between abortion and breast cancer. And the Justice Department, after hiring KPMG Consulting to assess the department's workplace diversity, would release the report only after it removed anything critical of the administration. Redacted from the report: all of the report's recommendations, the first five of its "key findings," and unhelpful conclusions such as "minorities are significantly more likely than whites to cite stereotyping, harassment, and racial tension as characteristics of the work climate." The only thing left in the report for the public to read were statements such as "The department's attorney workforce is more diverse than the U.S. legal workforce."

That worked out so well that the administration circulated a guide called "Redacting with Confidence," with information about "how to safely publish sanitized reports." Administration officials removed from the public domain some 55,000 pages of documents dating back to World War II, including a translated newspaper article from 1962. Administration officials went to the Nixon library to remove from the public domain information about American nuclear missile stockpiles—in 1972. President Bush himself issued an order blocking the automatic declassification of other quarter-century-old documents. And National Archives officials secretly agreed to keep the "reclassification" program under wraps.

What information the government did put out had to be carefully scrubbed. In 2006, the Agriculture Department decided that its annual report on hunger could no longer use the word "hunger." The eleven million Americans who sometimes couldn't afford to feed themselves would, the administration decreed, now be described as undergoing "very low food security."

With the speech controls going so well in Potomac Land, Bush asked Hughes to see if the rest of the world might be susceptible to the same techniques. She became undersecretary of state for public diplomacy and was given the challenge of dousing the raging anti-

Americanism in the Arab world. And Hughes set about the job as if it were another political campaign, creating a "rapid-response unit," and a plan to "forward deploy regional SWAT teams" to combat anti-American sentiment. And U.S. ambassadors would be given strict talking points. "If they make statements based on something I sent them," Hughes reassured State Department workers, "they're not going to be called on the carpet."

With her rapid responses and SWAT communications teams in place, Hughes set off on a "listening tour" of the Middle East, where she would address all those "things being said about us around the world that aren't true." As recounted by the *Washington Post*'s Glenn Kessler, one of sixteen reporters on the trip, she brought a prop—a Muslim intern—and a suitcase full of banal phrases: "I am a mom and I love kids. . . . I love all kids. And I understand that is something I have in common with the Turkish people—that they love children."

But this proved insufficient. In Turkey, a group of women assembled to talk about women's rights instead attacked Hughes over the Iraq war. One told her that the war brought "your positive efforts to the level of zero" and another said war "makes the rights of women completely erased." When Hughes voiced the Bush view that war is needed "to preserve the peace," her listeners told her they were "insulted" and "wounded." Nor did Hughes have sufficient facts at her disposal. When a reporter asked if she was meeting with an Egyptian opposition leader, she was stumped. She repeatedly, and falsely, told an Al Jazeera interviewer that Bush was the first president to propose a Palestinian state.

Clearly, the Hughes communication plan wasn't having the effect overseas that it did back in Potomac Land. The reaction in the foreign press was unequivocal: The problem with the American image wasn't about presentation, as Hughes supposed, but about U.S. policies. At home, *USA Today* condemned her "superficial PR blitz." But Hughes had a solution: She scheduled a second trip to the Middle East—this time, with no reporters on board.

Glossary

Just as modern French speakers who travel to Quebec often find the dialect of French Canadians to be archaic and quaint, English speakers who visit Potomac Land frequently are puzzled and amused by the language spoken here. Though the Potomac dialect shares the alphabet and grammar of English, it has developed a vocabulary all its own. A few examples of Potomac phrases, followed by their English equivalents:

You're doing a heckuva job.
You will be fired in ten days.

We have full confidence in his integrity.
We will cut him loose by nightfall.

I don't pay attention to the polls.
My job approval rating is 32 percent.

The only poll that matters is Election Day.
I am far behind my opponent in the polls.

Frankly . . .
The following statement is false.

I had some gals come over to the condo to give me a massage.
I used a prostitution service.

When we have something to announce, we'll announce it.
We know the answer, but we are not going to tell you.

I have great respect for the senior senator.
I am about to drill my elderly colleague a new one.

I didn't inhale.
I smoked marijuana.

I did not have sexual relations with that woman.
That woman performed fellatio on me.

There is no controlling legal authority that says this was in
    violation of law.
I did something bad.

You are either with us or against us.
You are against us.

We identified weapons of mass destruction–related program
    activities.
We could not find any weapons of mass destruction.

As I said in my *Wall Street Journal* op-ed last week . . .
I think I am so important that I am quoting myself.

I hope we can work together in a bipartisan way.
*I need to pick off one senator from the other party to pass this
    bill.*

I believe in an independent, free press.
The media are on my side.

The president has always said . . .
The president is announcing a new position.

I don't know how to get you to get it through your heads that
    it's not new.
I am disappointed that you noticed that I switched positions.

I am a uniter, not a divider.
I practice divisive leadership.

I am the decider.
My authority is in question.

I am a commander guy.
My authority is all but gone.

A suicider shows up and kills people.
I have problems with my vocabulary.

The senator will deliver a major policy address.
The senator is desperate to get on television.

We believe he has, in fact, reconstituted nuclear weapons.
I am talking out of my buttocks.

Mission accomplished.
Things are about to go south.

Pockets of dead-enders are trying to reconstitute.
The enemy is winning.

They're in the last throes, if you will.
The enemy has won.

Thank you for the very frank and candid discussion.
You just spit in my eye.

As long as needed and not one day longer.
We have no idea how long this will take.

War is my last choice.
The bombing begins in three weeks.

The American people don't want open-ended fishing
    expeditions.
A member of my party is being investigated for wrongdoing.

Congress must fulfill its constitutional oversight obligation.
A member of the other party is being investigated for wrongdoing.

I will continue to do the people's business.
I expect to be indicted.

This should not be a political issue.
My party has a winning political issue.

It's time to stop playing politics.
The other party has a winning political issue.

I actually did vote for the $87 billion before I voted against it.
I am trying to lose the election.

Author's Note

Let me begin with apologies to those anthropology Ph.D.s who bought this book in the mistaken belief that it contained genuine academic merit. Any resemblance to actual scholarship, living or dead, is entirely coincidental. I should also apologize to regular readers of the *Washington Post,* who may recognize some of the people and scenes in this book from my column, Washington Sketch. I'm indebted to my many coconspirators in the Washington press corps, some of whom have assisted me secretly with my Sketches even though they work for competing news organizations; I promise never to reveal them to their editors. This book benefits from their published work as well, and in those cases I have cited their reporting in the text.

I'm grateful to Bill Thomas, editor in chief at Doubleday, for convincing a journalist with adult-onset attention deficit disorder to attempt this book. *Homo Politicus* was his idea, and all bad reviews should be directed solely at him. Gratitude is also due Rafe Sagalyn, my agent, who convinced Bill to pay me more than I am worth. I'm obliged to my colleagues and editors at the *Post,* particularly Len Downie, Phil Bennett, Liz Spayd, Mike Abramowitz, Maralee Schwartz, Susan Glasser, Bill Hamilton, Tim Curran, Al Kamen, and

Chris Cillizza, for giving me the latitude and encouragement to offend the broadest possible cross-section of Washington. Above all, I thank my wife, Donna, and daughter, Paola, for allowing me the time to complete this project, and my mother, Ann, who, for better or worse, taught me how to put pen to paper.

Index

Speakers of Hebrew and Arabic, because their languages are written right to left, read books in a manner Western cultures regard as back to front.

Homo politicus follows the same procedure, but for entirely different reasons. Upon picking up a book, Potomac Man turns immediately to the index, where he searches for his own name and then reads those pages that mention him. He then repeats the process with the names of his rivals.

In a decision that will cause some disorientation for Potomac Man, this book has been published without an index. The author regrets the inconvenience.